Sing Always the Song of the Divine

Shankara

Published by Upanishads Sutras, 2024.

While every precaution has been taken in the preparation of this book, the publisher assumes no responsibility for errors or omissions, or for damages resulting from the use of the information contained herein.

SING ALWAYS THE SONG OF THE DIVINE

First edition. July 8, 2024.

Copyright © 2024 Shankara.

ISBN: 979-8227060235

Written by Shankara.

Table of Contents

Sing always the Song of the Divine

OH IDIOT! SING THE SONG OF THE DIVINE, SING THE SONG OF THE DIVINE, SING THE SONG OF THE DIVINE, SING THE SONG OF THE DIVINE, BECAUSE AT THE HOUR OF DEATH THE MEMORISATION OF GRAMMAR WILL NOT SAVE YOU.

O IDIOT! ABANDON THE DESIRE TO ACCUMULATE WEALTH, AWAKEN RIGHT UNDERSTANDING, MAKE THE MIND DESIRELESS, AND BE CONTENT AND HAPPY WITH WHAT YOU EARN BY YOUR OWN LABOUR.

DON'T BE INFATUATED WITH A WOMAN'S BEAUTY, BREASTS, NAVEL AND WAIST. THEY ARE NOTHING BUT CONTORTIONS OF FLESH AND FAT - CONTEMPLATE THIS OVER AND OVER AGAIN.

LIFE IS AS TRANSIENT AND UNSTABLE AS A DROPLET ON THE LOTUS LEAF. HE UNDERSTANDS WELL THAT THE WORLD SUFFERS FROM THE DISEASE OF THE EGO AND IS WOUNDED BY SORROWS.

THE FAMILY ONLY CARES ABOUT YOU AS LONG AS YOU ARE ABLE TO EARN MONEY. WHEN OLD AGE COMES AND THE BODY BECOMES DECREPIT, NO ONE IN THE HOUSEHOLD CARES ABOUT YOU.

ONLY AS LONG AS THERE IS LIFE IN THE BODY, THE PEOPLE IN THE FAMILY CARE ABOUT YOU. THE LIFE GOES OUT, THE BODY BECOMES LIFELESS, EVEN THE

WIFE HERSELF IS AFRAID OF THE BODY.

A CHILD IS OBSESSED WITH PLAYING, A YOUNG MAN IS OBSESSED WITH YOUNG GIRLS, OLD MEN ARE OBSESSED WITH WORRIES. MAN NEVER TURNS TO THE DIVINE.

The first basic sutra to understand is that truth is attained in emptiness and lost in words. Truth is attained in silence and lost in speech. Truth has no language; all language is falsehood.

Language as such has been created by man. Truth is not created by man, it is his discovery. Truth is. It does not have to be created or demonstrated, it only has to be unveiled. And this unveiling of truth only takes place when all the noise of language within ceases, because language is the veil. Thoughts are the only obstacle.

When a child is born it has no language. It comes with no scripture, no religion, no caste, no nation. It comes as a void. The sacredness of emptiness is unique. Emptiness is the only virginity, the rest is perversion. The child comes as a fresh flower, there is not a scratch on his conscience. It knows nothing. But the child's capacity to know is pure. It is like a mirror in which nothing is reflected yet, but the capacity of reflection is total and pure.

Later there will be many reflections; knowledge will increase but the capacity to know will continue to decrease. As that void will be filled with words the void will cease to exist. It is as if the reflections in the mirror will remain attached to it and will not disappear from it. So the mirror's capacity to reflect will continue to decrease.

A child is born; it knows nothing, but its capacity to know is pure. That is why children learn quickly and old people learn with difficulty. This is because the old man's capacity to learn has been reduced: he has had enough of everything. Much has been written on his blackboard; his paper is no longer blank. To write something new, the paper has to be left blank again.

You can only attain the truth if you can become like the newborn child. So the coming of the child into this world is the first birth, and the second birth is when holiness is born in him. The one who passes through the second birth is dwija, twice-born, and is the true brahmin.

The scriptures say that all are born as sudras, untouchables. It is very rare for anyone to become a brahmin. Most people are born as sudras and die as sudras.

Who is a Brahmin? Not one who knows the Vedas, for anyone can know the Vedas. Not the one who has memorised the scriptures, because anyone can memorise the scriptures. Memorising the scriptures is only memory, not true knowledge. Only the one who knows Brahma is a Brahmin.

You have come here. You may not know that your coming here is actually the quest to be a brahmin - the quest to know Brahma.

Shankara wrote the first verse of this sweet song when he was passing through a village and saw an old man memorising the rules of grammar. He felt pity for this old man who was on his deathbed: he had wasted his whole life and now he was wasting his last moment too. All his life he had never remembered the divine and even now he was busy with grammar. What would he gain by memorising the rules of grammar?

Swami Ramateertha went to America and the Americans were deeply impressed by him. He was a unique person, a living Vedantin. For him, the divine was not a borrowed idea, it was a real experience - he was luminous with his experience. The simple heart of America was very impressed by him. The heart of America is very simple; the reason for that is that America has no past, no history, no tradition. The country is only three hundred years old. Its heart is as simple as a child's; it is not covered with many layers of words of knowledge and scriptures. So the people of that country loved Ramateertha. They listened to his words so attentively, as if he had brought the message of the nectar, of the immortal. They danced and sang with him.

Ramateertha returned to India. He thought that if a country like America - which has no religious tradition, where people are absolutely materialistic - could be so impressed by his talks and his personality, what will happen in India? I am going back to my home country, whose tradition is thousands of years old. Its history is so ancient that no one knows when it began, it is hidden in darkness. The land where the Vedas, the Upanishads and the Gita were created, the land where people like Buddha, Mahavira and Shankara were born. With this background, the people of India will listen to me as eagerly as if I were handing out diamonds. If such a miracle can happen in America, where people are materialistic, where they cannot understand piety, where their connections with the divine are broken, what will not happen in India?

But what actually happened in India, Ramateertha would never have imagined. He thought it would be better to enter India through Varanasi, the ancient city of Kashi, because this is the city that has witnessed all of India's glorious past. Buddha delivered his first sermon there, Shankara declared his universal victory in the scriptural debate there, the Jaina tirthankaras were born there. There is no other city older than Kashi in the whole world. Even Jerusalem is new; Mecca and Medina are also new. Kashi is the oldest place of pilgrimage. It is the first city in the world to be civilised.

Ramateertha came to Benares and delivered his first speech there. But right in the middle of the talk a pundit stood up and said, "Stop! Do you know Sanskrit?" Ramateertha could not understand this interruption. He was an unconcerned man. He did not know Sanskrit. He knew Urdu and Persian very well. He had never thought what knowledge of Sanskrit had to do with the Vedas, with Brahma and with knowledge. One can realise the divine without knowing any language. Though illiterate, Kabir knew, the illiterate Mohammed knew; the flowers of that knowledge blossomed in the life of the carpenter's son, Jesus. For this you don't need to be a scholar.

So Rameertha was quite surprised by the question and replied: "No, I don't know Sanskrit".

This expert burst out laughing.

The others got up to leave and said, "If you don't know Sanskrit, how will you know Vedanta? First go and learn Sanskrit, then come and teach others".

After this Rameertha went to the Himalayas, and the sad part of the story is that he gave up the sannyasin's clothes. When he died he did not wear his ochre robes, because he thought why be part of the tradition whose religion has become stuck in mere words and whose sannyas has become only erudition and which thinks that knowledge of Sanskrit is necessary to know Vedanta? That is why, when he died, he was not wearing his ochre robe. He had even renounced sannyas.

Tradition has contaminated even sannyas. America could understand it but India could not. America is ignorant - that's why she could understand it. India is very knowledgeable - a little too knowledgeable.

Without knowing, India has the illusion of knowing too much. Its mind has become learned but not wise. It has become so full of words that there is no room left for what has no words, and religion has nothing to do with words. Therefore, you must be more attentive to what I do not say than to what I say to you. When I speak, do not pay too much attention to my words; be attentive to the empty space between them. It does not matter if you miss my words, but do not miss what is not said.

One has to read Brahma between the lines. One has to look for Brahma between the words. It only happens in the gaps. When I am silent for a moment you wake up, you look at me intently; it is then that you give me the opportunity to approach you so that I can caress your heart.

Religion is not in the rules of grammar, it is in singing the song of the divine. And it is not in your singing of the divine; when even the song is lost, only you remain. When all words disappear, only a void surrounds you. You don't even speak because there is no need to speak to existence; it knows without your speaking. Your speaking is not going to add anything more to this knowledge. Besides, what can you say? Whatever you say will be nothing but your crying, and if you have to convey unhappiness it is better to do it through crying, just because your tears will be able to express what your words cannot.

How can you express your gratitude in words? Words are too small and gratitude is too vast. It can only be expressed by dancing. If there is nothing to say, it is better to remain silent so that the divine can speak and you can listen.

Bhajan, devotional singing, kirtan, divine songs and dance are all means of expressing feelings. Shankara is implying that without saying anything you yourself should become a song, a divine song. These verses are very simple, these sutras are straightforward, and they are written by a genius like Shankara. In all of Shankara's literature there is nothing more precious than Bhaj Govindam. Shankara is basically a philosopher; everything he has written is very complex; it is all words, scriptures, logic, analysis and thought. But Shankara knows that godliness cannot be achieved through logic, analysis and thought. The way to attain it is through dancing and singing - through feeling and not through thinking.

Shankara's path of realisation is through the heart and not through the head. That is why, although Shankara has written commentaries on the Brahmasutra, the Upanishads and the Gita, you will find his innermost feelings expressed in these short verses; here he has opened his heart.

Here Shankara does not speak as a scholar or a thinker, here he expresses himself as a devotee.

OH IDIOT! SING THE SONG OF THE DIVINE, SING THE SONG OF THE DIVINE, FOR AT THE HOUR OF DEATH THE MEMORISATION OF GRAMMAR WILL NOT SAVE YOU.

OH IDIOT! SING THE SONG OF THE DIVINE. What is the idiocy? Shankara is not insulting you by addressing you as 'idiot'. In fact, it is his most loving expression. OH IDIOT! SING THE SONG OF THE DIVINE, SING THE SONG OF THE DIVINE, SING THE SONG OF THE DIVINE.

What does idiocy mean? Try to understand it. Idiocy does not mean ignorance. Idiocy means to think oneself knowledgeable when one is ignorant. The learned are idiots and not the ignorant. Why call the ignorant an idiot? The ignorant is simply ignorant; he does not know, that is all. Many times it has happened that the ignorant have come to know and the learned have got nowhere, because the ignorant have no ego. He is humble.

Since he does not know, he cannot claim to know. But the scholar who does not know, thinks he knows. Because he has learned words and scriptures and can repeat the rules of grammar, he is lost in all these things.

There is a Sufi story. To earn his living, a Sufi fakir worked as a boatman on a river. One day, a village pundit wanted to cross the river. The fakir offered to take him for free.

He charged one or two paisa for the trip. The pundit sat in the boat and the fakir started rowing. They were the only people in the boat.

The expert asked him: "Can you read and write? What else can an expert ask? He wants to teach others what he knows himself. We can only give to others what we have. Experts are obsessed with their supposed knowledge. He could not see the fakir's brilliance, he took him for an ordinary boatman. But the fakir was an extraordinary man. The pundit did not know that the divinity he had been contemplating, listening and discussing was present in this extraordinary man. It was peeping through him. Had he had eyes to see, he would have found in the fakir all that he had dreamt and read in the scriptures. Something was present there.

But the only thing the expert could ask was: "Can you read and write?

If an expert meets God, he is sure to ask: "Where is your certificate? What is your education?" An expert has his own world, lives in his own world of words and scriptures.

The fakir replied: "No, I can neither read nor write. I am absolutely illiterate and rustic". If there was a shred of conscience in the pundit, he would have seen the absolute humility of the fakir. Accepting one's ignorance is the first step towards self-knowledge. If one accepts one's ignorance wholeheartedly, then it can also become the last step. When you are fully aware that you know nothing, your ego will disappear, its foundations will crumble. The edifice of ego will collapse and you will slide into egolessness. That is the gateway from which one can be in touch with the divine.

The fakir said: "I don't know anything. I am absolutely illiterate.

Hearing this, the expert commented: "Then a quarter of your life is wasted.

The ship sailed a little further. Pundonor asked again: "But must you at least know arithmetic? You need it to keep accounts.

The fakir said: "I don't own anything, so I don't need to keep any accounts. What I earn during the day, I spend at night. I do not earn more than I need for my daily sustenance. At night I am a fakir again. In the morning I earn money again. Existence has provided me with enough so far, so why should I worry about tomorrow? If someone gives me money, nothing happens. If someone gives me nothing, nothing happens either. I have lived so far and I will be able to live in the future as well. Neither he who gives gives something that lasts forever nor he who doesn't give takes something that may be a loss forever: it's all a game."

Hearing this, the expert said: "Well, half your life is wasted". Just then a storm started, the boat began to toss about on the waves and it looked like it was going to sink at any moment. The fakir laughed because the pundit got very scared. Who doesn't get scared when death is imminent? The pundit used to talk about immortality, he used to say that the soul is immortal, but these erudite claims of the soul, of immortality, are of no use in the face of death.

The fakir asked him: "Can you swim?

The expert replied: "No, not at all".

The fakir said: "Then your whole life is a waste! I'm going to jump because this ship will sink".

OH IDIOT! SING THE DIVINE'S SONG, SING THE DIVINE'S SONG BECAUSE AT THE TIME OF DEATH - perhaps Shankara knew the story I just told you - MEMORISING GRAMMAR WILL NOT SAVE YOU.

When you are about to drown, when death surrounds you, you will only be saved if you know how to swim... swim in death. If you can't swim in death, death will drown you. It has also drowned you many times before, but you have not yet awakened, you have not yet learned to swim. At the moment of death your knowledge of languages - no matter how many languages you know - as well as your knowledge of grammar, will be absolutely useless.

Death is the criterion. What is useful at the time of death is wisdom and what is useless at the time of death is scholarship. Test everything you know by this criterion. Always carry this touchstone with you, just as a goldsmith goes about testing gold on the touchstone. All that is useful, useful at the moment of death, is true knowledge, and all that is useless and misleading is nothing but scholarship.

And can something that is useless in death be useful in life? What is useless even in death, how can it be useful in life? - For death is the ultimate culmination of life. It is the pinnacle of life. It is the festival of life. Whatever is useful in death is useful in life. While it is easy to cheat in life, it is impossible to cheat in death. Death exposes everything.

Who is Shankara calling an idiot? He is calling an idiot that person who does not know the truth but has memorised the grammar, who knows the words and the scriptures and can repeat them, explain them. Shankara calls the expert an idiot. His very words: OH IDIOT! SING THE DIVINE'S SONG, SING THE DIVINE'S SONG, FOR AT THE TIME OF DEATH THE MEMORISATION OF GRAMMAR WILL NOT SAVE YOU, prove that he was using the word idiot for pundit; otherwise, suddenly there would be no need to mention grammar. It is not the fool or the ignorant that we regard as such; it is the expert who memorises grammar, he is the idiot.

Pundonor is memorising grammar, and this has become a great burden in India, so much so that almost all people have this false notion that they know the divine only because they know the word God. Remember that the word God is not divinity, just as the word water is not water. When one is thirsty, the word water is of no use and real water is needed to quench one's thirst. At the time of death, the principles and theories of immortality are of no use; the real taste of immortality is needed.

Once I was on a trip during the summer. It had not rained that year in that area. The train stopped at a station where a man was selling water: ten paisa per glass. He shouted: "A glass of water for ten paisa". He went on selling the water and collecting the money.

A man sitting next to me asked him: "Won't you sell it for eight paisa?

When the water seller heard this, he didn't even stop and said: "Then you're not thirsty!

Yes, he was right. When you're really thirsty, you don't worry about eight paisa or ten paisa.

Only those who are not thirsty can think of bargaining. The water seller's comment appealed to me.

When you are thirsty you can't think about saving two paisa. In fact, one is ready to give everything at that moment. Bargaining continues only when one is not thirsty.

You say you are a Hindu, a Mohammedan or a Christian; that only means that you are not yet thirsty. When you are thirsty you don't care whether you are a Hindu, a Mohammedan or a Christian.

When one is really thirsty he asks for the divine; temples, mosques or gurudwaras mean nothing to him and these cannot quench his thirst. One does not bargain when one is thirsty.

The meaning of renunciation, the meaning of sannyas, is that you are thirsty and willing to gamble everything.

People say: "Yes, we want to know God, but at the moment there are many other things to do, there are many problems to solve". So they keep postponing religion to the last. God is the last on the list of your needs and the last of the needs is never fulfilled. He is still the last. One day you will be finished, you will never be able to reach him. When one need is fulfilled, ten other needs arise. When one ambition is fulfilled, a thousand others arise. Religion always comes last. The divine doesn't even come close. It all depends on whether religion is first or last on your list of life. An idiot is one who keeps religion at the bottom of his list, and certainly not an idiot is one who keeps it at the top of his list. He has begun to wake up. He has well understood that he can accumulate any amount of wealth, but in the end death will take it away from him. So there is no point in wasting time accumulating things that will be taken away from you in the end.

OH IDIOT! SINGS THE SONG OF THE DIVINE.

You also have to understand the meaning of bhajan. You will see many people doing bhajan, singing the song of the divine, but they are not really doing bhajan. They are doing it very superficially. It may be a kind of recreation for them, because they have not staked their life. It may be just an enjoyment for them, and this kind of enjoyment they can get from any other song or any other music.

Bhajan means that there is a deep agony in your inner being; a sound arises from your inner depths.

Your whole life is at stake, as if it were a matter of life and death. If you want to sing the song of the divine then you have to lose yourself. If you want to save yourself and be devoted to Govinda, God, then you are cheating yourself.

Bhajan itself is the climax. It is the ultimate. Ramakrishna's disciples used to be very careful that when he walked in the street no one should say "Ram Ram" or "Jai Ram", for even if a stranger greeted him by saying "Jairam-ji", he would stand there overwhelmed with emotion and ecstasy and start dancing in the middle of the street. The disciples would be embarrassed. The police would come and tell them to clear the chaos from the road. If he was invited to a wedding, no one cared about the bride or groom and everyone gathered around him.

Once, one of his admirers invited Ramakrishna to his daughter's wedding to give his blessings. The ceremony was about to begin when someone called out Govinda's name. There was a huge crowd and someone shouted, "Where is Govinda?". Ramakrishna heard Govinda's name and started dancing, and Govinda's bhajan began! That wedding place became a divine scene. The wedding feast was no longer a wedding feast. The wedding ceremony was no longer a wedding ceremony; it was something else altogether.

Bhajan means that there is a constant flow of the remembrance of the divine within you twenty-four hours a day. That constant flow existed in Ramakrishna, so that whenever anyone uttered the name of Ram, Krishna or Govinda, the inner flow would burst forth. The slightest external stimulus revealed the inner dance, the inner music, the inner sound. It is like a well full of water. If someone puts a bucket into the well, it will come out full of water. Similarly, if someone utters the name of Ram, the bhajan within, the inner remembrance will express itself outwardly.

Bhajan is not something you can do at your convenience. Bhajan is a continuous remembrance. When it starts it never ends, it goes on and on - a continuous remembrance within your being.

OH IDIOT! SING THE SONG OF THE DIVINE, FOR AT THE HOUR OF DEATH THE MEMORISATION OF GRAMMAR WILL NOT SAVE YOU.

Death will not ask you, "How much do you know of the Scriptures?". Death will reveal to you how much truth you have known. At the time of death only what you yourself have known will remain with you, and what was known by others and what was borrowed by you from others will be lost. If the scripture is borrowed then it is useless, but if the scripture is revealed to you then you have reached the very source where the rishis of the Upanishads had quenched their thirst. In that case the Upanishads are not mere scriptures to you; then they are the expression of your own realisation, of your own knowledge.

People ask me why I talk about Shankara, Buddha or Christ - I can also speak directly. I tell them I speak directly, because in this song by Shankara, he has said the same thing I would like to say, and he has said it so beautifully that it cannot be improved upon. He has said the last word, so there is no need to repeat it. I am not talking about Shankara because it seems to me that he knows it; the question of my believing in Shankara does not arise. It is because I too have drunk water from the same source from which he drank and this song was born in him.

O IDIOT! ABANDON THE DESIRE TO ACCUMULATE WEALTH, AWAKEN THE RIGHT UNDERSTANDING, MAKE THE MIND DESIRELESS, AND BE CONTENT AND

HAPPY WITH WHAT YOU EARN BY YOUR OWN LABOUR. O FOOL, SING ALWAYS THE SONG OF THE DIVINE.

Abandon the desire to accumulate wealth. Wealth' does not mean the wealth you know as wealth.

Here wealth means everything that you collect or accumulate... everything that you accumulate according to your desire is wealth, even knowledge. When you accumulate knowledge you are accumulating wealth.

One person is still counting how much money he has put in his locker, another is counting how much knowledge he has accumulated, how much information he has gathered and how many scriptures he has read, but both are accumulating. The third person may be accumulating renunciations, counting how many fasts he has done. The fourth may be accumulating fame, he may be counting how many people have faith in him, how many worship him and how many follow him. All that is accumulated and all that can be accumulated is wealth. And this wealth is very deceptive because on the outside you can keep accumulating, but you are still poor on the inside.

What accumulates outside cannot be carried inside, and death will take from you what you cannot carry inside, for only you can pass through death and nothing else. Only your being alone will pass through; flames cannot burn it, arrows cannot pierce it. Only you alone can pass through the gate of death, you in your purity and nothing else.

If you have accumulated only external wealth, you will still be poor when you pass through the gate of death. If death proves that you are poor, then it means that the wealth accumulated during life was only a delusion. Wealth is only that which can accompany us; otherwise, the rest is nothing but trouble. What you accumulate looks like wealth to you, but in reality it is not, it is only problems.

After accumulating you also realise that the problems have increased.

True wealth would bring contentment, true wealth would bring peace, it would bring fearlessness, it would ring a paradise in your life, it would bring relaxation in your life. It would bring the relief of arriving at the destination, of arriving home; a scent of relaxation would rise in your life.

But there is no such thing in you. With the increase of wealth your life sucks more, becomes more unhappy and more fearful. Accumulation of wealth creates a thousand worries. Wealth does not bring peace; it only disturbs peace.

OH IDIOT! ABANDON THE DESIRE TO ACCUMULATE WEALTH.

Yes, give up the desire to accumulate. Why are people so crazy about accumulating?

I once lived in a house whose owner was crazy about collecting things. He even collected things that were useless. His house looked like a storage room. I wondered how he could live in it. One day I was in the garden and while he was talking to me, his little son came out and threw an old, used and broken broomstick. He immediately became restless. He kept looking at the stick while talking to me. I knew my presence was bothering him, so I told him I would be back in a few minutes and went inside.

When I came out I found that the broomstick had disappeared. He had taken it with him. I followed him and caught him in the act. He was standing there with the broomstick. I asked him: "Why did you bring it?

He said to me: "Well, it might be necessary sometime".

I said, "But it's useless now".

He protested, saying: "No, no, it might be useful sometime. Why throw it away? Let it stay.

It is the mania for collecting things, what is the reason for this, why does man want to accumulate? There is really a great emptiness inside that has to be filled, and it has to be filled with anything, otherwise one feels very empty. If you have nothing, you feel very empty inside. Think: if you have nothing to possess, you will be free and empty inside.

Some friends come to meditate with me. When they have been meditating for a while, say a month or so, they start to see that emptiness inside. That emptiness has always been there, but they didn't notice it. Meditation makes you more aware, awareness increases and then you become aware of the emptiness. Then something very peculiar happens. The one who feels that emptiness inside starts to eat a lot. Every day I get one or two such cases. They say: "What are we going to do? We didn't eat so much before. The effect of meditation is such that we want to eat all the time.

I explain to them that the reason is that meditation has shown you the emptiness inside, and this emptiness hurts, so you have to fill it. Therefore, you fill this emptiness with money, position and fame. By accumulating things and sitting among them, you feel you have something.

Those who have nothing have the desire to accumulate. But those who have something do not accumulate, they are self-sufficient. Mere "being" is so satisfying that there is no need to accumulate anything.

That is why we worship Buddha, we worship Mahavira, we worship Shankara, because we realised that their wealth is within them; there is something in them by which the emptiness has disappeared. There is some light in them by which the emptiness within has become fullness, the emptiness within has become truth. Meditation brings emptiness.

If you are in a hurry you will have the desire to fill the emptiness. But if you are not in a hurry and you accept the emptiness and are willing to live with it, you will see that gradually the emptiness fills itself. Nature does not tolerate emptiness. You create emptiness, nature fills it. God does not tolerate emptiness; if you create emptiness, God fills it. Only emptiness is needed, fullness comes by itself. Just as when it rains, water rushes from all sides into the well; similarly, when you empty yourself, the divine rushes into you from all sides.

If you make a pit, existence will fill it. Half the work is done by you, the other half by existence. But your doing is not so important, the real work is done by existence. All you have to do is to be ready, to be empty. That's why all the enlightened ones insist: "Don't accumulate. Don't have the desire to collect things"... because if you fill yourself, then you are not giving the divine a chance to fill you.

I have heard a story. Once Krishna sat down to eat. Rukmani was serving the food. Krishna had hardly tasted the first mouthful when suddenly he got up and ran out. But as soon as he reached the door, he came back and sat down.

Rukmani could not understand this behaviour. He asked him: "Why did you run, what for, and why did you come back from the door? You ran as if some house was on fire and you had to put it out before eating. But then you came back as if nothing had happened".

Krishna replied, "Yes, indeed something was burning, but by the time I reached the door it had gone out, so I went back. One of my devotees was walking down a street in the capital. People were throwing stones at him, his forehead was bleeding and he was shouting, "Govinda, Govinda! He did not react and did not try to save himself. He had totally entrusted himself to me. So to save him I had to run.

When one becomes helpless like that man, existence has to take care of him. When a person becomes so empty that despite being stoned he does nothing to save himself, does not even run away and does not even react, then the whole existence comes to save him. When there is a well, water rushes in from all sides to fill it. Rukmani asked, "Then why did you come back?".

Krishna replied, "When I reached the door, I had changed my mind. He had taken a stone in his hand. He was reacting himself, so he didn't need me any more.

God is needed when you are helpless, and in that helpless condition, when you utter "Govinda, Govinda!", that is bhajan, devotion. There is no need to say the word Govinda aloud; the inner emotion is enough. When your eyes full of love look towards the sky, when your heart is open towards the sky and you make no effort to do anything on your part, that is the moment when the divine rushes towards you. If you become a well, he is always ready to fill it.

Muhammad used to say that if you take one step towards Allah, he takes a thousand steps towards you. But if you don't take even one step, and that step is very necessary, because until you give him the invitation, how is he going to come? Even if he wants to come, how will he come? Even though you don't invite him, even though you don't ask him to come, if he comes to you, your doors will be closed. Even if he knocks, you will think it is the mind. Even if he calls out loudly, you will not be able to hear him because of your inner turmoil.

O IDIOT! ABANDON THE DESIRE TO ACCUMULATE WEALTH, AWAKEN YOUR RIGHT UNDERSTANDING.

Intellect means your cunning; right understanding, your wisdom. So as the world becomes more and more intelligent, it also becomes more and more cunning. It was hoped that education would make people simple and innocent, but the amazing thing is that with increasing education man is becoming more cunning, more dishonest and more hypocritical. He has become adept at exploiting others.

Intelligence means efficiency in this world and common sense means efficiency in the inner world. Worldly people may think that the person of good sense is stupid. They are bound to say so because he will ask, "What are you doing?". Buddha gave up his house, his palace, his kingdom, because common sense prevailed. The charioteer who had come to see him off at the border of his kingdom was an ordinary servant, but even he said to him, "Forgive my impertinence, but I cannot help telling you that what you are doing is absolutely stupid. Have you gone mad? The whole world longs for such a palace and kingdom. You are lucky enough to have them, but you are giving up all these things. Where else could you have such a beautiful wife? Where else are you going to get this wealth, these comforts, these luxuries, this kind of family and this respect? You'd better go back.

Certainly the old charioteer is more worldly wise than the Buddha, so he gives this advice.

Buddha said: "I understand perfectly well what you say. But where you see the palace, I see only flames of fire; where you see beauty, I see death; what you see as wealth, to me is only a delusion of wealth. I seek true wealth, I seek a true home that cannot one day be taken away. My search will continue until I get it. For this quest I am willing to gamble everything, because why not gamble something that in the end will be taken away from me, it is only a matter of time. If I get something that cannot be lost by betting something that will be lost, then this deal is not bad. It's just a matter of time. If I can bet what is going to be taken away from me tomorrow anyway for something that can never be taken away from me, it's not expensive.

Common sense has prevailed over Buddha and the charioteer is, in effect, a worldly sage.

Buddha became enlightened and returned home after twelve years. But his father got angry. He said, "Don't be stupid! Go back home. You have cheated me, you have cheated your wife and your newborn child. In spite of everything, I will forgive you, because I have a father's heart.

Go back, your begging on the road doesn't look good. And why are you begging? You can give alms to thousands of beggars every day".

Even now Buddha seemed stupid to his father. Religious intelligence always seems stupid to worldly wisdom, and people generally think it is utter folly. But to the person who possesses this religious intelligence, this worldly wisdom seems stupid.

And it is you who has to make the decision. Without this decision you cannot enter the world of religion. Until worldly wisdom appears to you as foolishness, you cannot attain sanity. When you see that worldly wisdom is foolishness, when you see that worldly cunning is deceit, when you see the futility of worldly fame, position and reputation, then it means that the seed of right understanding has sprouted in you.

AWAKEN THE RIGHT UNDERSTANDING, MAKE THE MIND DESIRELESS, AND BE CONTENT AND HAPPY WITH WHAT YOU EARN BY YOUR OWN LABOUR.

This is true with regard to all kinds of wealth - also with regard to the external wealth that one obtains by one's own efforts. Whoever is satisfied with it, his life will be full of morality. And the same is true about inner wealth as well: when inner wealth is obtained by one's own effort one will be religious within.

Memorizing scripture means you are committing theft. You are stealing the knowledge hidden in the scriptures; you didn't get it by your own effort or hard work. It is all borrowed and stale, you are just holding on to someone else's knowledge. Don't build your building on it.

Its foundations are on sand, so it will collapse at the slightest gust of wind.

A few days ago I was telling a Zen story. One night, a Zen monk knocked at the door of a Zen monastery. It is a tradition in Zen monasteries that if a travelling monk wants to rest there he has to give the correct answer to at least one question. He has to earn the shelter to rest by giving a correct answer to one question; otherwise, he cannot stop at the monastery, he has to continue his journey.

The head of the monastery opened the door and asked the guest an ancient riddle of the Zen monks.

The riddle is: What is your original face, the basic face, the true face, the one that was yours even before the birth of your father and mother? This question refers to the soul. What you have received from your mother and father is the body; your face you also received from them. But what is your basic face, the original face? What is your nature?

And Zen monks say that the answer to this question cannot be given in words, its answer must be a living expression. As soon as this question was asked, the travelling guest monk took off his shoe and hit the face of the monk who had asked the question.

The host stepped aside, saluted and said: "Welcome! Come on in.

After dining together, they sat by the fire in the evening and began to talk. The host said to the guest, "Your response was wonderful.

The guest asked: "Have you experienced this response yourself?

The host replied: "No, I have not experienced it. But I have read many scriptures and I have learned from them that the one who gives the right answer does not hesitate. You have answered without hesitation and your answer says it all. Based on the scriptures I have understood that you have come to know the answer, because through your answer you have said: "Idiot! You are asking the question with words and you want the answer without words; you are asking for the original face that you also have. Therefore, by hitting your face with the shoe, I am saying that this face is not your original face - it deserves a shoe.

The host said: "So I have understood your answer. I too have read the scriptures and such answers are written in them."

The guest said nothing. He continued to sip his tea. The host began to hesitate. He looked carefully at the guest's face and what he saw did not please him at all. He said: "Friend! I ask you one more time: Have you really experienced the answer or not?".

The guest replied: "I too have read many scriptures. I have read that this is an adequate answer to the question you have asked. But the fact is that I have not experienced the answer".

Scripture can be very misleading because the answers are also written there. But repeating the answer from the scripture is like using the answers written at the back of the arithmetic book. You read the problem, then turn the book over and see the answers at the end. In this way you will give the correct answer but you will never know the method by which that answer is arrived at. The answer will be correct but you will still be wrong, because if you had gone through the method you would have evolved, you would have developed.

Someone else's answer is of no use. The answer must be your own. No one is going to test your knowledge of the scriptures; existence is going to test you existentially. No one is going to ask you, "What have you heard? What have you read?" Existence will ask you, "How have you lived?". If the answer comes from your life, it means it has come with your own effort. With the outer wealth, if you earn it by your work, by your hard work, then your life will be full of morality, and if you earn the inner wealth by your work then your life will be religious - it will be real religion. That is why Ramateertha called this authentic religion. Yes, there is borrowed religion and there is authentic religion.

Borrowed religion means that the answers are correct but impotent; they are like empty, spent cartridges, not usable in a gun. People will laugh at you, but that's what most people do: they repeat other people's answers, they repeat them mechanically. How can they get their own answers if they don't even have their own questions? They don't even know what exactly they want to know. They don't know the question they are looking for.

O IDIOT! ABANDON THE DESIRE TO ACCUMULATE WEALTH, AWAKEN RIGHT UNDERSTANDING AND BE CONTENT AND HAPPY WITH WHAT YOU EARN BY YOUR OWN LABOUR. OH IDIOT! SING ALWAYS THE SONG OF THE DIVINE.

DON'T BE INFATUATED WITH A WOMAN'S BEAUTY, BREASTS, NAVEL AND WAIST. THEY ARE BUT CONTORTIONS OF FLESH AND FAT, CONTEMPLATE THIS AGAIN AND AGAIN. OH IDIOT! SING ALWAYS THE SONG OF THE DIVINE.

The man is attracted to the woman and the woman is attracted to the man. Opposites always attract, and this attraction is like hypnotism. Let us understand this.

When a child is born, its first contact with this world is the mother's breast; the first contact with the other is the mother's breast. His journey in this world begins after he becomes familiar with the mother's breast. That is why man is always obsessed with the breasts of the woman; that is the first impact, no other impact is more profound than this. That is why all paintings, pictures, statues, films, stories, everything revolves around women's breasts. Breasts are the part of a woman's body that most mesmerises a man's mind. Women keep trying to hide breasts and men keep trying to uncover them. Women know what attracts men and men also know what interests them in a woman's body.

As civilisation develops, this problem is also increasing. The fact is that uncivilised tribes are not attracted to breasts because their female bodies and breasts are not covered. Every child is free to suckle from its mother's breast as long as it wants. He can even continue to suckle until he is ten years old. In civilised societies, attempts are made to wean the child from the mother's breast as soon as possible. The earlier the child is weaned from the breast, the greater the attraction to it. People go on writing poetry, painting pictures, making statues, etc. about the beauty of breasts. Their mind is totally obsessed with breasts.

This means that the child was not satiated, he was still dissatisfied. This dissatisfaction creates dreams. This dissatisfaction creates an inner hypnotism. But now there is no means of satisfaction until common sense awakens.

Shankara says to remember this continually - the previous impact can only be eliminated by remembering it again and again.

Scientists have made some discoveries; one of them is very important. One scientist was experimenting with chickens. When a chicken hatched from a hen's egg, he did not let the chicken see the hen, but kept it with a duck. When the chicken opened its eyes it saw the duck, and this was its first footprint. And an interesting thing happened: it ran after the duck and did not recognise the hen. The hen couldn't stand the chicken running after her all the time, so she kicked it, she hit it, but still it followed her everywhere. The hen tried in every way she could to win him over, to bring him closer to her, but he was afraid of her and stayed far away. At night, too, the chick wanted to sleep in the same place as the ducks, but the ducks chased him away. The hen wanted to take him to the henhouse, but he was not ready to go there.

The first imprint, the first conditioning, is very important. It haunts you all your life. The first event in life, whatever it is, always haunts a person, and the mind keeps dreaming about it. What is attractive about a man's or a woman's body? There is certainly something. Your body is the result of the union of the bodies of a man and a woman: the man gives half to your body and the woman gives the other half. Every person is half woman and half man, a mixture of both.

Your whole existence is half male, half female; it is incomplete.

The feminine half in you still longs for the man and the masculine half in you still longs for the woman.

According to the latest research in psychology, in the unconscious mind of every man hides the woman and in the unconscious mind of every woman hides the man. They keep looking outside until their inner man and their inner woman meet.

Until your inner man and your inner woman are united, until your conscious mind and your unconscious mind become one by being united, the attraction to the opposite will always be there. A man will be attracted to a woman and a woman will be attracted to a man.

Surely you have seen the statue of Ardhanarishawara in which Lord Shiva is shown as half woman and half man. Until the half man and half woman within you become the image of Ardhanarishawara, until you become complete within yourself, you will keep looking outside feeling lost and thinking that meeting a woman will bring you fulfilment. But the woman is there in your unconscious mind.

That is why all yogas and tantras are basically the process of uniting your inner energies. When you unite and become one within yourself, then your outer desire ceases to exist. But at the same time, when the outer desire ceases to exist, only then can you become one. These two things are interdependent. That is why Shankara says:

DON'T BE INFATUATED WITH A WOMAN'S BEAUTY, BREASTS, NAVEL AND WAIST.

Shankara is addressing men, because in those days, especially in this country, religion was monopolised by men. But the same has to be said to women too, that there is nothing special about a man's body that should obsess or hypnotise her.

These words of Shankara and other such words of other saints have created a misunderstanding. It seems that there is nothing in a woman's body, but there is something special in a man's body. Actually, there is nothing in any body. Men look down on a woman's body saying, "It is nothing but bone, flesh and fat". But what about a man's body - is it made of gold, silver or diamonds? As long as you do not see the bones, flesh and fat in your own body, you cannot see them in a woman's body. Because of the misinterpretation of these words, it has become a tradition to condemn women.

Men think that women are the cause of their slavery. But who has enslaved women? Men think that women are the main obstacle to achieving liberation. But the question is: if women are the obstacle in achieving liberation, then who is the obstacle for a woman to achieve liberation? Then it means that women can attain liberation without any obstacle. If there is no obstacle in their life, then they can attain it directly without any difficulty.

No, it is not about a man or a woman. Attraction on the contrary is of no avail. You must contemplate again and again that these are the perversions of the flesh. It is necessary to contemplate again and again in this way to remove this imprint that is there in the mind. Continuous remembrance is like the waterfall breaking the stone, a strong stone. No one can imagine that a small trickle of water falling for the first time will be able to break the stone. Over time, the stone turns into granules of sand and the water continues to fall in the same way. This footprint is very strong and very deep, but if the thought continues like the trickle of water, drop by drop, one day the stone will break and disappear. And the day your footprints disappear, you will be free.

OH IDIOT! ALWAYS SING THE SONG OF THE DIVINE. Shankara is saying: Remain devotional to Govinda continuously. Whatever you do, you should always remember Govinda. Never forget Govinda.

Govinda's bhajan means that what is visible is not enough, is not enough, is not all, is not everything. Remember that there is also that which cannot be seen. Don't let the invisible get lost in the visible, always remember the invisible.

You see me, I see you. As far as you can see me, that is visible. When you pass men, animals, trees as you walk along the road, all that is visible is the world. These things are visible. But if you can remember the invisible within me... the invisible hidden in the visible is Govinda. The meaning of Govinda bhajan is that the visible should not deceive you, you should not get lost in the visible; you should always be able to remember the invisible.

During the revolution of 1857, a soldier mistakenly killed a sannyasin. A naked and silent sannyasin was passing by the cantonment of a British battalion. The soldiers grabbed him and asked him: "Who are you? But as he was silent he did not answer. As he remained silent, they began to suspect him and an English soldier pierced his chest with a spear. The sannyasin had taken a vow to speak only once at the moment of death: he had been silent for the last thirty years.

When the spear pierced his chest and the blood gushed out, he then uttered only one sentence from the Upanishads: tattvamasi, shvetketu - you too are that, Shvetketu.

The people gathered around him and asked him: "What do you mean?

He said: "I mean that the divine can come in any form, he cannot deceive me. Today he came with the spear in his hand. The spear has pierced my chest, but I can see that inside the soldier there is only him. He cannot deceive me. Blood oozed from his chest, but the sannyasin danced because he could see the mercy in his killer.

OH IDIOT! SING THE SONG OF THE DIVINE, SING THE SONG OF THE DIVINE.

This means that whatever happens, in all circumstances, the divine must be visible.

It must be seen in the enemy, it must also be seen in death when it comes. It must be seen in a friend and also in the enemy.

But at the moment you cannot see it even in a friend. Right now you can't even see it in the person you love; you don't even see it in your beloved or lover, let alone others. You don't see it in yourself, how can you see it in another?

OH IDIOT! SING THE SONG OF THE DIVINE, it means that, come what may, the divine is seen everywhere. Even in a rock it is there, perhaps fast asleep. You can see it even in a tree, it is mute, but it is there. Even in the lunatic, it is mad, but it is there. You should be able to recognise it in any form.

There is an anecdote in Sai Baba's life. A Hindu sannyasin lived about three miles from the mosque where Sai Baba lived. This sannyasin used to come daily for Sai Baba's darshan, taking his food only after seeing Sai Baba. Sometimes there was a big crowd and he could not enter the mosque, so he would spend the whole day without his darshan. But the sannyasin never took food without touching Sai Baba's feet. Sometimes he had to sleep without taking food because he only ate during the day, that was his rule.

So one day Sai Baba said to him, "There is no need for you to come here daily. I will come to you, but you must recognise me. Do not allow me to come and not recognise me. I will come just when your food is ready, you can have my darshan there. For you to come here from a distance of three miles and then go all that way back is too much. It pains me to think that sometimes you have to go without food."

The sannyasin was very happy. He said, "It is my good luck. Tomorrow I will wait for you.

The next day he prepared food early and waited happily for Sai Baba. No one came except a dog. The dog must have smelt the food. He chased the dog away with a stick and chased it away saying, "I am waiting for Sai Baba, go away from here". He hit the dog with the stick twice and made it run away. After that no one came.

In the evening he ran to the mosque. There was a large crowd there. He asked Sai Baba, "Why didn't you come? You are sitting here surrounded by people but you had promised me to come".

Sai Baba said, "I came but you did not recognise me. I was hit by your stick.

The sannyasin was perplexed. He said, "But only one dog has come".

Sai Baba said: "Didn't I tell you that I will definitely come, but you must recognise me? I cannot say in what form I will appear; it all depends on the form that is readily available. At that time it was only appropriate to appear in the form of a dog. On that sunny day there was no other form available. There was only this dog, so I used it".

Hearing this, the sannyasin burst into tears. He said, "It was my fault, but please give me another chance. You must come tomorrow. I will definitely recognise you.

If the dog had come the next day I would have recognised him. But the dog did not come. He kept waiting for either one of two things: for Sai Baba to come directly or for him to appear in the form of a dog. But the dog did not appear. Well, dogs are not very reliable, they may or may not come. The dog didn't come, but a beggar came who was a leper. He stank terribly.

The Sannasin thought the food would be spoiled by the stench; no one would want to eat it.

It was nauseating to see the beggar, so he said, "Please get out of here. Don't come in.

For a moment he hesitated, but then he thought: "How can this leper be Sai Baba? Compared to this leper even the dog was better to look at, he seemed nice and healthy.

In the evening he went to Sai Baba again and said, "I waited for you and the dog, but you didn't come".

Sai Baba replied, "I came, but you could not stand the stench. You threw me out.

The man began to cry and said: "Give me another chance.

Sai Baba said: "Even if I come a thousand times you cannot

recognise me. You can recognise me only when you are awake; only then is it possible.

Singing the song of the divine means that everything you see will become a song of the divine.

Anything from anywhere will become a message - when the breeze blows it is your memory, the sound of the waterfall is your memory, when the birds sing it is your memory, if there is silence it is your memory. The noise is his, the silence is his, the market is his and the emptiness of the Himalayas is his. His remembrance, his message, comes from everywhere: the flower, the leaf, the stone, everything reminds you of the divine. His memory will surround you everywhere; whenever you look into someone's eyes you will see the divine.

And this is not imagination or poetry, it is a fact, because it is looking from all eyes. If you haven't seen him, it's your fault. If you have not recognised, it is your stupidity, but he is looking from all eyes. Go back and look into the eyes of your wife or look into the eyes of your son. Soon you will realise that the child disappears and the formless is there. Wherever you look deeply you will find mercy. But you will still miss the inner world as long as your sight is shallow.

LIFE IS AS TRANSIENT AND UNSTABLE AS A DROP ON A LOTUS LEAF.

This must be well understood: that the world suffers from the disease of the ego and is sick with unhappiness. So, O IDIOT! SING ALWAYS THE SONG OF THE DIVINE.

Nothing is stable here. Everything flows, everything changes. So don't make a building on the unstable. Even sand is more stable than this. This world is like the flow of water: don't build on it, otherwise you will regret it. Seek the stable, the permanent. Always look for the one who is stable in this flow.

A wheel turns with the movement of the vehicle, but the axle does not move. So look at the axle, you will find the divine in the axle. The wheel signifies the world; that is why we call it sansar chakra, the wheel of the world. The wheel keeps moving, but the axle, on which the movement of the wheel depends, is stable. The existence of the unstable depends on the stable. Even a lie has to depend on the truth to exist. A seer is needed for a dream to exist; otherwise a dream cannot be dreamt.

LIFE IS AS TRANSIENT AND UNSTABLE AS A DROP ON A LOTUS LEAF.

Don't get too entangled with life, otherwise you will regret it and be unhappy. Nothing stops here; even if you want to stop it, it will not stop. Everything flows. You are young, but this youth will pass. You will try to hold on to it, but you won't be able to. Then you will regret it because you will have spent time in the effort to hold on to it. Today it is this body; tomorrow it will perish. Many such bodies have existed and perished. The world is transient, unstable and ever-changing. Don't make this your home, this is only a night shelter. One spends the night here and has to leave in the morning. If you have settled here, you will be unhappy, that is why you are unhappy.

People ask me: Why are we unhappy? You are unhappy because you are building your house where it cannot be built. You don't see where it can be built or where it is already built. You are unhappy because you are looking in the wrong direction. Unhappiness is the result of being associated with the wrong, of being in the company of the wrong. To be in the company of truth is happiness.

Your family will love you as long as you have the energy to earn money. When you grow old and your body weakens, no one will care about you. Therefore, O IDIOT! ALWAYS SING THE SONG OF THE DIVINE. If you have to have a family, make it with the divine. If you have to marry, marry with the divine. The marriages of this world are nothing but divorces. All the relationships of this world are superficial. There is no depth in them.

Mulla Nasruddin was in love with the daughter of a billionaire. He used to tell her: "I can live or die, but I cannot leave you. If ever I have to, I will die for you.

One day the girl was very sad. She said to Nasruddin: "Listen, my father has gone bankrupt".

Nasruddin said: "I knew that your father would create some trouble to prevent our marriage".

The very reason they were getting married had disappeared.

This is your kind of relationship. You don't mean what you say. You cheat most of the time and sometimes you also cheat yourself. You don't only deceive others, but also yourself.

Man is very cunning; he deceives even himself.

Family members keep asking about your welfare as long as there is life in the body. When the body becomes lifeless your own wife becomes afraid of that body. Therefore, O IDIOT! ALWAYS SING THE SONG OF THE DIVINE.

It is better to be in the company of those who can always be with you. The company of those you meet for a short time while travelling together or while crossing a river by boat does not count for much. Such company is momentary: for some time travellers are together, they move together, but soon each goes his own way. Don't make too much of this. In this world people are together for a short time. It is like meeting someone in a dream. When the dream ends, the meeting will end.

A CHILD IS OBSESSED WITH GAMES, A YOUNG MAN IS OBSESSED WITH YOUNG WOMEN, OLD MEN ARE OBSESSED WITH WORRIES. MAN NEVER TURNS TO THE DIVINE.

SO, O FOOL! ALWAYS SING THE SONG OF THE DIVINE.

Childhood is spent in play, in games; youth is spent in the game called love; old age is spent in the worries of the old days, in thinking of the past, and all life is wasted in this way. The divine is never remembered. We keep postponing until tomorrow, and tomorrow brings death. We hardly ever remember the inner world until we die.

OH IDIOT! ALWAYS SING THE DIVINE'S SONG... before death comes. Every time you are a little conscious, wake up. Think, what are you doing? What are you involved in? What is the result of your actions? Your actions, your money, your reputation will be worthless in the end. So don't spend too much time on what is going to be useless. The sooner you wake up, the better.

You cannot be in love with the divine until your infatuation with life is over. If you are too infatuated with life you cannot recognise the divine. How can you recognise the formless if you are obsessed with form? You cannot understand the formless with a materialistic attitude. If you look at the earth all the time, how can you see the sky? You cannot get rid of your infatuation until you wake up and realise that this infatuation is the cause of your misery. The essence of life is misery.

All temptations of happiness end in misery. All hopes of happiness end in misery. All plans to achieve happiness are as futile as the plan to get oil from sand. You are left empty-handed. If you are willing to go away empty-handed from this world, then there is no need to remember the inner world. But then you will go away crying. If you want to leave here fulfilled, then the sooner you remember the divine, the better. You should spend as much time and effort as possible in remembering it; that is virtuous, that is the only thing that can realise you. But you don't bother to remember and you go on worrying about things that can never fulfil you.

Mulla Nasruddin's wife was about to die. She was lying on the bed. She opened her eyes and asked him: "Do you really mean that you will go mad if I die?

Nasruddin said: "I will certainly go mad if you die".

The wife laughed and said: "You are lying, I know you will

remarry after my death.

Nasruddin said: "It is true that I will go mad, but not to the extent of remarrying".

If you look at this life carefully you will not want to be born again, you will not want to remarry, because from them you have gained nothing except misery. The quest of the East is how to free oneself from this cycle of birth and death. Those who have seen life in the right perspective, their only desire is how to get rid of this life.

I have heard that when a unique sannyasin named Bodhidharma went to China with the Buddha's message, Emperor Wu said to him, "I do not have much time. My kingdom is vast; I cannot spare time to be with you any longer. Please tell me in a few words what is the most valuable thing in life? What is the greatest fortune?"

Bodhidharma said, "You will not be able to understand ...... The greatest good fortune is not to be born.

Wu was shocked: what a thing to say! Is it fortunate not to have been born? But Bodhidharma is talking about good fortune. Buddhas certainly wish not to be born again.

Bodhidharma said, "But this is not possible now, for you are already born. But the next good fortune for you is to die as soon as possible". It is said that Wu never went to see him again.

I also want to tell you the same thing, that the best luck would have been not to be born, but since you have already been born, the next best thing is that you can die while you live. Let the attraction to life end.

The meaning of dying while alive is to live as if you were not alive. Sit in the market, but as if you were not there. Take care of your wife and children as if you were not there. Absent yourself and you will soon discover that your absence is not empty; pity will appear little by little.

OH IDIOT! SINGS THE SONG OF THE DIVINE.

Enough for today.

The attraction of the transient

The first question:

Question 1:

BELOVED MASTER, SHANKARACHARYA TEACHES METAPHYSICS AND AT THE SAME TIME SINGS THE SONGS OF GOVINDA. IS THERE ANY INTERRELATION BETWEEN KNOWLEDGE AND BHAKTI, DEVOTION?

Knowledge is negative, devotion is positive. Knowledge is like preparing the soil by removing the weeds and weeds and then pouring the manure, and devotion is like sowing the seed.

Knowledge in itself is not enough. It cleanses the soil but does not sow the seeds (it cannot be sown). It is necessary but not sufficient, for knowledge is of the mind and devotion is of the heart. All obstacles in the way of the divine can be removed by knowledge. But the rungs of the ladder can only be climbed with devotion. That is why knowledge is negative. It is very effective in eliminating the meaningless, but it is not capable of creating the meaningful.

Shankaracharya speaks of knowledge so that the layers of ignorance accumulated within you can be cleansed. And once the soil of the mind is cleared of all wild grass and unnecessary plants, the seeds of devotion can be sown. Then it is possible to sing the song of the divine.

There is no contradiction between the two. Devotion is the culmination of knowledge and knowledge is the beginning of devotion, because man has both heart and mind, and both have to be addressed, both have to be transformed. If you get stuck only in knowledge then you will be like a desert - very clean but nothing will grow there; clean but without seeds; vast but without any height or depth.

Knowledge is dry and lonely. And if you remain a devotee, a bhakta only, then there will be trees, flowers and greenery in your life, but you will not know how to protect that greenery. You will not be able to protect those plants. If someone puts the seeds of doubt in your fertile soil, they will also sprout.

If a devotee has not gone through the process of knowledge, then his construction will be unstable.

Anyone can question him. He knows how to believe the believers, those who guide him along the way, and he believes even those who deceive him. He has no sense of discrimination and discretion. He clings to the wrong just as he clings to the right. The devotee is like a blind man and the pundit is like a lame man. If the two come together, then things work wonderfully.

I'm sure you've heard this story. A blind man and a lame man were trapped in a fire in the jungle. The blind man couldn't run away because he couldn't see. He had strong legs and feet and could save himself by running away, but he had no sense of direction. The lame man could see the path, he could see which part of the jungle had not yet caught fire, but he could not run away because he was lame. As the story goes, the two came together. The blind man carried the lame man on his shoulders. As they became one, they overcame their shortcomings. With the combined efforts of the blind man's feet and the lame man's eyes, they were able to get out of the jungle safely. The fire could not destroy them.

You cannot save yourself from the flames of life until the intellect and the heart are united. The intellect has eyes, but no feet; the intellect is lame. The heart has feet, but no eyes; the heart is blind. That is why it is said that love is blind. When they meet, there is perfume. When they unite, there is attainment, there is enlightenment, there is nirvana. If they oppose each other, both will destroy each other. Then it will be impossible to get out of the burning jungle. Alone, both are crippled. United, both become whole. And if you have both, you have to use them. Therefore, make knowledge a support of devotion; make devotion a support of knowledge.

You can fly in this sky if you make them your two wings. No bird can fly with one wing, no man can walk with one foot, nor can you row a boat with one oar; you need both oars. There is no contradiction, and those who have told you there is are wrong. They made this mistake because they did not know this great harmony. Either they were mind-dominated people who possessed only dry thoughts and logic and never experienced the dance of the heart, or they were heart-dominated people who could dance but had no understanding.

It will be a fortunate moment when you can dance with understanding. It will be a fortunate moment when you can love with understanding. And never reject anything that existence has given you, because if you do you will be incapacitated to that degree. You are complete, but everything has to be adjusted and matched properly. It is as if there is a musical instrument, a veena:

the ropes are there, and they have to be attached to the vein, tightened and adjusted.

Everything is within you but the coincidence is not there. The name of that coincidence that can adjust your inner vein and its strings is sadhana.

Sufis tell of a man who was starving. In his house there was flour, water, fuel, an oven, but he did not know how to knead the flour, how to light the fire and how to bake the bread. Everything was there, but he was hungry. The raw food was there. But these things didn't match, so he died of hunger.

This story applies to everyone. You have all the means but you are hungry. You have it all; existence sends everyone with all the means. But these means must be adjusted in the right proportions, the right harmony and the right music; only then will the light of the divine shine within you.

You must not allow yourself to be dominated either by the intellect or by the heart; your consciousness must flow like a river between these two banks. If you become the Ganges, the sea is not far away. But do not insist on flowing with the support of only one bank, for the support of both banks is needed. In the end both shores will be abandoned. But this end is possible only through that support. In the ultimate condition, in the ultimate realisation, there is neither devotion nor knowledge.

When a river flows into the sea, both banks disappear and the river becomes the sea.

Therefore, there are three types of people in this world. The first are the people dominated by the mind: philosophers, metaphysicians. They keep thinking and arguing but they get nowhere. Their life is filled with the dry sand of logic.

The second type are people dominated by the heart. They sing and dance a lot, but they do it without understanding or discretion. They do not do it out of freedom; it is a kind of madness or intoxication. The heart is like intoxication for those who have no conscience and no discretion.

The third type are those who have made full use of the mind and the heart and have gone beyond both.

Your goal must be the third. You must desire, you must aspire to this great transcendence.

In the end, the Ganges has to leave the two banks and flow into the sea. But don't be in a hurry, you have to reach the sea with the support of the two banks, and you can leave the banks as soon as you get there.

The second question:

Question 2:

BELOVED MASTER, RELIGIONS TRY TO DISINTEREST US FROM WORLDLY HAPPINESS BY SAYING THAT IT IS TEMPORARY AND TRANSIENT. BUT ISN'T THIS VERY TRANSIENCE THE CAUSE OF ITS ATTRACTION?

This is certainly so. Transience is the cause of attraction. And religions do not create detachment by saying that life is transitory. Religions say that all that is transitory will be followed by misery.

Transience is not the cause of detachment: misery follows transience like a shadow; the cause of detachment is misery. It is transience that attracts and invites.

As life goes by, the mind says: "Enjoy it as much as possible, it may end at any moment. No one knows when you will die. So make the most of every minute by enjoying it. Live as intensely as possible: not a moment should be empty. Suck it up, enjoy the possibilities of every moment".

Yes, transience is the attraction. Death is coming, so we cling to life. If death were not approaching, no one would cling to life. No one would have cared if happiness came and never disappeared.

The cause of attraction is transience. Everything that disappears quickly seems precious. The stone is not as precious as the flower because the flower blooms in the morning and withers in the evening. So you had better contemplate its beauty well and satisfy your eyes, because everything that has blossomed has already begun to wither. It won't be long before it does. The sun is already in the middle of the sky. The flower has begun to fade, half its life has passed.

That is why there is so much attraction to beauty. If beauty could remain forever, no one would care about it.

Another interesting point is that ugliness is more permanent than beauty. An ugly person remains ugly all his life, but a beautiful person does not remain beautiful all his life. He is beautiful for a while, in youth, and then he withers. Have you ever noticed that if a person is very beautiful, he withers quickly? The more delicate the flower, the more quickly it fades.

The mind keeps saying, "Hurry up, don't waste your time sitting and chanting in the temples. This can be done later. Enjoy now as much as you can". Not only the other is changing, your capacity to enjoy is also weakening day by day."

Indeed, transience is the cause of attraction. If things were permanent, no one would care about them. Maybe that's why you don't care about the inner world. It is eternal, so there is no hurry. It is not going to be lost, so we can keep postponing it until tomorrow. If not in this birth, it will be in the next, and if not in the next, then later still. Wherever you go, the divine will be at home. The mind says, "But these passing flowers of life, the beauty of the eyes, the rosy colour of the cheeks, this youth and your capacity to enjoy, all these are withering and weakening. So don't delay, enjoy them".

Indeed, transience is the cause of attraction. There is no attraction to anything that is eternal.

How can there be attraction in what is and always will be? Dreams always seem beautiful: they are over as soon as you open your eyes.

Religion does not try to create in you a feeling of indifference or detachment by saying that life is fleeting. In saying that it is fleeting, it tries to ask you the question: What will you do after that moment? After dancing for a moment you will cry. Life is fleeting; you will enjoy it for a moment, but afterwards you will regret it. You will be finished in this futile pursuit.

Just as children chase butterflies, you run after small pleasures that will tire you out completely, and one day you will fall down and die. You haven't really gained anything by running after the transient, you've only wasted your time, because all transient things wither before you even get them, flowers are dead as soon as you hold them in your hands. And by the time you bring them home, happiness turns to anguish.

The awakening of detachment is due to misery and distress. Religion says that you should try to see that momentary pleasure is followed by unlimited misery. And you also know very well that whenever you have found happiness, misery has followed. Whenever you were happy, later your eyes filled with tears. You fell whenever you were vain. Bad luck started as soon as you thought good luck was smiling on you.

Religion says that if you want happiness that is not lost and does not turn into misery, seek the eternal, the immortal, and awaken from this passing world. Time spent in dreams is time wasted. Seek the truth.

What is the definition of truth? The definition of truth is what always was, what always is and what always will be. The definition of untruth is what was not yesterday, but is now and will not be tomorrow. Falsehood means the existence of that which is momentary between two not - the illusion of being, between two not.

Think about it: if it is not on both sides, how can it be in the middle? That is why Shankara says that the world is maya, an illusion. The meaning of maya is that it was not yesterday, it is today and tomorrow again it will not be. So what is not at both ends cannot be in the middle either, even if it seems to be. How can "is" be born out of "is not"? And what is, how can it not be?

There was a time when you were not. Where were you before you were born? Where will you be after death? It is only a short-lived dream. You see the dream while you sleep, but it is lost as soon as you wake up. Sahajo has said that this world is like the morning star. Yes, the morning star is there for a short time and disappears soon. It will disappear while you watch it.

Yes, all life is like the morning star.

Mahavira has said that life is like the dewdrops on the blade of grass. Have you noticed the dewdrop on the grass? It is about to fall at any moment; it will fall while you are still watching it, just a breath of breeze. It will evaporate with the sunrise. A little push of the breeze and it will disappear. But during its existence it is so beautiful that not even pearls can match it; even the pearl envies its lustre. But its existence is momentary, it is like non-existence.

If life is fleeting, it cannot be true. Whatever you have known, if it is then lost, then it cannot be true. It must have been the imagination of the mind or the projection of the mind. It is not the truth, but you believed it was. That is your belief.

Belief is an illusion. You are still seeing the projection of your inner desire on the screen of life.

Have you ever noticed that a woman or a man you think is very handsome at one moment is no longer so after a few days? It's the same woman or the same man? What happened? Actually, a few days before you had projected your own desire. Now that desire is gone, so there is nothing on the screen, no image on the screen. With the mind full of desire you cannot see what is; you only see what you want to see.

Only the pure eye can see what is. The impure eye sees what it wants to see. If you look for beauty, you will see beauty. Everyone has his own definition of life. Because of this definition, life is an illusion.

Mulla Nasruddin manufactures and sells medicines. He has written on a packet that he will refund the price of the medicine if it is not beneficial. I was sitting in his shop when a very angry man came in. He said, "I have been taking this medicine since last month, but it has done me no good, no benefit. So give me back the money I paid for it".

Mulla said: "It is written on the package that the money will be returned if it is not beneficial. Well, you may not have benefited from it but I have, so why should I return the money.

It all depends on one's definition. One sees life as one wants to see it. Consequently, the meanings of words and the meanings of truths change. One constructs one's own world of beliefs and continues to live in it. In order to maintain those beliefs, one finds one's own reasons to strengthen them so that they do not break down.

Mulla Nasruddin had an argument with someone in the market. The man got very angry and said to Mulla: "I will slap you so hard that all thirty-two teeth will fall out of your mouth.

Mulla was also furious. He said, "What do you think? If I slap you, your sixty-four teeth will fall out".

A third person who was watching this fight said: "My dear friend, you should know that a man does not have sixty-four teeth".

Mulla said: "I knew you would interfere. That is why I said sixty-four teeth. With one slap, all sixty-four of your teeth will fall out".

Man is like that. He cannot accept his own mistakes. He finds reasons and logic to justify his mistakes. Actually it takes a lot of courage to admit one's mistakes. If you admit the mistakes then gradually the mistakes disappear.

You are in love with a woman - you dream of heaven, you write poetry and you think you have reached heaven, but a few days later heaven disappears. You don't realise that it was you who made a mistake, you think it was the woman who deceived you. You don't see that your imagination, your conception has been broken. You don't realise that your idea, which was like the morning dew, has disappeared. You think that this woman has deceived you, that this woman was wrong. So now you look for another woman. You start looking for a new woman again. You will go on projecting your ideas, and again you will make the same mistake, you will have the same hangover!

Again the same dream that will be shattered again in a few days.

There is a very old and sweet story in the Mahabharata. The four Pandava brothers lived deep in a forest. One day they got lost; it was in the evening and they could not find water anywhere.

One of the brothers went in search of water and came across a lake. But as he bent down to get the water from the lake, a voice said to him: "Stop! You can't get the water until you answer my question".

He was a yaksha, a spirit, who possessed the lake.

"What is your question?" asked the Pandava.

The yaksha said: "If you do not answer the question or if you give a wrong answer, you will die immediately. But if the answer is correct, you will receive water and innumerable gifts from me". The question was: What is the greatest truth of man's life? But the answer - whatever it was - was not correct, so the first brother fell down and died.

One by one, the four brothers went in search of water and died. Eventually Yudhishthira followed them, wondering what had happened to them all. He found all four dead. Then the yaksha shouted: "Be careful! First answer my question, otherwise you will also die like them. You can drink water only on one condition: that your answer is correct, because my salvation depends on that answer. I will be free the moment I get the right answer; the bondage of being a yaksha will be broken.

The question is: what is the greatest truth of man's life?

Yudhishthira said: "The greatest truth is that man does not learn from his experiences".

The yaksha was freed from the curse. The four brothers came back to life: the yaksha was so happy to be freed that he revived all four of them.

Yes, men never learn from their experiences. He barely gets rid of one woman when he starts running after another. One problem is over and he is ready for another. He is always running after something or other. After satisfying one desire, he will desire ten more. He cannot see the illusion of desire. He never realises his mistake and justifies his every mistake with reason and logic. He holds another responsible for his own faults and then happily falls back into the same mistake.

To blame the other for your mistake is to set yourself up to repeat it over and over again.

Whenever you hold the other person responsible for your mistake, you are rejecting your own responsibility.

That responsibility could have woken you up, because in that moment of responsibility you could have realised that you were making a mistake.

There is no fault in any woman or man; the fault is in the desire or the imagination you projected on that man or that woman. That desire is fleeting, that desire will be broken. Think, how long can you keep a thought in your mind? Even the morning star remains for some time, even the dewdrop remains for some time. But how long can you hold a thought? It is there for a second and disappears. Even if you try to hold it, it disappears. You cannot catch it in your fist. Even if you run after it, you can't find it. It comes and goes like a breeze. The life you live in this world on the basis of such a mind is fleeting. Don't think that the world is transient, it is just a figure of speech. The world is not transient. The world was when you were not and will continue to be when you are not. The world is eternal. But the world you create out of your mind is transient.

In fact, there is no such world, there is only pity.

These images of your own desires that you make on the screen of existence, these images are the world, and that world is full of misery. Every day you suffer, but you keep waiting for the happiness that tomorrow will bring. Many times you fall down, but you get up again. Many times life tells you that you will never get what you are looking for, but you always find one excuse or another saying that now you will not repeat the same mistake; you will not make the same mistake anymore.

I heard that a prisoner was released from prison. He was there for the thirteenth time.

The jailer felt sorry for him - half his life had been spent in prison - so, on releasing him, he said, "Be sensible now and don't go back to prison again."

The prisoner replied: "Every time I try not to come here, but I come again and again. But this time I won't come back.

The jailer said: "I'm glad to hear this".

The prisoner said: "From your happiness you don't seem to have understood. I say that now I will not make the mistakes that got me caught. I do not say that I will not steal, but that I will not repeat the old mistakes that got me caught. I will not repeat the mistakes I made thirteen times. I will steal, but now I won't make any mistakes".

Actually, stealing is not the mistake; the mistake is getting caught! People who are sent to prisons come back as hardened criminals because they meet even bigger criminals. They learn all the tricks from them, benefit from their experience, train with them and return to crime.

It seems that it's not stealing that's bad, it's getting caught that's bad. Yes, think about it: if you are sure you won't get caught, will you steal or not? Your mind will say: "Why not?

Stealing is not bad, but getting caught is". You will sink into misery if you keep thinking like that.

For in reality misery is not in being caught but in being a thief; misery is in stealing and not in being caught.

If you could see that misery is in my being wrong, then you would realise that misery is because I am wrong. This is the meaning of the theory of karma. It means that if you are in misery it is because of your own actions, and if you are happy it is because of your own actions.

If you want bliss, you have to go beyond actions: where there is neither happiness nor misery, you are beyond both. There is absolute peace and your inner balance is absolutely right, just as when both sides of the scale are balanced, they are on the same line. In the same way, when you have the capacity to go beyond happiness and misery, you attain supreme bliss.

Religion does not try to detach you from the world by calling it transitory. By calling it transitory is meant: Don't lose yourself in happiness; distress quickly follows. As soon as happiness comes, misery enters through the other door and sooner or later you will meet misery.

The attraction is to the transient, not to misery. If you are able to see the misery behind every happiness, then a revolution will take place. You will try to free yourself not only from misery but also from happiness. If every pleasure is definitely followed by misery, then one has to be free from pleasure as well as misery.

This is the difference between a sannyasin and a householder. The householder wants to be free from misery and cling to pleasure. The sannyasin has understood that every pleasure is followed by misery. He wants to be free from both misery and pleasure. And whoever wants to be free from both can certainly be free from both, but whoever wants to be free from only one of them cannot be free from it. It is as if you have a coin in your hand and you want to get rid of one side and keep the other side. That is not possible. Either you keep the whole coin with its two sides or you lose the whole coin. Either happiness and misery disappear or both remain. If this kind of clarity comes into your life, only then will there be non-attachment, only then will there be sannyas.

The third question:

Question 3:

BELOVED MASTER, YOU HAVE SAID THAT WHEN THE SELF SURRENDERS, ALL EXISTENCE THEN

PROTECTS. THEN WHY WAS THE FAKIR WHO COULD SEE THE FORMLESS EVERYWHERE, OR WHO COULD FEEL THE PRESENCE OF DIVINITY EVERYWHERE, KILLED BY THE ENGLISH SOLDIERS?

It looks like murder to you, but not to him. You see it as murder because you are under the illusion.

He saw only the divine in that spear; he saw that death was an encounter with the divine. Existence protected him in the sense that even death did not seem like death to him. Death became the gateway to ultimate bliss. It seems to you that he died, that he was finished.

When the Ganges flows into the sea, it seems to you that it is finished. But ask the Ganges: it will say: "I have disappeared and so I have become the sea". The Ganges will say, "Once there was the fear of annihilation, but now it has disappeared. Before it was very narrow, bounded by the two banks. I could have been finished. I was limited, so I could have died. But now I have become unlimited, now there is no death. The Ganges has become the sea.

Ask that sannyasin: he saw the divine even in that soldier, even in that murderer. Even in that spear he saw the arrow of the divine piercing his heart. It looks like death to you, but not to that sannyasin.

He reached the ultimate life.

You asked: "You said that when the ego surrenders then the whole existence protects".

It will not really protect you, and if you try to surrender to get this protection then this surrender will not be true, it will not be real. Surrender means that there is no one left in me who can be protected.

If you think, "Existence will protect me, so I will surrender," then you are not surrendering at all, you are only appointing the divine to your service. Surrendering means that now I am not me, only you are; now there is no question of my protection. Now you are just a plain sky, an empty house. There is nothing left to finish. I am finished long before you. The meaning of surrender is that I am finished; now there is no need for you to finish me. I will not give you that job, I will do it myself.

The real meaning of surrender is suicide. The suicide that you consider suicide is only the death of the body. The soul does not die, only the body dies and a new body is acquired. But in reality, surrender is suicide. You destroy your ego. You say to it, "Now I am not, only you are". Now there is no question of your protection. Who are you now, from whom do you want protection? And when you don't exist, only then the whole existence protects you. Now it is no fun to annihilate yourself, what is the point? When you annihilate yourself, death becomes meaningless.

When the spear pierced the sannyasin's chest, the soldier must have thought he had killed him. It must have seemed to the onlookers also that he had died, but ask that sannyasin: he announced: "Tattvamasi - you are that too". He said, "You can come in any form but you cannot cheat me, I will recognise you. Today you have come with a spear and enacted the drama of death, but I recognise you, I am looking at you. You can come disguised as an enemy or as a friend, I will recognise you in any situation."

The sannyasin did not die. His Ganga had become the sea.

But I understand your difficulty. Even when you do the right thing, you do it for the wrong reasons; your reasons are not right. Even if you go to the temple it is for the wrong reason. Someone goes there asking for a job, someone goes there asking for money, someone goes there asking for a wife and someone goes there asking for a child. Don't you realise that you never go out of the market. Is that how you go to the temple? You take the whole market with you to the temple. If you are like that, the temple will not be able to purify you, you will defile the temple.

The temple is not a place, it is a state of mind. There can be no temple as long as there is demand.

You keep asking for insignificant things that are available in the market, as if it were a supermarket.

You couldn't get these things in the shops, so you want to get them in the temple. You couldn't get them in this world, so you'll get them in heaven! But why do you ask?

Only the person who has realised that asking for anything is in vain, who has realised that asking gets nothing but misery; who has realised that in spite of all efforts the beggar's bowl remains empty, it is never full, can reach the temple.

Only that person comes to the temple who goes there not to ask, but to be grateful. The day you are full of gratitude - flowers bloom and you are grateful, it rains from the clouds and you are grateful, a child cries for joy and you are grateful, even your breath, your being is so peaceful that you feel grateful - this state of gratitude, this feeling of gratitude that is within you day and night is actually the song of the divine. There is no need to chant: one does not become devoted by chanting. Devotion is the continuous inner state of mind. The day you realise that existence has given you more than you deserved, will you go and thank it or ask for more? You have not even earned what you have. It has showered its grace upon you, it is in abundance so it has distributed it, but it has not given it to you because you deserved it.

People ask me: "Why did God create the world? They think that this creation must be out of some desire, because we don't do anything without desire. Even an ordinary man has a reason to make a small house. Then why has God made this whole world?

And it's not just ordinary people who think like that. Someone asked the great German musician Wagner: "Why have you created such marvellous music?

He replied: "I was unhappy. So to keep me busy, to keep me

involved, I created this music". And Wagner said: "I tell you that God must also have been unhappy to create this world". What Wagner says is true about man. Man writes poetry to cover his wounds; to hide his tears he sings, he smiles so as not to cry; he walks merrily along the road because his inner poverty hurts him.

Others must not know your inner poverty, so to fool them you smile. When someone asks you: "How are you?", you answer: "I am fine, I am happy". Have you ever thought about what you are saying?

You, and happy? But of course you have to say this, otherwise it doesn't look good. Saying this is just a formality. You don't have to tell the truth. You only say the words that are appropriate and not the truth.

Each one has different masks on his face and hides behind them deep anguish and hell.

You have to do a thousand and one things to forget that hell. Someone paints... look at Picasso's paintings. It seems as if anguish and misery are spread everywhere. There is a very famous painting by Picasso called "Guernica". It's nothing but madness spread out. You will go crazy if you look at it for half an hour.

Wagner is right in saying this about man: that man is in misery, therefore he creates. But this is absolutely wrong about existence. The world was not created for any reason. That is why in this country we call creation leela. Leela means without any reason; leela means play; leela means energy is so much! - What else to do? The bliss is so much that it overflows, so it has to be distributed. There is so much water in the lake that it overflows, not for any reason, just because it is too much, so it has to be distributed. When the flower is full of fragrance, it opens and the fragrance flows. In the same way godliness flows in this world: it has so much in abundance, it has so much left over that there is no choice but to distribute it.

Creation is bliss and not anguish, but you are mean even to give thanks. It has given you eyes that you may see beauty; it has given you ears that you may hear music; it has given you hands that you may feel the touch of life; it has given you mind that you may understand; it has given you heart that you may rejoice; it has given you life that your life may become a great festival. But you are stingy even to give thanks. When you go to the temple you don't even say, "You have given me so much without any reason. If you had not given it to me, we would not have complained even if you had not created us. In what court could we have complained that you had not created us? What you have given us is too much. We did not deserve it.

The meaning of prayer, the meaning of Bhaj Govindam, singing the song of the divine, is that you are singing from your bliss. You are saying, "You have given us too much and it will be discourteous on our part if we cannot even thank you".

But whenever you go to the temple you will always complain: "My son is sick, why hasn't he recovered yet?

My son has no job, are all our prayers and devotion in vain? Why don't you hear anything? Are you deaf?".

Whenever you go to the temple you are always going to complain. Going with a complaint means that you have never entered the temple, you have stayed outside the temple. If you are asking for something, then you cannot enter the temple. Only those who are going to give thanks enter. Even your giving is with the motive of asking for protection. Who are you, that you need protection? You want even the divine to be your bodyguard. You want him to stand near you with a weapon to protect you.

Surrender means, I have nothing worth saving in me; I surrender my emptiness at your feet. And in surrendering you don't feel that you are doing something great. You simply return to existence what he had given you: "Your gift is returned to you".

But what else do you do? You must return it after you have soiled it some more. There are very few blessed ones like Kabir who can say that they have returned the sheet as clean as it was. Certainly it is very difficult to keep the sheet clean, because it always gets a little dirty. So when you offer yourself at the feet of the divine, you do not do so in the hope that he will be pleased with this act and be grateful to you. In fact, you will feel sorry that you have soiled the sheet; you will feel bad that you have not returned to him only what he gave you. You will say, "I am not even giving you back only what you gave me, I could not add anything to it, I could not fill that sheet with pearls and diamonds". At that moment the whole existence protects you.

Do not surrender to seek protection. The essential outcome of surrender is protection.

The fourth question:

Question 4:

BELOVED MASTER, THERE IS AN EMPTINESS SO INTENSE WITHIN ME THAT I FEEL EVEN MORE FRIVOLOUS THAN THE DUST BEFORE MY VERY EYES. AND WHEN THERE IS NO CAPACITY LEFT I CANNOT BELIEVE THAT GOD WILL EVER SIT ON THIS EMPTY THRONE. BECAUSE OF THIS FEELING LIFE SEEMS INSECURE. IT SEEMS THAT I HAVE NOT ARRIVED ANYWHERE. I AM NEITHER HERE NOR THERE.

"There is such an intense emptiness inside me that I look worse than dust in my own eyes".

If emptiness becomes so intense, then you will not be aware of your being. Then you will not be able to say that emptiness has become intense within me; you will only say "emptiness has occurred". You will not be able to say "within me", because as long as you are, emptiness cannot be.

You are full of yourself.

And you say that you feel more frivolous than dust in your own eyes. Who told you that dust is insignificant? Who taught you this condemnation? You are made of this dust and in the end you will end up in this dust, and you say that dust is insignificant.

Man's ego is marvellous. Just because dust remains under his feet he thinks he is insignificant. But this very dust is your heart and mind. Every particle of your body is made of this dust. The earth is the mother. You came out of it and you will return to it.

"More frivolous than dust" - this language of 'great' and 'frivolous' is the language of the ego. The day you empty yourself you will see the divine in every particle of dust and it will no longer seem insignificant. Then nothing will be insignificant because he is great, he is present everywhere and in everything and in every way. Then you will kiss even the dust and see his feet there.

The dust is insignificant? This is your ego talking. There is no emptiness inside you yet. You have only thought about it. Man is very clever in thinking. If one becomes empty then there is nothing left to do.

And you ask "when there is no capacity left....". What kind of capacity can there be? In order to attain the divine, the question of capacity does not arise. If capacity is necessary to attain the divine, then it is like getting a government job. Then Kabir could never have got it; he was illiterate and had no certificate. Even Muhammad could not have got it; he could neither read nor write.

When Muhammad heard the echo of God for the first time he became nervous. He began to tremble and became feverish, because he thought: "How can God shower on me? Impossible. There are so many capable people in this world, how can he choose me? Impossible! I must be under some illusion.

At that moment a voice rang out: "Lee". Mohammed said: "This is crazy. I can't read or write.

He came home, covered himself with a blanket and went to sleep.

His wife asked him: "What happened? You were fine when you left here in the morning.

He said: "I have the illusion that the voice of God has spoken to me. But it can't be: I don't have the capacity.

But this was capacity. As long as you think you are capable, you are incapable. Until then the obstacle is there, until then the ego is there. Capacity means ego. You are in front of the temple and not in front of the labour exchange. Here certificates will be of no use. In fact the more certificates, the more difficult it will be to enter the temple. Only the incapable can enter there.

You must understand well what I am saying, because you are so deluded that you can make even incapacity a capacity. You will say: "I am incapable, why has God not known me yet? You can make incapacity look like capacity. No, the meaning of denying capacity is that you cannot claim the divine; you cannot ask Him why you have not been able to reach Him yet.

Any pretension is ego. If you don't reach it, you know there is no reason for you to reach it. But if you do reach it, you will dance out of gratitude, because you reached it for no reason, only by its grace.

Capacity means that you have confidence in yourself and not in the divine. Capacity means you are also willing to buy it. Capacity means you are saying I have acquired all the virtues, so why is there this delay? I have prayed, I have worshipped, I have lit so many clay lamps, burnt so many incense sticks, offered so many flowers at your feet. I have fasted, meditated and subjected myself to so much austerity. I have done all this, but you have not yet come. Through these words your ego is announcing: "I have earned it and he is being unjust to me". You have come to other people who have done nothing. You have come to those who have no claim on you and you have not come to me". This very claim is the obstacle.

Only those people have attained godliness who have renounced all pretension. They say, "We are very insignificant, very small, so whatever we do will be insignificant, very ordinary; we are ordinary.

We cannot reach it by doing anything or by our own efforts; our doing is like trying to grasp the sky with our hand. A sky so vast and a fist so small.

It is so ridiculous: you can only achieve mercy when you accept your worthlessness and helplessness in its entirety. Then you become an empty vessel claiming nothing. Only the one who does not harass the divine to come to him and merely waits can attain divinity. Even to say that you have to come to me is selfish.

You write: "And when there is no capacity left I will not be able to believe....".

If there is no capacity, belief will arise at that very moment. Even now there is some capacity.

You are actually thinking that your so-called intense emptiness is your capacity. You say you have become more insignificant than dust; you think that is your capacity. Now you are waiting for him and if he does not come to you, you think he is being unjust to you. "I have done so much and still you have not come. It is too much.

Remember, the divine dawns in your emptiness. That is the condition. When you are totally empty then there will be no delay. As soon as you empty yourself, the divine will appear. These two things happen simultaneously.

So what you think is emptiness is just a thought of your mind. Beware of the tricks of the mind. The mind is very cunning, very efficient, very calculating. It does everything with complete calculations and keeps track of everything, even religion. Beware of this mind.

It is this mind that says, "I am neither here nor there". Well, what's the need to be here or there, what's wrong with being in the middle? But you think you have gained neither the divine nor this world. I have understood what you mean. The ambition to attain this world is still suppressed in you, therefore you are neither here nor there. Otherwise, freedom exists in the middle. What difference does it make to the washerman's donkey whether he is tied up at home or on the river bank? In fact, there is some freedom in the middle: he can run away from there because the washerman is at home in both places.

The mind says that if the time spent in meditation had been spent doing business, some money would have been made, or "I would have become a leader by standing for election".

The whole world is busy doing one thing or another and I am meditating. I am not attaining the divine and I am also losing the world".

This thought arises only because you still have attachment to this world. Therefore, you had better go back to the market because your sannyas will not be real and your meditation cannot be real either. Your attraction for money is still there. You are only curious about meditation. You are not thirsty, you are not yet a seeker.

That's why I say it's better for you to go back to the market rather than sit back and think that existence is being unfair to you. Maybe it is not yet time; you are not yet ripe. You are raw. To become mature, you will have to go through a lot of misery and anguish. You haven't suffered much yet.

When a person has suffered all his life, when he has experienced only unhappiness in life, then he comes to the conclusion that there is nothing worth gaining in this world. Then he says: "Now it does not matter whether I find the divine or not, but one thing is clear, that I will gain nothing from this world. As for the attainment of godliness, it does not matter now and the question of going back to the world does not arise - that door is closed, that bridge is broken, that ladder has been pulled down so the question of going down does not arise.

The fifth question:

Question 5:

BELOVED   MASTER,   SHANKARACHARYA
EMPHASISES THE SENSE OF INDIFFERENCE, THE

NON-ATTACHMENT TO MALE AND FEMALE BODIES. BUT IN THIS ASHRAM YOU APPROVE OF THE FREE MIXING OF MEN AND WOMEN. PLEASE SAY SOMETHING ABOUT IT.

For you to grow up, for you to grow up... I don't want to separate you from the world. I want to set you free from this world.

Detachment and release are two different things. Detaching is like plucking the raw fruit and releasing is like the falling of the ripe fruit. Outwardly they are similar because in both cases the fruit is detached from the tree, but there is a basic difference between them. When a raw fruit is plucked, the pain of being plucked remains in the fruit and there is also a wound left on the tree. There is no need to pluck the ripe fruit; the ripe fruit falls off by itself without any pain, without any longing to be with the tree a little longer. When the fruit ripens, the work of the tree is completed, so there is no pain left in the tree. A ripe fruit absolutely forgets the tree, it doesn't look back. And after the fruit falls the tree also becomes lighter, it is not hurt.

I do not want to separate you from this world because he who is deliberately torn away from this world remains attached to the world. You must be free from this world and you must not be torn away from it. And where can you go after a forced break? You have a wife, children, family, a shop. Even if you leave them, where will you go? You can go anywhere, but if the shopkeeper remains in your mind, you will open a new shop! It won't make any difference.

If the attraction to women remains in the mind, then running away from your wife will not help you; some other woman will attract you. If you are interested in money, giving it up will not make any difference. You will start collecting coins in some other sense - maybe this time the coins will be of renunciation and austerity, but coins are coins. You will start amassing another kind of wealth. First you used to announce how much money you had. Now you will announce how much you have renounced. Your vanity will remain the same. I want to free you from the world; I do not want to separate you from it. In this commune I try to make you free to live.

If you can be free while you live in this life, then that is true freedom. You walk on water, but your feet must not get wet. You must be like the lotus leaf: you can touch the water, but the water will not touch you. You live in the water, but you are free from it.

The ultimate conception of sannyas is: sannyas is not non-attachment, vairagya, as opposed to attachment, raga. Sannyas is beyond attachment and non-attachment. It is veetragata, beyond attachment and non-attachment.

The sannyas that Shankaracharya talks about is non-attachment. But the sannyas I am talking about is veetragata, beyond attachment and non-attachment. Shankara sannyas will not take you very far. After Shankara sannyas, you will still have to search for the sannyas I am talking about. Shankara sannyas can be the beginning of the journey, not the end. What I am telling you is the end.

I don't tell you to run away from a woman; I say, "Wake up from attachment to women". I don't say, "Give up money"; I say, "Understand money". In that understanding is freedom.

Money does not hold you back, it is you who holds it back. It is your inner condition, it is your attraction. You can only free yourself from this attraction when the experience of life tells you that it is useless. If you don't learn from the experience of life, then you can go on thinking in your mind, "It's useless, what's in the world? But deep down, somewhere in the back of your mind you will think, "Who knows, maybe there is something worthwhile in this world and I have given it up. Maybe I've made a mistake.

Many sannyasins have come to see me, some in their seventies or eighties. They say: "Sometimes we wonder if we have wasted our lives because we have not attained the divine and have renounced the world also. So now this doubt wavers in the mind.

This doubt arises because you fled the world when you were

still attracted to it. You didn't leave the world because of your own experience, you left it because you were influenced by someone else.

When people like Shankaracharya and Buddha are in this world, their influence is unlimited and all-pervasive. Like magnets they attract thousands of people. Their life is beyond attachment and detachment.

They are quite right when they say: "This world has no meaning; there is no meaning in men, women and children".

They are like the ripe fruits of the tree. But hearing his words, the unripe fruits begin to think that, since they are meaningless, let us give up this world. They separate from the tree, then doubt arises because they don't even have the fragrance of the ripe fruit. The ripe fruit has a fragrance, its own smell; they don't even have that and they have already detached themselves from the tree. They have not related either to the earth or to the sky. They are hanging in the middle.

This was exactly the meaning of the previous question: "I am neither here nor there, I am hanging in the middle". This hanging in the middle is a very miserable condition. That is why I tell you that there is no need to run away from anything. Wake up wherever you are. Forget about leaving the world; call the divine, ask it to come and let it appear in your innermost space. As soon as its rays begin to penetrate you, you will begin to ripen. The sun ripens the fruits, existence ripens you.

And don't run away from life, because if existence has given you life there must be a reason for it. It is not a coincidence. There is total planning behind it, because no one can be free without going through the experience of life.

There is a great statement in the Upanishads which says: Ten tyakten bhunjeetha. I have not found a more revolutionary sentence than this in any scripture in the world. It is a unique statement. It has two meanings. The first meaning is: only those who renounce experience. The second meaning is: only those who experience renounce. Both meanings are very valuable; both meanings are really like the two sides of a coin. Only those who experienced renounced renounced: how can you renounce unless you experience it? The understanding of renunciation can only come through experience. The lotus of renunciation can only blossom from the mind of experience, there is no other way. So don't denounce the experience of pleasure, because the lotus will grow out of it. Don't condemn the experience, don't run away from the mud, otherwise you will be left without the lotus.

And how different the lotus is from the mud!

Divinity will arise in you, the lotus will blossom, how different is the divine from you! Even where you are living with your wife, your children, the shop, the market, one day suddenly the divine nectar will start flowing in you. All you have to do to get its nectar is to empty yourself. When you receive diamonds and precious stones, you will automatically get rid of the pebbles and stones. Don't insist on giving up, insist on receiving. But, of course, it is not certain that you will get diamonds and precious stones by simply throwing away the dirt and pebbles. But one thing is for sure, that after getting diamonds and precious stones no one accumulates dirt; it is automatically given up. And that giving up has a beauty of its own, it has a different music. Why? Because when you renounce without knowing that you are renouncing, then there is no trace of renunciation, then there is no pretence of renunciation.

Every morning you sweep the house and throw the rubbish out. Do you inform the newspapers that you have given up so much rubbish today? If you do, people will laugh at you. They will think you have gone mad. If it is rubbish, then throwing it out does not mean renunciation. And if it was not rubbish, then why did you give it up?

When you announce your resignation, you are actually saying

that I had money but I gave it up under someone's influence. You were not yet ready, you were not yet mature; you were still raw and you took the step in haste. Nobody is transformed by haste. I don't want you to be in a hurry. If you are attracted to women, live that experience. Enjoy it thoroughly. Ten tyakten bhunjeetha - renunciation will be born out of that indulgence. When you go on indulging and find that you have gained nothing from it, then you realise that with this indulgence you only get misery, nothing flourishes in life. Then indulgence has given you the key to renunciation.

Indulgence is not your enemy, it is your friend. My only condition is that you live indulgence with awareness. You must not go on experimenting without learning anything; experience must teach you a lesson. Experience is always worthwhile. Even going through hell is useful, if you do it fully awake, because in that wakefulness you find the way to heaven.

That's why I don't want to cut you off from life on any level. Stay where you are and sow the new seeds of consciousness in your heart. That is why I do not emphasise renunciation, but meditation.

I say nothing against the world, but I say much in favour of piety. Shankaracharya's emphasis is against the world.

The old conception of sannyas was that people should renounce the world in order to reach the divine. My idea is that people must come closer to the divine in order to renounce the world.

The last question:

Question 6:

BELOVED MASTER, MY MIND IS EXTREMELY SCEPTICAL. THAT IS WHY, IN SPITE OF ALL EFFORTS, IT DOES NOT SETTLE ANYWHERE. SINCE MY BIRTH I HAVE KNOWN ONLY THE MATERIAL - AND YOU SAY THAT EVERYTHING IS GODLINESS. SHOULD I BELIEVE IT?

IS IT HONESTY?

Just understand these words, "My mind is extremely sceptical ....".

You can be sceptical but not extremely sceptical, because an extremely sceptical person starts to doubt from doubt. That kind of doubt has not yet arisen in you. Your doubt is lame, rather impotent.

You have doubted, but you have not yet reached the climax of doubt. The climax of doubt is faith...

because when you keep on doubting everything, eventually you start doubting doubt. You start to think: "Will I get anything out of this doubt? Has anyone else got anything out of this doubt?

When you start doubting doubt, then it is the extreme of scepticism. But at that point doubt cuts doubt and a virgin faith is born.

You are sceptical but lame; you have not come all the way. If you were not lame you would not have come to me. There was no need to come to me to doubt, the whole world is there to doubt. In fact, you are tired without having completed your doubt, and now you want to have faith, that is why you have come to me. But you have come too soon, you should have waited a little longer. Keep doubting a little longer and remember, just as a thorn is removed by a thorn, so doubt is removed by doubt.

"My mind is extremely sceptical. That's why, despite all efforts, it doesn't settle anywhere".

No, it will not settle. Has any sceptical person ever achieved renunciation, meditation or realisation of the divine? No, because a sceptical person can do nothing. What he does with one hand, he takes away with the other.

I have heard:

A great thinker joined the army during the First World War. It was a compulsory conscription where everybody had to go to war, so he went too. But he became a problem because he was a great thinker, a philosopher, and he was always doubting. When his commander would order "Turn left", the whole regiment would turn left, but he would stand as he was, thinking whether he should turn or not.

His commander asked him: "What's taking you so long? Are you deaf? All the lines have moved but you are still here".

He replied: "Excuse me, but I don't do anything without thinking about it first, and thinking takes time.

First of all the question is: Why turn left? What is the need to turn? What is wrong with turning right? Just because it has been said: "Turn left", why do you have to turn left? I don't understand the purpose of all this turning left and right. What is the point of this parade? In the end we go back to where we were before. But I am already there. All these people will also come back here after all their left and right turns".

He was a famous thinker. So the commander realised that such doubts were his old habit and that he would be of no use in the army, so he was sent to the military kitchen. On the first day he was given peas and asked to separate the big ones from the small ones. When, after a while, the commander arrived, he was standing in rapt attention over the peas, just as they had been given to him. The commander said to him: "You couldn't even do this?

It is very difficult. There are large and small peas, but there are also medium-sized peas.

Where should they be placed? I don't start any work until everything is very clear. I was waiting for you to tell me what to do with these mediums".

This type of personality can do nothing. It cannot do any work. Every action is full of doubts, which destroy him like poison.

Meditation is the ultimate act. Meditation is the ultimate. At this moment you are hesitating. When you hesitate even to turn left, then turning is going to be very difficult.

"Since I was born, I have only known material things".

What you say is also wrong. If you were really a sceptical person then you could not have said that you have only known matter. True sceptics say: "Nobody knows whether matter exists or not". And it is not certain.

I am sitting here and you are listening to me. You may be dreaming: is it true that I am here and you are sitting there? In your dreams you have also seen people many times, so this can also be a dream. And have you ever seen matter? You are hidden behind the brain and the matter is outside the brain. Have you ever seen the matter inside the brain? You have never seen matter; only the images of matter enter the mind. Do you see the tree there? No, you have never really seen it.

The rays coming out of the tree fall on the eyes; these rays carry an image inside them. Just as an image is created in a camera, an image enters your brain. You have only seen that image. It is not certain that a tree like the one in the picture exists. There is no proof; there is no proof that the tree exists outside.

A person who doubts cannot even believe in matter, let alone the divine. But I tell you that it is difficult to know matter but easy to know the divine, because matter is outside and the divine is inside. The divine is near and matter is far away. You yourself are the divine and matter is the world.

The divine is not something that can be known. It is not an object to be known, it is the knower. You are that; it is your consciousness. It is that divinity that is doubting. Try to understand this:

if the one who doubts is the divine, how can you doubt him? - because the one who doubts is within. Even if you doubt, he is there.... because even to doubt is necessary. If he is not there, then who will doubt? Try to understand.

One evening Mulla Nasruddin returned home with his friends. As they were sitting in a hotel, one of them remarked: "You are a great miser.

Mulla said: "Who says that? I am a charitable person.

When the friends heard this, they said, "Well, if that's the case, you'd better invite us to your house today.

On hearing this Mulla replied: "Yes, let's go, let's all go". And a crowd of thirty or thirty-five friends accompanied him. But by the time he reached home he had realised his mistake. In his excitement he had forgotten that his wife was sitting at home; his wife didn't like to have a single guest at her house, and here were thirty-five people! So he said to his friends: "You are all men with families, you know the reality of a man; you must understand my problem. My wife is inside. You'd better wait outside, I'll go in first, I'll explain to her and then I'll call you all to come in. He went inside and closed the door, leaving them outside.

His wife lost her temper when she heard that he had brought so many people. She said, "There is no food, no vegetables, nothing to eat. Where have you been all day? You didn't bring the food from the market.

Mulla said: "You'd better tell me what to do. It's already dark, even the market is closed. How am I going to deal with these people?"

He said, "You brought this problem, so now you'd better deal with it".

He said: "Go and tell them that Mulla is not at home".

He came out and told them that Mulla was not at home. "How can that be," they argued, "He came with us. He came in and we never saw him leave.

Mulla was listening to the discussions and in his excitement forgot that he was inside. He looked out of the window and said: "Well, I might as well have gone out the back door.

You cannot deny yourself. Through the back door or the front door, you can't say you're not there. If someone knocks at your door you cannot say: "I am not at home". If you say it, it means you are, because even to deny yourself, you are needed.

The divine is not a thing, it is not a commodity. It is not outside of you, it is your inner being, your inner nature. It is your inwardness. It is your swaroopn, your being. But don't believe this just because I say so; that would be dishonest. You yourself must go in search of it. And you know, yesterday I was reading the words of a poem that I liked:

"Years went by; I didn't even remember you, But it's not that I forgot you".

"Centuries have gone by; I didn't even remember you, but I haven't forgotten you. The divine is like that.

The years may have passed, you may not remember it.... but you haven't forgotten!

It is just a matter of sitting with peace within and that is meditation.

The meaning of meditation is: to have inner peace and to know the all-knowing One. Be aware of your consciousness.

The divine is not sitting in the sky. It is surrounding your inner heaven. "You are the divine" - this is the announcement. You have to seek the essence of this sutra within you. You have not only to believe in me. When you find it, only then will you have faith in me. Your experience will give you faith. Your faith in me cannot give you the experience.

When you have a little fragrance inside you, then you will have faith in me, because then you will be able to understand what I say.

"Years went by, I didn't even remember you, But it's not that I've forgotten you".

Enough for today.

Loneliness through Satsang

WHO IS YOUR WIFE? WHO IS YOUR SON? THIS WORLD IS VERY STRANGE. WHO ARE YOU? WHO ARE YOU? WHERE DO YOU COME FROM? REFLECT ON THESE ESSENTIAL QUESTIONS.

FROM SATSANG COMES SOLITUDE, FROM SOLITUDE COMES DETACHMENT; DUE TO DETACHMENT THE MIND BECOMES STABLE AND DUE TO THE STABLE AND UNSHAKABLE MIND LIBERATION IS ATTAINED.

WHAT IS SEXUAL DESIRE WHEN OLD AGE COMES? WHAT IS A POND ONCE ITS WATER HAS DRIED UP? WHO IS THE FAMILY ONCE ITS WEALTH IS GONE? WHERE IS THE WORLD AFTER SELF-REALISATION?

TAKE NO PRIDE IN WEALTH, PEOPLE AND YOUTH, FOR DEATH TAKES THEM ALL AWAY IN A MOMENT. ABANDON ALL THESE ILLUSORY MATTERS, KNOW THE DIVINE AND ENTER INTO IT.

DAY AND NIGHT, EVENING AND MORNING, WINTER AND SPRING COME AND GO AGAIN AND AGAIN. SO GOES THE PLAY OF TIME AND ONE'S LIFE COMES TO AN END. AND YET THE BREEZE OF HOPE DOES NOT LEAVE ONE ALONE.

OH, MADMAN, WHY ARE YOU CAUGHT UP IN WORRIES ABOUT YOUR WIFE AND YOUR WEALTH? DON'T YOU KNOW THAT EVEN A MOMENT OF

COMPANIONSHIP WITH GOOD PEOPLE IS THE ONLY BOAT THERE IS TO CARRY YOU ACROSS THE OCEAN OF THIS WORLDLY WORLD?

Before beginning the sutra it is necessary to understand an essential complexity of the human mind.

Because of this complex many people, in spite of understanding, do not understand anything. Because of this complex they are saved from the abyss but fall into a pit. The mind prevents itself from going to one extreme, but in the process it goes to the other extreme.

Someone eats a lot: he is a glutton, his only interest is food. But one day or another, without anyone telling him, he will understand that he is torturing his body. The body will get sick and feel pain. It will not be difficult for him to realise that eating too much is unhealthy, but then the danger is that he will start fasting - from eating so much he may go to the extreme of giving up food altogether.

If the attachment to the world and to money is too strong, it is easy to run away from the world. Instead of interest there can be disinterest. Attachment can create detachment. Near and dear ones can seem like enemies instead of one's own people. There is hardly any difference between the two conditions. This is what it means to fall into a pit while saving oneself from the abyss.

These Shankara sutras are not meant to help you understand detachment, they explain the futility of attachment. If attachment loses its meaning, it is enough; if attachment disappears, it is enough. The disappearance of attachment is detachment, nothing else is needed except this. But the opposite is always the case. After reading these sutras many people, innumerable people, have taken hold of detachment without giving up attachment. Attachment continued but under the guise of detachment. First you were standing on your feet, now you are standing on your head, but nothing changes by standing on your head; things remain as they were. But when attachment stands on your head it becomes detachment - the detachment of ordinary people, the so-called detachment of the sannyasin. But when attachment disappears, then the detachment of Mahavira, Buddha and Shankara is born.

Mulla Nasruddin was mentally ill. Every time the phone rang, he would panic that his landlord had called to collect the rent or that his boss had fired him from his job - a thousand anxieties. Because of these imaginary fears, he couldn't even pick up the phone.

So I told him to consult a psychiatrist. He took the treatment for two or three months.

One day, when I went to his house, I saw him talking on the phone and he was not shaking. He was not afraid at all. So I asked him: "It seems that the treatment has been good for you, you are not afraid anymore?

Mulla replied: "The treatment has helped me more than necessary.

I asked him: "What do you mean by 'more than necessary'?

He said to me: "You know, I am very brave now. I pick up the phone and start talking even if it doesn't ring. I used to be scared when the phone rang. But when it didn't ring, I picked up the phone and started to scold the landlord. He got so scared that he was absolutely silent on the other end of the phone; I couldn't even hear him breathing.

This is the irony of human life. It is easy to go from one extreme to the other.

There is a Hindi proverb that says that a person who has burnt his mouth drinking hot milk is afraid even of drinking cold milk. Similarly, a person who is afraid of the world is also afraid of the divine. One who is burnt by the world is afraid of drinking the divine.

You have to detach from the world, but not out of fear. If you leave something out of fear, you won't really leave it, it will chase you, it will follow you. If you are afraid of something, it will scare you more. If you run away from something, it will follow you because the fear is inside you.

Where will you flee to, who will you flee from? If the world were outside, you could run away. But you will find the world wherever you go. Even in a Himalayan cave you will be the same "you" that lives there, the same "you" that lives here. So the real issue is not to change the place or the way of living; the real issue is to change the inner state of mind. At present, the state of your mind is tilted too much to one side. So don't tilt it too much to the other side.

The extreme is disease. He who balances in the middle is free, that is why Buddha has called his path majjhim nikaya, the middle way. He who remains in the centre has found the way.

A person who is in the middle, who doesn't lean one way or the other, is there. As long as you lean to one side life will be unstable, there will be no stability, you will not be healthy and you will keep wavering. Just as the light of the clay lamp goes on burning steadily in the middle undisturbed by the breeze, so when the light of consciousness becomes steady in the middle, when neither desire nor detachment is able to shake it, in fact when nothing shakes it - when it is neither on this side nor on that side, when it is steady right in the middle - then Krishna calls it stithapragya, one who has become steady in his wisdom. You sit, you stand, but within you no one sits or stands. You eat or fast, but within you no one eats or fasts. You can live in the world or in sannyas, but there is neither sannyas nor world within you. This last intermediate condition is detachment.

If detachment is the opposite of attachment, then it is wrong. But if detachment is freedom from attachment, then it is right. This is a very delicate difference. If detachment is the opposite of attachment then there is something wrong somewhere, because that which is the opposite of attachment is definitely connected with attachment. All opposites are interconnected. If you love someone, you keep remembering them. If you hate someone, you also keep remembering them. Love and hate are opposites but they are connected. You may be able to forget a friend, but you can't forget your enemy. It keeps pricking you like a thorn. You are related to the friend, just as you are related to the enemy.

Never think that an enemy is one with whom all relationships have been broken. No, if all relationships were completely broken, then he would not be the enemy. You do not have a friendly relationship with the enemy, but you have a relationship of enmity with him - the relationship is not broken. If the relationship is really broken then the friend is not a friend and the enemy is not an enemy. If the relationship changes, the friend becomes an enemy and the enemy becomes a friend.

How long does it take for a friend to become an enemy? It can happen in a moment. How long does it take to turn an enemy into a friend? Why doesn't it take a long time? - Because they are both relationships. It's just a matter of changing direction a little bit. You were going East - you turned West. You were going West and you've turned East. Both are movements, only the direction has changed a little bit.

I have heard that in England there was a great thinker called Edmund Burke. He was once invited to give a lecture in a church in a little village near London. But he was a very absent-minded person, so he very often used to forget the time and date of his lecture, and sometimes he used to arrive at the place the next day. But this time the host had insisted again and again that he should arrive at the church on time on the right date, so he too tried to be very careful about this invitation.

It was some church anniversary and I had to be there at seven o'clock in the evening.

He left his house at two o'clock. It was barely an hour's ride. He got on his horse and arrived at the church at three o'clock, but there was no one in the church at that time because the performance was to begin at seven p.m. What could he do? He took out a cigarette, put it in his mouth and tried to light a match, but because of the breeze he could not. He turned the horse so that he could light the cigarette. The cigarette was lit and the horse began to trot.

At four o'clock he was in front of his house. What had become of the church? Where had it gone? Then he remembered that in order to light the cigarette he had changed the direction of the horse. He had started smoking and the horse had turned towards his house.

This is only the difference in the change of direction. Any small incident, like lighting a cigarette, can be the reason for changing direction. Then a friend can become an enemy and an enemy can become a friend. You can turn from East to West or from East to West. Any small incident - one becomes bankrupt or one's wife dies or one's child dies - can make a person renounce the world and become a sannyasin. These incidents have as little value as lighting a cigarette, but they can change the direction. But this kind of renunciation will be false. This renunciation will be full of hatred and not of understanding. It will have a sense of failure, agony, and will be devoid of understanding and freedom.

There is another kind of renunciation in which you don't change direction. You don't turn your back on the world, you look at the world with care, with attention, and in looking at it with attention, the world disappears. In that realisation, in that state of meditation, we realise that all the relationships in the world are meaningless. Then we do not create any new relationship with the world. Until now our relationship with the world was one of attraction, but if we only change direction it will now be one of detraction; until now we were running towards the world and now we start running away from the world in the opposite direction. This kind of detachment is wrong. This becomes the new disease and you have to get rid of it too. This is not health. It is like a sick person who has recovered from his sickness but has become dependent on medicines. He carries his medicines with him everywhere. He is not willing to give them up.

Buddha used to explain this situation by telling the story of the five stupid men who crossed the river in a boat and then carried the boat over their heads. People would ask them why they did this.

They said: "We are very grateful to this boat. Thanks to her we crossed the river, so how can we give her up? We are not ungrateful.

They carried the boat to the marketplace on their heads. The people said to them, "This boat has taken you across the river, but now it has become a burden on your heads that you will carry all your life and you will not be able to do anything else".

The so-called sannyasins, mahatmas and saints you know, if you look at them closely, you will see that they have a boat on their heads! They gave up attachment but they took hold of non-attachment because they awakened the opposite of attachment.

What Shankaracharya is saying is something completely different. He is saying: "Watch attachment carefully, with discretion". In that state of awareness of true reality, the clouds of attachment will disperse - not that detachment will take their place.

Non-attachment is detachment; it is not the opposite of attachment. It is not that attachment disappears from your heart and detachment takes its place - attachment will disappear and nothing will take its place. This is the ultimate detachment.

So do not make a mistake in understanding these sutras, because this mistake is very easy to make.

WHO IS YOUR WIFE? WHO IS YOUR SON? THIS IS A VERY STRANGE WORLD. WHO ARE YOU? WHO ARE YOU? WHERE DO YOU COME FROM? REFLECT ON THESE BASIC QUESTIONS.

Shankara asks you to reflect, to contemplate, to awaken and to observe, with awareness. Do not be in a hurry to borrow detachment. Borrowing detachment will not do any good.

If right thinking creates the light of understanding in your heart, then attachment will disappear. So don't try to cast out the darkness - just light the lamp.

So Shankara says: "Who is your wife?" Yes, who is your wife? "Who is your son?" They are like strangers meeting on the road. Did you know your son before he was born? Did you call this son to be born from you? You didn't even know him, what were you going to call him? You didn't know his address. You didn't even recognise his face.

It's just a chance meeting between strangers. But the human mind creates illusions: "This is my son, this is my wife, this is my sister, this is my brother". How do you create these relationships? How?

It is a very strange fact. It is as if two strangers were walking on the same path.

They will walk together for a short time and then, after saying goodbye, they will go their separate ways, but in that short time all sorts of relationships will be established. There must be some other profound reason for this. These relationships are not true, because we are all strangers. Despite living together for years, we do not know each other.

Do you know your wife? You have lived with her for thirty or forty years, but do you think you know her well? Can you prophesy what she will do tomorrow? Even after living with your wife for forty years you cannot make a prophecy about what she will do in the next moment. A moment ago she was smiling, she was happy, and now she is angry. It is difficult for you to say what her mood will be in the next moment.

Does your wife know you? This "knowledge" is only superficial. No one can peep inside the other person. It is so difficult to even enter into oneself, how can it be easy to enter into the other? But there must be some deep reason why we establish so many relationships: because man is alone, because he is afraid of being alone, because he gets scared and worried when he is alone. It is very painful to be alone.

We are alone. The whole earth may be crowded, but each individual is alone. Even when you are in a crowd you are alone. This loneliness is unbearable and you want to get rid of it, so you create these relationships to forget yourself and your loneliness. For some time you feel that you are not alone.

Have you ever noticed it? If you walk down a dark street at night, the loneliness scares you and you start singing a song. Normally you don't sing when people ask you to because you are embarrassed, but at night, in a lonely street where the darkness is absolute, you start humming a song or whistling. What is the reason for this humming or whistling? While humming you hear your own voice and you feel that you are not alone, that someone is with you. Your own song creates the illusion that there is nothing to fear. The song gives you courage.

In solitude, a person starts to talk to himself. Psychologists say that if a person is absolutely alone for three weeks, he will start talking to himself. You also talk to yourself, but not out loud. If you watch someone carefully, you can see even the slight movements of the lips, because when you talk inside your lips move a little. But if you stay in a lonely place, the loneliness is so terrifying - to be alone in this vast world, to be alone in this great emptiness - that one begins to tremble.

So you start talking to yourself.

Have you seen crazy people talking to themselves? They are an enlarged copy of yourself. The difference between you and them is only in quantity and not in quality. You speak softly; they are a bit braver, that's why they speak loudly. The madman also talks to himself because he is afraid, he is nervous. He forgets himself by talking to himself. These are methods of self-forgetfulness, self-forgetfulness.

I was reading the memoirs of a German writer about his stay in Hitler's prison. He wrote that he was alone in his room, but that there was also a lizard. Lizards frightened him. He was very frightened when he saw them, but now, in prison, he was happy to see one. When he looked at it he thought: "I am not alone, there is someone with me", and little by little he began to talk to the lizard. Sometimes he laughed at his own madness. But he got so used to it that he felt as if the lizard was talking back to him. Then he spoke for himself and also on behalf of the lizard.

Man is alone, very alone. With this loneliness there are only two things you can do: either you make a world of your own or you enter sannyas. To make a world means to make relationships so that the loneliness can be forgotten. And the meaning of entering sannyas is to accept this loneliness because it is your nature. Don't run away from it, don't avoid it; accept it, embrace it. This is your nature.

You won't get anywhere by running away from it. You have done it in countless lifetimes and failed. You have gained nothing except failure.

Sannyas means: one who has accepted his loneliness - now he does not whistle, chant, or make any connection - he is absolutely satisfied with himself.

It is very interesting to note that the more you run away from yourself, the more you will have to run away, the more you will be afraid of loneliness. The more you accept being with yourself, the more you will discover that loneliness is not loneliness, but solitude. There is a difference between loneliness and solitude. Loneliness means that you miss the presence of the other. Being alone means that it is enough to be alone. Loneliness is painful but there is joy in being alone. When Shankara is alone, he is alone, but when you say you are alone, you are alone.

Being alone means that you feel the absence of the other.

Loneliness means that you are happy being with yourself. Loneliness means that you have fallen in love with yourself. Meditation means being in love with yourself. Meditation means to establish such a relationship with yourself that there is no need to establish a relationship with anyone else.

Meditation means self-realisation. Your world, your whole world is in you. You lack nothing. You are complete, you are everything, you are the divine, there is no need for you to go anywhere. This inner state means sannyas.

We make the world because loneliness hurts us. We try to fill this loneliness with money, with friends, with family, with religion, caste, nation. We make so many efforts to fill this inner emptiness because this wound is painful. But it is a mistake to think that it is a wound; it is not a wound.

Last night a sannyasin came to see me and told me that since she has started meditating her heart seems to have died. She has no desire to relate to anyone, she doesn't seem to be interested in love; even friendship seems to be meaningless. He was very sad... because he came from the West and in the West if love starts to disappear people think that all life is finished, if feelings disappear and relationships break down, then people think that now life is meaningless.

This is his definition. So I was sad.

We, in the East, have made a deeper investigation. We have discovered that when a person remains totally within himself, all relationships dissolve. It is a very fortunate thing to happen; it is not something to be unhappy about. When a person becomes stable within himself, sex dissolves and so does the urge to enter into relationships with others. The feeling of gratitude is so great that one does not want to relate to anyone. He will no longer beg others to have a relationship with him, he will no longer say "I can't live without you". Now he can live alone. And the person who can live alone, really lives! The other kind of life is just a delusion, an illusion.

If you cannot live alone, how can you live with others?

So I said to that young lady, to that sannyasin: "Don't be afraid, don't be unhappy. This definition of yours is wrong. This definition of the West is wrong. Be happy, be blissful; how fortunate you are because you don't want any relationship.

The relationship only gives you pain and anguish. This is also quite natural, because when two unhappy people meet, how can they give each other happiness? The mathematics is quite clear: when two unhappy people meet, the unhappiness is not only doubled, but multiplied many times over. You look for the other person because you are unhappy. You are not happy alone, so you look for the other person. The other person is not happy being alone either and also looks at you with the same expectation. So, two unhappy people meet in the hope of being happy. But they do not achieve happiness. It is not possible because two beggars are begging from each other and neither of them is a giver, both of them are beggars. Both of them are still waiting for each other. Whenever you love someone you expect them to love you back.

People say to me: "We give a lot of love to others, but others don't love us". How can you love? Love only flows from the heights of bliss. The river of love flows only from the heights of bliss. You are not happy, you are not blissful, you are begging, and the other person is also begging. Neither of you has anything to give to the other, but you keep expecting to receive some love in charity! While you are waiting, the disappointment begins.

Until a person is happy within himself, no one else can make him happy.

There is a very old story. God made man. Man was alone and got fed up with his loneliness.

He asked God to give him a companion, for he was alone. But God had used up all the material, everything was finished. He had made forests, mountains, birds and animals, and at the end he had made man - now there was no material left. But the man wept and wept, so he asked him to wait and tried to make a woman. However, there was no material available at that time, so God asked the animals, birds, flowers and plants for some. He told the moon to give a little of its light, the peacock to give its arrogance, the doves to give their sweet murmur, the parrots to give their voice, the rivers to give their restlessness and movement, the flowers to give their delicacy.... thus he made the woman!

After seven days, the man came back and said: "This woman is a nuisance. I thought she'd have a companion, but she won't stop fighting. The voice the parrots give her is very sweet - she certainly is when she's affectionate, but she's arrogant like a peacock. She is very kind and very cruel at the same time. It's very contradictory. I am fed up. It was better to be alone. You must take her back.

God took the woman away, but after seven days the man came back and said: "Yes, she has made my life miserable, but I miss her, I can't live without her. During these seven days I have not been able to eat or sleep. I still remember her. Please give her back to me".

After seven days he was again at God's door. He said: "I cannot live with it and I cannot live without it.

God turned his back on him and said, "How long am I going to listen to your nonsense? You can't live with it and you can't live without it, so you'd better figure it out for yourself.

Since then, man has been trying to solve it, but so far he has not been able to. It is not possible, because when you are alone you are afraid of loneliness. When you are with another person, their presence bothers you. When you have company you want to be alone, when you are alone you want company. When you are with someone you start to notice the bad points in him or her. When you are alone, loneliness scares you like death.

Both companionship and loneliness are bothersome to him. That is why man establishes many kinds of relationships. He brings a wife home so as not to be lonely. Then, in his effort to be away from his wife, he sits in the hotel or in the club. Becoming a member of a club means that he is trying to escape from his wife. He makes one mistake and then tries to rectify it by making another.

So begins the chain of errors, and you call this life!

WHO IS YOUR WIFE? WHO IS YOUR SON? THIS IS A STRANGE WORLD.

You are all strangers here. You don't know each other. If you don't know yourselves, how will you know the other? The one who knows himself will also know the other. But if you don't know yourself, you can't know anyone else. You have established relationships without knowing. All relationships are casual. Your whole life, your whole world, is based on chance. When you fall in love with a girl you say that God has made you both for each other - but it was by the coincidence of living in the same house or going to the same school. It was just a coincidence that you knew each other, not that you were made for each other. In fact, no one is made for each other. But the man tries to justify a mere coincidence with the theory of fate.

Mulla Nasruddin went to Africa for a safari. When he returned, all his friends gathered around him to listen to his adventures. He would narrate with great enthusiasm and exaggeration, saying: "There is a certain animal over there. When the male animal has to call the female he squeals and the female, wherever she is in the jungle, comes running to him".

A friend asked him to copy the sound of the animal's squeak. He copied it, screeching loudly. At that moment, the door to the next room opened and his wife asked him, "Well? What's wrong?"

He said to his friends: "See, now you understand the theory".

It's just a coincidence. There is no theory in it. But if a person thinks that his love is mere coincidence, then there is no place for poetry. If you tell Majnu that his meeting with Laila was a coincidence, then poetry dies, romance dies. Majnu will say, "No, this is not possible. Laila was made for me and I was made for Laila. And even if the whole world puts obstacles in our way we will definitely meet". If Majnu had lived in some other village then some other girl would have been his Laila. Majnu would have definitely found some Laila who would have been different from this one.

What you think is the structure of life is not a structure at all, it's just a coincidence, a few incidents, a few coincidences. You have a child. Don't delude yourself that you have given birth to your child. While you were having sex, a soul was waiting anxiously to be reborn. You were close, you were available, so that soul entered your womb. You had dug a pit, it was raining, so the water that was nearby entered that pit. Water that was further away went into other pits.

It is a coincidence.

It is a coincidence to be a child, it is a coincidence to be a mother, it is a coincidence to be a father; friendship is a coincidence and enmity is a coincidence. If you can see this correctly, then suddenly your deep relationships will weaken, their depth will disappear.

WHO IS YOUR WIFE? WHO IS YOUR SON? THIS WORLD IS VERY STRANGE. WHO ARE YOU? WHO ARE YOU? WHERE DO YOU COME FROM? REFLECT ON THESE ESSENTIAL QUESTIONS. OH IDIOT! ALWAYS SING THE SONG OF THE DIVINE.

... Because nothing will happen by thinking alone: thinking alone is lame. You must think, but you will not be able to get there by thinking alone. All obstacles will be removed by thought, but you will not be able to travel. The journey is possible only by bhajan, devotion. The journey is possible by emotion and not by thought. ALWAYS SING THE SONG OF THE DIVINE.

FROM SATSANG COMES SOLITUDE, FROM SOLITUDE COMES DETACHMENT; DUE TO DETACHMENT THE MIND BECOMES STABLE AND DUE TO THE STABLE AND UNSHAKABLE MIND

LIBERATION IS ATTAINED.

Try to understand this. It is a very valuable sutra: FROM SATSANG COMES SOLITUDE. This is the definition of satsang. Satsang is that which creates loneliness. Satsang that creates relationship and attachment cannot be satsang. The meaning of satsang is that you begin to see the truth. The meaning of satsang is that your eyes must be open and your dream is over.

The search for the master is intended to awaken you from your dream. The master will awaken you and tell you that all the relationships you have established are illusions; do not waste your life in these dreams and do not let your soul be lost in them. These relationships are but formalities to be observed in this world, so do not attach too much importance to them, do not attach too much importance to them to the point of destroying yourself. They may be necessary in this world, but for the inner world they are not necessary at all.

You cannot take with you there your father, your son, your brother, your wife, your friend - you go there alone. Therefore, in spite of living in all relationships, you must know that your true self is in being alone. Don't forget that. Don't let the sun of loneliness be covered by the clouds of relationships.

FROM SATSANG COMES LONELINESS, FROM LONELINESS COMES DETACHMENT.

And when you discover that you are alone, then there is no attachment.

DUE TO DETACHMENT THE MIND BECOMES STABLE.

And when there is no attachment the mind does not waver.

I heard that a house was on fire and the owner of the house was watching and weeping. But then someone from the crowd said to him: "Don't cry! It is not necessary. Perhaps you don't know that your son had sold this house yesterday".

The man stopped crying at once. The house was still burning, the flames were spreading everywhere, but the man was no longer crying because the house did not belong to him. But at that moment his son came running up and told him that the preliminary discussion to sell the house had started, but that the final sale had not yet been made.

Hearing this, the man cried his eyes out again. The house is still the same. He is not crying because the house is on fire, he is crying because of his relationship with the house. If it's not his, he doesn't care whether the house is burning or not.

If someone's child dies but it is not your child, it makes no difference to you. It only affects you if it is "yours". You cry because it is "yours", not because of anything else. If you come to know that no one is "yours" then there will be no anguish. When attachment disappears, misery disappears too.

If it becomes clear to you that no one is "yours", that you are alone, the mind becomes stable, then the mind is not restless; then you become stable, unshakable. That stability, that unshakeable condition is the ultimate experience. In that unshakable condition you come to know who you are. Then the fundamental question of life is resolved: "Who am I? As soon as the flame becomes unwavering you get the answer, you get the solution. This stability, this unshakeable condition, is called samadhi.

Samadhi means the solution to everything.

THROUGH A STABLE AND UNSHAKABLE MIND LIBERATION IS ATTAINED. OH FOOL! ALWAYS SING THE SONG OF THE DIVINE.

Where is the sexual desire when the time for sex is over? Where is the pond when the water dries up? And no one is near you when you've lost your money.

Likewise, after the realisation of truth, where is this world? Try to understand this.

When Shankara, Buddha or Mahavira speak of the world, you

make the mistake of thinking that they mean this sprawling expanse. No, that is not what they mean.

Whenever they talk about the world they mean the world made by your attachment, created by your attachment, the world made by your unconsciousness, the illusions you have created. Even when you wake up, these trees will still be there; they will not disappear.

People often ask: "When a person becomes enlightened and this world disappears for him, what then happens to these trees, mountains, the moon, the stars, the sun? They do not disappear. In fact, for the first time they appear in their purity. That purity is the divine. Then you don't see the moon, then you see the light of the divine in the moon; then you don't see the trees, you see the greenery of the divine in the trees; then you don't see the flowers, you see the divine blossoming. Then all this becomes unlimited piety.

Right now you don't see the divine. You see the world and the world is not one. There are as many worlds as there are different minds, because each individual has his own world. If your wife dies you will cry, no one else. Others will try to explain to you that the soul is eternal, it doesn't die, so don't cry. They will use the occasion to show off their knowledge. They will see you in a pitiful state and start lecturing you. They will say, "Why are you crying, who really belongs to us?" Tomorrow, when their wives die, then you will have your chance, then you will go and preach to them that this world is an illusion, all these relationships are an illusion.

Each individual's world is his own. Your attachment, your unconsciousness, your ignorance, your infatuation, your love, your love, that is your world. What you have seen through this infatuation, love, attachment, unconsciousness is not true, it is all false. It is as if your eyes are covered with clouds of smoke.

Shankara says: After knowing the essence, the reality, there is no world. WHERE IS THE WORLD AFTER SELF-Realisation?

The truth remains, but whatever you have added to the truth is lost.

ALWAYS SING THE SONG OF THE DIVINE.

TAKE NO PRIDE IN WEALTH, PEOPLE AND YOUTH, FOR DEATH TAKES THEM ALL AWAY IN A MOMENT. ABANDON ALL THESE ILLUSORY MATTERS, KNOW THE DIVINE AND ENTER INTO IT.

I was reading a song this morning and a few lines of that song attracted me: JOR HE KYA THA JAFA-E-BAGVAN DEKNA KIYE ASHIAN UJRA KIYA HUM NATWAN DEKHA KIYE. The meaning is: The garden was being destroyed and I watched helplessly. Yes, your whole life is the same story. Your garden will be destroyed daily. Spring will soon be over. Youth will also pass away.

This speed and this energy will gradually diminish. The house will be destroyed and death will draw nearer and nearer. Life is only a momentary dream; death is approaching every minute. You are dying from the day you were born. A birthday is actually also the day of death. You cannot postpone death, you cannot run away from it. It is getting closer and closer.

DON'T BE PROUD OF WEALTH, PEOPLE AND YOUTH.

This ego is superficial. In fact, all egos are shallow; shallowness is the nature of the ego. It thinks of what is not its own. That which is transitory seems permanent to it, and that which flows seems static to it. You not only deceive others, you deceive yourself.

One day Mulla Nasruddin came home. He knocked on the door but there was no answer. He knocked again, but no one answered. Then he shouted: "I am Nasruddin, not the landlord asking for rent, not the milkman, not the vegetable seller".

Even then there was no response. So he shouted again: "I say that I am the real Nasruddin".

He must have told his family not to open the door when someone knocked because he owed money to many people. So when he himself knocks on the door of his own house nobody opens it. So he has to explain that he is the real Nasruddin. But still no one believes him.

We continue to deceive others and create a world of deception around us. Then we deceive ourselves, and so we become inauthentic. Everything we do in life is false.

The person who wants to awaken must stop sowing lies and say goodbye to all his false beliefs. He must know that this body is not permanent, it is not static, it is dying every moment, and death is not going to happen tomorrow, it is happening now. We are dying. Death is not going to happen after seventy more years - we are dying gradually and there will be nothing left after seventy years.

Life is running out drop by drop. Don't call it life, it's a lie. You can call it gradual death. Don't celebrate birthdays, they are all days of death. The day you see death on your birthday and hear the footsteps of death in life, you will know the truth. That truth will give you freedom.

As soon as you know that truth you will begin a new search: money will seem meaningless, the body will seem meaningless; the relations of body and money will seem meaningless and even the world based on money and body will seem meaningless. And before knowing the truth it is necessary to know falsehood as falsehood, the false as false.

DAY AND NIGHT, EVENING AND MORNING, WINTER AND SPRING COME AND GO AGAIN AND AGAIN. SO THE GAME OF TIME GOES BY AND ONE'S LIFE IS OVER. AND YET THE BREEZE OF HOPE DOES NOT LEAVE ONE ALONE.

Hope is poison, and because of this poison you have mistaken death for life. Today you are unhappy, but the mind says that tomorrow all will be well. Today there is no happiness, but the mind says, "Wait, tomorrow everything will be all right". That is how the mind has been guiding you so far: it has been giving you hope. The day you give up hope you will wake up. Hope is a dream.

Have you ever thought about how hope affects you in life? Hope says: "Don't worry about today. Whatever happens doesn't matter. But tomorrow you will definitely reach heaven. This very hope has made you realise that there is nothing to worry about even if this life is lost because you will get heaven after death. This is the expansion of hope. Hope says "tomorrow". Hope says "future". Hope says "more life". But if the revolution of life is going to happen, it will happen right now and right here.

Don't depend on tomorrow; tomorrow never comes. Tomorrow is a lie. And the hope that is giving you the security about tomorrow is the cause of creating these dreams in you. Whatever has to be done, has to be done today. Whatever has to be, will be today. Don't wait for more than today.

At first it will be quite shocking. With the disappearance of hope you will feel absolutely despondent.

You will feel that you have become totally hopeless. But if you are willing to live without hope, you will discover that if there is no hope in life, there is no hopelessness either.

Hopelessness is the reverse of hope and will disappear with hope. Life without hope is life without despair. Then there is neither hope nor despair. That is stability. The flame remains in the centre. Then there is no wavering. That is the condition of unwavering consciousness.

DAY AND NIGHT, EVENING AND MORNING, WINTER AND SPRING COME AND GO AGAIN AND AGAIN. SO THE GAME OF TIME GOES BY AND ONE'S LIFE IS OVER. AND YET THE BREEZE OF HOPE DOES NOT LEAVE ONE ALONE. THEN, OH FOOL! SING ALWAYS THE SONG OF THE DIVINE OH FOOL! WHY ARE YOU CAUGHT UP IN WORRIES ABOUT YOUR WIFE

AND YOUR WEALTH? DON'T YOU KNOW THAT EVEN A MOMENT OF COMPANIONSHIP WITH GOOD PEOPLE IS THE ONLY BOAT THAT EXISTS TO CARRY YOU ACROSS THE OCEAN OF THIS WORLDLY WORLD?

Who is a holy person? The one in whose company you wake up. An unholy person is one in whose company you enter into a deep sleep and who helps you to increase your illusions and attachments.

But in this world the opposite is true. The person who tries to wake you up doesn't seem friendly to you. The person who puts you to sleep seems like a friend. The one who gives you alcohol to drink seems like a friend and the one who tries to bring you back to consciousness seems like an enemy. That's why the wine bars and pubs are crowded and the temples are empty. There are long queues in the bars, and God is still waiting in the temple but no one shows up. Yes, the priest comes, but he is already a servant; he gets paid and comes to worship. His worship is not from the heart, it is professional. He is not a lover. What is the reason?

Wherever there is intoxication, there will be crowds. There is a crowd in front of a cinema: people get drunk for three hours, they lose themselves in the film for three hours. They forget their miseries, their sorrows, their worries and anxieties. For three hours they forget themselves. This kind of intoxication is not the solution to your problems. After three hours the film is over, the lights come on and you are back to where you were: full of worries and miseries. Alcohol makes you forget yourself for two or three hours, but when it wears off you are unhappy and suffering again.

Going to the temple is also going with the expectation of getting some kind of intoxicant. This is the difference. You can sing the song of the divine in two ways. One is like alcohol: lose yourself in it.

For the moment you forget the worry, the misery; you forget that you have to go home, that you have a wife and children, that the wife is ill, that the children have to be admitted to school and that you have no money. You forget your worries while you are lost singing the song of the divine.

If you lose yourself in singing the song of the divine, then this too is like alcohol.

If it wakes you up, only then is it the song of the divine. Even temples are like bars and under the pretext of religion people are still seeking unconsciousness and not consciousness. It is very difficult to wake up. Sleeping is very relaxing, you keep dreaming beautiful dreams. You will be disturbed if you are woken up and brought to consciousness.

Knowing the truth of life is a great challenge. You will have to fight for it. You will have to work hard for it. You will have to go through sadhana and austerity. This journey can only be undertaken with open eyes, for the path is very difficult and full of thorns. It can also deceive you.

Those who never walk are never afraid of getting lost on the road. Those who always lie in bed will never have an accident. But those who walk the path may get lost on the path or have an accident and face many difficulties. This journey is laborious because you have to climb the mountain. Going towards the divine means going towards the summit. It becomes more and more difficult. Only those who are willing to go through all these difficulties will reach the bliss of the summit.

Happiness is not free. It has to be earned, it has to be worked for. Of course, it is not achieved by work alone, it is achieved by grace, but you have to work for it. Divinity can only come to the person who has worked and prepared himself.

AND YET THE BREEZE OF HOPE DOES NOT LEAVE ONE ALONE.

You start to hope for the divine as well. When people come to me, I tell them to give up hope and meditate. They tell me: "If we give up hope, what are we going to meditate for? For hope we have come to meditate - hoping that through meditation the mind will be at peace, that we will attain samadhi and realise the divine".

Now this is very complicated. The hope will create the obstacle. Because when you hope you don't meditate, you just hope, you can't do both at the same time. Even if you meditate for a while, you will still wonder why you have not yet found peace: three days have passed and nothing has happened, you have not yet experienced bliss.

Try to understand it this way. If I tell you to come to the river to swim because swimming is very pleasant, you will come. But if from the beginning of the swimming you go on waiting for the pleasure, then you will not get it. Because of your impatience, your anxiety to attain it, you will not get it, because the very nature of bliss is that it seeks you when you are not seeking it. You will not get it while you are looking for it, because when you are looking for it you are not in the present; your mind is in the future waiting to get it. And it is now.

You get it when you are purely in this moment without any hope, without any expectation, without any desire or longing. When you are present in this moment you find that it has rained everywhere.

It was raining, but you were not present, you were absent, you were lost in the future because of your hope, and here the bliss was being distributed. You were wandering elsewhere, so you couldn't receive it. You receive it the day you are in the present, and being in the present means being without hope and without desire.

So I say to you: "Meditate. Have no hope. Meditation is not the means, but the end. Meditation itself is joy, bliss, and don't ask for more bliss, don't expect the result. If you can do any action without expecting any result, then that very action will become meditation".

In the Gita Krishna has only said this to Arjuna. He has said it repeatedly in different ways: don't expect any result. This desire for the result, the expectation for the return, is the world. Abandonment of desire for the result is salvation. There is no need to run away from the world, just do away with the expectation of the result. Then you will live here, but the world will disappear for you.

OH, MADMAN, WHY ARE YOU CAUGHT UP IN WORRIES ABOUT YOUR WIFE AND YOUR WEALTH? DON'T YOU KNOW THAT EVEN A MOMENT OF COMPANIONSHIP WITH GOOD PEOPLE IS THE ONLY BOAT THERE IS TO CARRY YOU ACROSS THE OCEAN OF THIS WORLDLY WORLD?

But people go on worrying about nothing until the last moment of their lives. All worries are meaningless. You have to contemplate what is meaningful and not worry about it.

I heard that a Marwari merchant was dying, he was on his deathbed. He asked his wife, "Where is the eldest son?". The wife told him that he was standing by the bedside. "Where is the middle one?" he asked. She told him he was also nearby. "And where is the youngest?"

She said, "Don't worry, He is at your feet. Relax and sleep with peace in your mind".

The Marwari trader got up and said: "How can I sleep peacefully? Who is looking after the shop?

They are all here.

Their father was dying. Thinking this, all the sons had gathered there. They had closed the shop.

But death is not the concern of the dying father: who tends the shop? He does not ask about his children out of love: where is the eldest, where is the middle one, the youngest? He asks who tends the shop. They are all there, does that mean that there is no one in the shop?

Yes, even at the last moment your mind is full of shops! It will be so, because whatever you have done in your whole life, you will think about it also while you die. You cannot change suddenly at the moment of death. Don't believe that false story.

A man was dying, his son's name was Narayan which is another name for God. So he called his son Narayan, and God thought he was calling him. Such stories are created by the pundits to comfort the sinners. On the basis of such stories the pundits are able to take some money from the sinners - nothing else will happen.

If God is deluded, then surely he is not God. Did this man go to heaven just because he called "Narayan" while dying? It is not worth getting such a cheap God. This kind of heaven or salvation is absolutely false. This story cannot be true.

Death is the summary of your whole life; at the moment of death your mind will be full of what you have done during your life. If you have been counting money all your life, you will also be counting money at death, because death is the essence of your life. If you have been restless all your life, you will also be restless at death. If you have been peaceful then your death will be very peaceful. Each individual has a different death because each individual lives a different life. Neither your life nor your death can be the same as another person.

When a buddha dies, the greatness of his death is different: the greatness of his death is much greater than the greatness of your so-called life. Your life is nothing compared to his death. The greatness of his death is a million times greater than the greatness of your life, because at that moment of his death all life shrinks and comes closer, the music of his whole life condenses, as if the essence of all the flowers of his life had been taken and turned into a fragrance. At the moment of death, the fragrance that emanates from a buddha is the essence of the flowers of his whole life. The stench that will come out of you will be the essence of all the dirt and rubbish of your entire life.

You can't suddenly change with death. So don't believe the experts who tell you to become religious at the end of your life. If you want to be religious you have to do it here and now; don't leave it for the end. If you are careful now you can be careful in the future. If you wake up today, you will gradually become awake. If you sing the song of the divine from today, perhaps at the moment of death the divine will hear you.

Do not think at the time of death that a borrowed pundit will save your soul by reciting mantras in your ears, pouring the water of the Ganges in your mouth, reading the Gita near you. That pundit will keep repeating the Gita but you will not be able to hear it inside you at that time. Only a person who has learnt the art of correct listening throughout his life will be able to hear the Gita at the time of death. If one has sung the song of the divine all his life, then at the time of death he will not have to hear it sung by a borrowed servant or a pundit; every breath, every beat of his heart will be singing the song of the divine.

In that moment of death you will go dancing towards the divine full of gratitude. Your death will become the gateway to a greater life; you will change death. Death kills you now, then you will kill death.

And religion is the art of killing death, it is the science of becoming nectar.

Therefore, O IDIOT! ALWAYS SING THE SONG OF THE DIVINE.

Enough for today.

Every step is destiny

The first question:

Question 1:

BELOVED MASTER, IT IS SAID THAT SHANKARA WAS A HINDU VEDANTIN, AND YOU HAVE SAID THAT SHANKARA IS AN OCCULT BUDDHIST. PLEASE CLARIFY THIS.

Shankara is a hidden Buddhist, a hidden Jaina, a hidden Mohammedan, in the same way that Buddha is a hidden Hindu, a hidden Jaina, a hidden Christian... and in the same way that Christ is a hidden Hindu, a hidden Mohammedan, a hidden Buddhist.

Those who have known, have known only the one; two are not there to be known. Hindu, Mohammedan, Christian... these are only the surface names, the outer identity; the inner truth is one. The language may be different, but what is said is not different. The style of saying will be different, the process of explaining will be different, but there is no possibility of the taste being different, it is the same.

This has to be understood. This misunderstanding, this stupidity creates a lot of unpleasantness. The Hindus fight with the Mohammedans, the Jains fight with the Buddhists... and you must understand that truth is lost whenever and wherever there is any kind of conflict. Truth is killed in your struggle, falsehood is created in your conflict, because conflict means violence. So it does not matter whether the violence is expressed in physical conflict or in mental conflict. Violence is violence, whether the effort to destroy the other is physical or mental. The desire and the mentality to find fault with the other is the expansion of violence. Know that until you can see yourself in the other you have not gone beyond the mind, nor have you entered the temple of consciousness. That temple has many doors and entry is possible from every door. And whoever enters the temple forgets the door. Nobody remembers the door after entering. Before entering, the door seems very important because one has to enter through it, but afterwards it becomes useless. Before entering one was facing the door and after entering the door is at your back.

All faiths are doors. You must know that you have not entered the temple if the faiths - Hindu, Mohammedan, Jain - still seem very important to you.... That means you are still looking at the door. When you have entered the temple and you turn your back to the door, then the words Hindu and Mohammedan become meaningless.

The great meaning that will appear inside the temple will not only destroy your creed, your scripture, but it will also destroy you, and in that flood everything will be drowned.

What remains after that flood is your own nature. In that flood whatever was the other element will be swept away, in that flood whatever were the outer coverings will be lost; in that flood your relations will be broken with whatever was alien to your nature and only you will remain in your pure virginity, in your innocence.

And you cannot understand that inner being without experiencing it; you have to taste it, you have to drink it and become intoxicated. Until you become intoxicated, until you lose yourself in it after losing everything, only then will godliness begin. The world will remain as long as you remain.

The divine is not until you are not. And the divine begins only when your ego, your separate identity dissolves. Shankara is an occult Buddhist because he says the same thing the Buddha said.

Buddha was also an occult Vedantin because he said the same thing as the Upanishads. The robes are different, and sometimes even seem contradictory.

Try to understand this. Buddha opposed the Upanishads and the Vedas and yet he proposed the Upanishads and the Vedas. One has to oppose. When the Upanishads were born, when the Ganges of the Upanishads was born, then the Ganges was very clean, pure; it was the Gangotri, the source.

After that, the Ganges flowed on, thousands of people bathed in it, it passed through thousands of villages, it became dirty, rubbish got into it, rivers and streams joined it. In Varanasi, the Ganges does not have the mercy it has in Gangotri. It cannot be like that. With the passage of time, the original source loses its purity.

Two thousand five hundred years before the Buddha, when the Upanishads were born, their grandeur was unique. Each and every word they contained was luminous, each line filled with the divine!

But that greatness was lost in the Buddha's time: the mirror was there, but a lot of dust had accumulated on it. Now the mirror had become blind and nothing could be reflected in it. A great belief system had risen up near the mirror. Even if Buddha tried to clean the mirror, that creed would not allow him to do so, because what Buddha calls dust, the masses call religion. The communal mind does not know the mirror, it only knows the dust accumulated on it and thinks that this dust is the decoration, it is the jewel. The communal mind cannot accept the wiping of the dust; it thinks that this will destroy its religion.

Because of this dust Buddha had to deny this mirror. People could not accept another mirror until this one was denied. But the other mirror is exactly the same as the first one; the only difference is that the first one had grown old, deteriorated and dust had accumulated on it.

When the truth is organised, it dies. Now the other truth is new again, newborn, fresh as the morning dew. The new truth will also become old in a few days.

The truth of Buddha had grown old when Shankara was born. Time spares no one and covers everything with dust. What is new today will be old tomorrow, today's newborn will be old tomorrow; today he is welcomed into this world, tomorrow he will be bidden farewell when he dies.

Just as men are born and die, religions are born and die. In time everything becomes old, weak, dilapidated and useless. When someone dies in the house - your mother dies, how much you loved her... but when she dies you have to take her to the crematorium. If some foolish person keeps his mother's corpse in the house, it will be difficult for the living to live there. It can be very painful to cremate your mother whom you loved, but there is no way out: a corpse cannot be kept in the house, it has to be cremated.

But we do not treat belief systems with that understanding. Religion means living religion; when it becomes a creed it becomes a corpse. But we guard the corpse very carefully; because of the stench of the creed it becomes difficult to breathe. Religion unites, but creeds fight and make others fight. Creeds break and make others break. There is much enmity between a temple and a mosque, but there can be no enmity in the divinity of the temple and the mosque. There is much enmity between the worshippers of the temple and the mosque, but the one who is worshipped in the temple and in the mosque - someone calls him 'Rama' and someone calls him 'Allah'... these addresses may be different but the one who is called is one.

When the Buddha stream reached Shankara it had become dirty, it had lost its purity: the Ganges had reached Benares. Shankara had to object because there were now many Buddhists, followers of the Buddha, and it was a large creed. They would not allow the dust to be wiped off, so again a new mirror had to be made. Today the condition is the same: dust has accumulated on Shankara's mirror. It will always be like that.

Don't worship the dust. Always look for the mirror. Then you will find the same mirror in everyone.

When you can see the same mirror in everyone, only then is wisdom born in you.

This is the only difference between intelligence and wisdom. Intelligence criticises, opposes, debates, but wisdom communicates. Intelligence tells where the difference is and wisdom shows where the unity is.

Intelligence analyses: wisdom synthesises. Intelligence draws the limits; wisdom destroys all limits. When all limits disappear, the unlimited is obtained.

Do not think you can know the unlimited by remaining limited. Who will know it? If you are bound and limited, who will know the unlimited? Everything you know will be limited. To know the unlimited you will have to break all your limitations. If you see the sky from the window, you will only see what is visible through the structure of the window, not more than that; the window also limits the sky. If you want to see the whole sky, you have to go outside.

Abide under the open sky where you will be neither Hindu nor Mohammedan, for these are the names of the windows. Only you alone will abide under the open sky and only your abiding means pure existence.

There is a way to know the unlimited. To know the unlimited one has to become unlimited - this is the only condition, because only the like can know the like. How can you, the limited, know the unlimited? If you try to see the unlimited, you will only see what your limitations can show you.

Not only is Shankara a hidden Buddha, Buddha is also a hidden Vedantin. All that is defiled has to be destroyed; that which has become perverted has to be destroyed. Everything that has become ruinous has to be put into the fire so that there can be room for the new. The mind says, "Save the old"; the mind says, "Take care of the old". But if you go on taking too much care of the old then there will be no room for the new. The old has to go so that the children can come in. The old and rotten tree will fall so that a new seed can sprout.

I heard that there was a very old and dilapidated church. It was in such a bad state that it could fall down at any moment. The people who used to pray in it were also afraid to go in. Finally, the administrators called a meeting to decide what to do with it, because now even the priest was afraid to go in. People were afraid to go in and even passers-by were afraid that it would collapse at any moment: anyone could die. So no one was passing that road, it had become a lonely place. So they passed three resolutions:

The first was that the old church should be demolished. It was unanimously approved with great regret.

Secondly, a new church had to be built. This was accepted with a lot of pain because the attachment to the old is always there. The new is not yet born, the new is not yet known, so there can be no attachment to the new - the attachment is always with the old. That's why if a small child dies, the anguish is not much. But the distress increases with age, because the relationship, the attachment increases proportionately. The old has to be demolished, with great pain. The new has to be built, just out of sheer helplessness.

And they passed a third resolution according to which the new church will be built on the same site as the old one, and until the new one is built we will continue to use the old one. For the new church we will use the stones of the old church. And until the new one is built we will continue to use the old one. This was also approved unanimously. That church is still there. It cannot be demolished, because there is a deep attachment to it.

I only call a person religious who, after renouncing the old, always turns towards the ever new, and thus is able to retain his innocence and purity; someone who comes out of the past at every instant, just as the snake comes out of its skin, and does not look back. If you tune into what is always new, if you live in what is always new, if you refuse to carry the old rubbish, then you will find in the new what is eternal. In the eternal is hidden godliness.

The second question:

Question 2:

BELOVED MASTER, BEFORE YOU TELL US TO SING THE SONG OF THE DIVINE, WHY DO YOU AND SHANKARA ADDRESS US AS 'IDIOT' EVERY TIME?

Because you are! To call you otherwise would be a lie! When Shankara says: O IDIOT! SINGS THE SONG OF THE DIVINE, he says it with great love, he says it out of compassion.

He is not cursing you, he is not insulting you, because Shankara cannot curse or insult; it is impossible for him. He is shaking you, he is waking you up. He is saying, "Get up! It is morning and you are still sleeping". He is calling you "idiot" because until he uses strong words your sleep will not be disturbed and you will not wake up. He is calling you "idiot" because it is true, it is a fact.

Idiocy means unconsciousness. Idiocy means to live asleep. Idiocy means lacking discretion.

Idiocy means not being awake, not being aware when you are angry. Then you become more idiotic because you lose even more consciousness. But sometimes, when you are conscious, you are not such an idiot. And you also know that sometimes you are less of an idiot and sometimes you are more of an idiot.

When the mind is full of attachment then idiocy increases, when there is passion you become more idiotic. In Tulsidas' life story it is said that when his wife went to her parents' house, he followed her at night. It was raining and dark. He went up to his room clutching a snake. He must have been in a very deep state of idiocy to mistake the snake for the rope. It must have been a very strong passion. That passion left him almost blind; he couldn't even see the snake!

People often mistake a rope for a snake out of fear. Death scares man. A rope on the road always looks like a snake. But this was just the opposite: Tulsidas thought the snake was the rope. He grabbed hold of it and climbed up. He didn't even notice it by touch; he must have been absolutely unconscious. Passion must have driven him mad.

Seeing his condition, his wife said to him, "If you had loved God as you love me, you would have attained deliverance by now!". He turned around, saw the snake and realised that passion had blinded him. A revolution took place in his life. The wife became the teacher. Passion had pointed him to the non-passionate state. He became a sannyasin and went in search of the divine: the energy that was spent in passion turned to Rama. The energy that expressed itself in sex began to become Rama.

Idiocy is that energy that today is asleep but tomorrow it will awaken. Today it is hidden, but tomorrow it will be revealed. This foolishness will become your wisdom. Your dream will become your awakening.

So don't get angry with him, don't condemn him and don't try to hide your idiocy. Most people do. They try to hide their idiocy, so they are even more idiotic! You collect information and try to hide your idiocy with that information. You cover internal wounds with flowers.

Knowledge borrowed from the scriptures is like these flowers, information borrowed from others is like these flowers with which you cover your idiocy to help you forget it. Idiocy must not be forgotten. Idiocy must be remembered because it can only be destroyed if it is remembered. That is why Shankara keeps repeating: SING THE SONG OF THE DIVINE, SING THE SONG OF THE DIVINE, O IDIOT!

Seeing your unconsciousness, you keep repeating it out of pity so that you don't forget that you are an idiot. You do your best to forget it. You try your best to forget that you are an idiot. You think you are a very knowledgeable person. Only a person who knows a lot knows that he knows nothing. All ignorant people think they know.

The ignorant are unwilling to accept that they do not know. Only the more knowledgeable person is willing to question his own knowledge.

Edison has said: "People say I know a lot. But the reality is that a child on the seashore who has picked up a few shells.... My knowledge is just that: a few shells in my hands and there is this vast sea that I don't know".

Your small knowledge seems great to you. You have lit a small lamp; its dim light is able to illuminate a small place and you think it is a great knowledge. But you are not aware of the boundless darkness that surrounds you. When you realise your idiocy then you will say, "Is this knowledge, this dim light? I have collected some seashells in my hand and I think I have become a knower. But the journey of knowledge is endless, the search is limitless". Then you will also renounce that knowledge.

The day you become aware of your idiocy, the day you become aware that you are an idiot, your idiocy will begin to dissolve, because that awareness will bring you out of it. Idiocy is unconsciousness; it will begin to dissolve with consciousness.

Psychologists say that a madman will recover if he realises he is mad. A madman never knows he is mad, he thinks the world is mad.

Kahlil Gibran has written that one of his friends went mad, so he went to visit him in the asylum. The friend was sitting on a bench in the garden of the asylum. Gibran sat down next to him and said, "I am sorry to see you here.

The friend looked intently at Gibran and said: "Sorry for what?

Gibran replied: "To see that you had to come to this madhouse".

That crazy friend laughed and said: "You are wrong. Since I came here I have found the company of sane people. Outside they are all mad; I am lucky to be free of them. Do you think this is a madhouse?

No, the madhouse is outside these walls. Only a few sane people live here.

An insane person cannot understand that he is insane. If he had that understanding he would not have gone mad. If he understands that he is mad, the madness will disappear.

If at night, while you are sleeping, you realise that you are dreaming, you stop dreaming. To dream it is necessary that you do not remember that you are dreaming. In the morning you will remember it when the dream is over. As long as you are dreaming it will seem real to you. But if right in the middle of the dream you remember that it is a dream, it will be over.

Gurdjieff used to tell his disciples that before they could break the big dreams they must learn to break the little dreams. This big world is an illusion, a big dream; you cannot break it until you break the small dreams. How can you stop the day dream if you cannot stop the night dream? That is why Gurdjieff used to tell his disciples, when they went to sleep at night, to remind themselves that whenever they began to dream, they should immediately remember that it was a dream. It takes about three years to break the night's sleep. For three years in a row, every night when you go to sleep, if you keep thinking, contemplating, meditating on this thought, then there comes that moment - that fortunate moment - when you suddenly remember that this is a dream. And this memory breaks the dream and the consciousness even enters the dream. From that moment the dream stops.

Then the dreams are over.

Only after this can you wake up in the great dream - this dream of the open eyes is the great dream.

The night's sleep is personal, private, solitary. It is absolutely private. Not even a husband can call his wife to his dream. Not even a friend can call another friend to his dream. This dream is solitary; no one else can participate in it.

But this great dream is collective, public. It is very difficult to break it because it is not only yours, it belongs to everyone, collectively and together. But if the first dream is broken, then that memory can break this dream too. That memory is enough. Even while awake one should be able to remember that this is a dream. Just think, if someone has cursed or insulted you and you remember that this is a dream, then it will be impossible for you to lose your temper. If something valuable is broken and you remember that it is only a dream, you will not be unhappy. If your wife or your husband or your child dies, then it will be difficult to remember that this is all a dream, but if you can do it then your agony will disappear.

The person who has realised that this is a dream becomes a buddha, a jinna; neither death nor life is capable of shaking him. Happiness, then, does not seem to him to be happiness and unhappiness does not seem to him to be unhappiness. This is the supreme wisdom: neither happiness nor agony affects him!

Shankara is reminding you again and again that you are an idiot, so don't get angry. If you get angry then you are proving that Shankara is right in calling you an idiot. Maybe you are a big idiot and Shankara is just calling you an idiot, he is doubting. Don't insist on proving that you are not an idiot, otherwise this insistence will reinforce your idiocy. You must accept it. Your acceptance will dissolve your idiocy.

You must not only accept it, but you must also remind yourself every moment that you are an idiot: you are unconscious, ignorant and insane. Then your consciousness will move in a new direction, your inner quality will change, your actions will change. If you could only remember that you are not sensible, then that would be the beginning of you becoming sensible.

Realising one's ignorance is the first step towards knowledge. The effort to kindle the fire, the light, begins only after understanding the darkness. If one does not know darkness as darkness and blindness as blindness, he will not try to cure his eyes. When you go to the doctor, he does not give you the medicine immediately. He first tries to diagnose the disease and then administers the medicine. If the diagnosis is correct, then it is easy to administer the treatment. That is why all the big doctors charge for diagnosis and not for treatment, because after diagnosis anyone can give the medicines. Once the disease is diagnosed, its treatment will be easy.

Shankara tells you again and again: OH IDIOT! SING THE SONG OF THE DIVINE. He has diagnosed your disease. Idiocy is your disease and SING THE SONG OF THE DIVINE is the treatment. But if you are not an idiot, what are you going to sing the song of the divine for? If you don't consider yourself sick, then why would you take the treatment? If you keep protecting your illness, if you keep claiming that your illness is your health, then of course you are incurable, no one can treat you.

The third question:

Question 3:

BELOVED MASTER, DURING CATHARSIS I EXPRESS ONLY NEGATIVE EMOTIONS, ANGER, JEALOUSY, ANGUISH AND SO ON. WHY DON'T I EXPRESS LOVE, DEVOTION, JOY AND RELIGIOUS EMOTIONS? DON'T I POSSESS THEM?

They are in you, but they are a little deeper. When you dig a well, the first things that come out are stones, pebbles and mud, not water. It also depends on the terrain. Somewhere the water is thirty feet and somewhere the water is sixty feet deep. The water is certainly there. All land has water under it, but the difference is the depth.

A simple-minded person will get the water soon, perhaps two, three or ten feet, and if a complicated person digs, he may get it fifty or sixty feet. An innocent-minded person will get it quickly, but a violent and angry man will take a long time to reach the water level.

The difference is in the layers of the earth. The water is underneath all the earth. Soul is there in everybody, godliness is there in everybody - the difference is in the layers of past actions. When you start digging you cannot get the divine directly, you will only get the layers of actions because they surround it. When you start digging the well, you only get stones and pebbles. Don't be discouraged by this. In fact, this is a good start; these things give the signal that the journey has begun. Yes, first you will get stones and pebbles, then rubbish, then good soil, then wet soil. You are getting closer every day. When you see the wet ground you should know that water is not far away.

Water is inside everyone, because you cannot live without water. Life is inside everyone, how can you exist without life? You may have hidden it, you may have covered it, but you cannot destroy it.

The soul can be covered by your activities but it cannot be destroyed. We have suppressed the soul in birth after birth, so the catharsis has to be done according to the degree of suppression. Therefore, do not be discouraged.

"During catharsis I only express negative emotions, anger, jealousy, anguish, etc.".

It is good. These are good signs. Throw them away. When you get absolutely catatonic then you will meet the other hidden currents. The day anger is uprooted and expelled from you, from that day onwards you will get compassion, because compassion is the other side of anger. The moment violence ends in you, non-violence will be born in you.

Keep digging as long as you keep having these negative emotions - the positive emotions are hidden somewhere underneath them. But you have to dig and you can't be lazy.

It takes continuous work, continuous vigilance, because you may keep digging with one hand and re-laying the stones and soil with the other.

In the morning you will expel anger while meditating, but you will accumulate anger all day in the marketplace. Then this digging will be useless. It will be like digging a well during the day and filling it with stones at night and having to dig it again the next day.

There is a story that Jesus used: A man sowed wheat in a field, but someone put seeds of wild plants and weeds in it to destroy the field. The servants became very worried. The head of the servants called a meeting to think about what to do and how to save the crop. They asked the master. The master replied: "If you start pulling up the wild plants, the wheat plants will also die. The two can be separated at harvest time".

But this did not please the servants. They said that the field had to be weeded soon.

The evil had to be destroyed as soon as possible. They decided to look for the person who had done the mischief. "Who could be the enemy of our master, who is an honest knight? They tried to find out but to no avail.

One night, a servant came to the head servant and said: "Forgive me, but I can't keep this secret any longer. I know who has sown the seeds of these wild plants in our field. I myself have seen that person because I was awake at the time and saw him enter the field. But maybe he was not conscious at that time, because I was standing in front of him, but he did not see me and did not recognise me; maybe he was asleep. I have kept this secret for a long time but now it is difficult to keep it".

The chief servant was very angry and asked him why he had kept the secret until now. Why had he not told him before? The servant replied: "Even now I don't have the courage to tell you, but I can't keep it to myself any longer. So you had better hear the whole story first.

The chief servant said, "You must tell me the name of that man. He will be punished. The servant sat with his head bowed. The chief asked him: "Why don't you tell his name? Why are you afraid?

The servant replied: "You won't believe me. It is our master who has thrown the seeds of the wild plants into the field. It is our master." So they both decided to keep the secret to themselves.

This story of Jesus says that whatever you build by day you tear down by night. Everything you build during the day when you are conscious, you destroy at night when you are unconscious.

There are people who walk in their sleep. There have been cases in court: a woman gets up at night, sets fire to her clothes and goes back to sleep. She is not fooling anyone because it is her clothes, which are very valuable and she likes them very much. But in the morning, when she wakes up, she screams that someone has burnt her clothes. But no one has entered the room; only the husband and wife are sleeping in that room and no one else has entered. The husband could not have burnt them and how could the wife do such a thing? Yes, it could be the work of a ghost! But after much investigation it was discovered that it was the wife who was burning her own clothes; she had the habit of sleepwalking. There are some people who go to the kitchen in their sleep, eat something and go back to sleep. If you ask them in the morning, they will deny it and say that they never got up in the night. At most they may remember that they saw a dream; they do not remember that clearly either.

In reality, all individuals suffer from this disease. What you do with one hand you destroy with the other. You hate the person you love. You disrespect the person you respect very much. You are contradictory; you are divided into many pieces, into many parts within yourself. You destroy your love with your hate and you destroy your compassion with your anger.

You go to the temple to remember God and you start remembering the market, the shop. There was no need to go to the temple, you could have sat in the marketplace. But the problem with you is that when you are sitting in your tent you keep remembering the temple, and when you are in the temple you keep thinking about the tent.

I heard that a sannyasin died. On the same day a prostitute also died. They had lived in opposite houses. When the angels came to take them away, they were taking the sannyasin to hell and the prostitute to heaven. The sannyasin said, "Stop! You seem to have made a mistake. You are doing just the opposite: taking me, the sannyasin, to hell and taking this prostitute to heaven! You must have misunderstood your instructions and it is quite natural.

Even ordinary governments make mistakes, so there may be a mistake in the administration of this universe. You'd better find out first.

The angels also began to doubt. They said there had never been any mistake "...but it is quite clear that you are a sannyasin and she is a prostitute". They went to check and there was no mistake: the prostitute should be taken to heaven and the sannyasin to hell. "If she insists on knowing the reason then tell her this reason...."

The reason was that the sannyasin lived in the temple but he was always thinking about the prostitute. While worshipping God his mind was thinking of the prostitute. And when at night there was singing and dancing, drinking and merrymaking in the prostitute's house, this sannyasin would miss all that and think that he had wasted his life sitting in that empty temple. He would say to himself: "What am I doing sitting in front of this stone image? I don't even know whether God exists or not". He doubted God. He couldn't sleep all night; he kept dreaming of having a good time with the prostitute.

And the mental attitude of the prostitute was just the opposite. She was a prostitute, so she had to entertain people by dancing, but she was always thinking about the temple. When the temple bells rang, she would think, "When will that lucky day come when I can enter the temple? I am the most unfortunate person. My whole life is wasted, it is dirty. Oh God! Please make me a priestess in my next birth. I will consider myself very fortunate even if I turn into dust on the temple steps so that people who come to worship me will touch me with their feet. That will be more than enough for me.

When she smelled the aroma of incense from the temple, she was lost in ecstasy. She thanked God for keeping her close to the temple. She thought that there are many people who live far away from the temple, but "I am lucky to be so close, even though I am a sinner". She would sit and close her eyes every time the priest worshipped.

The priest thought of the prostitute and the prostitute thought of the cult. The priest went to hell and the prostitute went to heaven.

Man is always in a dilemma. He thinks of the temple when he is in the market. The head of the family, the father of the family, thinks of becoming a sannyasin, and the sadhus keep repenting and thinking that maybe they were wrong in renouncing the world: maybe this life is all there is and we are dreaming of the other life. Heaven and liberation, who has seen them?

Sometimes some old sannyasins come to see me, honest sannyasins, because the dishonest ones never say this to anybody, they keep it to themselves. Yes, honest sannyasins sometimes come and say to me: "We are seventy years old now; we became sannyasins forty years ago but so far we have not achieved anything, and now we have started doubting whether there is anything worth all this effort. Have we wasted our life? We did not enjoy what we had and we have wasted our life in the hope of getting something that is not. These are honest people. What they say is authentic, they don't hide anything.

If you get to know the inner stories of your sannyasins you will be surprised, and you will find it difficult to bow your head at their feet. You think they have attained bliss, they have attained peace, they have attained God, but most of them have attained nothing, they are in a worse condition than you. There is no doubt that they have lost their world and have not attained God.

This is a complicated issue. Renouncing or forsaking the world does not realise the divine. The fact is that if you realise the divine then the world is lost. Light cannot be created by eliminating darkness; the coming of light eliminates darkness.

Therefore, Sannyas is not negative, it is positive. First one has to attain, then one gives up, and this is also right. And this is also correct, how can you give up the futile until you have seen the meaningful?

The vision of the significant gives the courage to give up the non-essential. After seeing the significant, you automatically give up the non-essential. You will not have to make the effort to renounce, you will not have the pain of renouncing; your steps will go towards the significant with great joy, you will never look back. It is only the sannyasin who does not look back. Looking back means that the sannyas is immature.

At first you have to bring out the negative emotions that are hidden in you. In the beginning you have to expel the disease. When the disease has been expelled, when the catharsis has been done, then health will appear. Don't be afraid. You are fortunate, you have the opportunity to expel the disease. If the disease is expelled, then the water of health is not far away. You have dirt in the upper layer; once removed, the water in you is as pure as that of Mahavira, Buddha and Shankara. Your innermost nature, your being, is exactly the same. There is no difference, there cannot be. The "meaning" of nature is that there is no difference.

But to get to that nature you have to do a lot of digging. The sooner you do it, the better. And you have to be careful about one thing, and that is that whatever you throw away you don't put back into the pit. Otherwise you will work all your life and you will get nothing. A lot of people start digging a lot of times.

There was a great Sufi fakir, Jalaluddin Rumi. One day he took his disciples to a nearby field. He showed them how the field had been spoiled by the owner; it was full of big holes. He had started digging a well, but found no water after digging four or five metres deep, so he started digging elsewhere. Finding no water even in the second place, he started digging in the third place. So he dug in eight places and now he was digging in the ninth place. Thus he had spoiled the whole field.

Jalaluddin said: "Look at this man! If he had concentrated on one place and worked hard only in one place, he would surely have found water, however deep it was. But he digs only three or four metres and thinks there is no water there, so he tries somewhere else. He has dug eight holes and in all he has dug a hundred and sixty feet deep, and even then he has not been able to find water. But if he had dug one hundred and sixty feet deep in one place, he would certainly have found water.

You will also start digging many times in life. Sometimes you start meditating and out of enthusiasm you do it for a fortnight or a month and then you forget about it. Then you think about it again after four years, you start digging and become a little peaceful and then you forget about meditation again. So you will dig many holes but you will not reach the water level. Your field will be spoilt.

If you get used to giving up after digging for a few days, you might as well not have dug at all, because you will have wasted the work. If the water level is not reached, all the work is wasted. Continuity is needed. And remember that just as the continuous dripping of water breaks the stones, so the continuous dripping of meditation will certainly break the big rocks around you.

Today it may seem that your anger is too strong, how can meditation break it? But it breaks, it has always broken. The rock is very strong and meditation is very delicate, but this is the mystery of life: the continuity of the delicate can break the strongest and the hardest.

The fourth question:

Question 4:

BELOVED MASTER, YOU SAY THAT GETTING LOST IN SINGING THE SONG OF THE DIVINE IS INTOXICATION. YOU ALSO SAY THAT JOY IS LOST WHEN YOU ARE SEEKING JOY WHILE SWIMMING, PLAYING, MEDITATING, AND JOY SEEKS YOU WHEN YOU ARE IMMERSED IN THEM. PLEASE EXPLAIN AND CLARIFY THE LIMITS OF IMMERSION, CONSCIOUSNESS AND UNCONSCIOUSNESS.

To sing the song of the divine in order to lose oneself is intoxication, but to lose oneself singing is not intoxication.

Let me repeat: it is a bit complicated. It is subtle but understandable. To get lost, singing the song of the divine is an intoxicant. If you just want to get lost.... Life is full of worry, anguish, pain, sorrow, tension, disturbance, misery; to forget about this, to save oneself from all this, one has to occupy oneself or get involved somewhere so that one can forget oneself. So somebody sits in the cinema and forgets himself; somebody sits in the wine bar and forgets himself for two hours; somebody goes to the temple, starts singing the song of the divine and forgets himself. These are all different methods of forgetting oneself. But the aim of all three is the same: to forget your worries. But the worries are waiting for you to come home. When you go home you will be the same.

Those two hours were wasted, they were useless. For those two hours the worry is not going to go away.

The search for something with which you can forget yourself is intoxicating, it is like alcohol. For that you can make religion like alcohol. But to lose yourself in singing the song of the divine is something else altogether. You didn't go there to lose yourself, you had no desire to forget yourself, you didn't go there to save yourself from worry; you had gone there to wake up from worry.

Worry is not to be forgotten, but destroyed. You went to destroy worry, to understand the essence of life; you went to create a time in life when worry would become impossible, a time when there would be no disturbance, no restlessness; you had gone in search of your nature.

You had gone in search of deep springs of water. You had not gone to forget, but to awaken. But you got lost while meditating. This kind of getting lost is not an intoxicant. If this is an intoxicant then this intoxicant is of consciousness. In this you will lose yourself and yet remain awake. You will find yourself absolutely finished and at the same time, for the first time, you will be finished. On the one hand you will find that everything is lost and on the other hand you will find that everything has become new.

You are and yet you are not. This you can only understand by experience.

In meditation there is a moment when you are not - there is no "I" in that moment; only existence is, only your being is. The "I" is lost, there is only existence. There is no thought, there is no ego; the mirror of the mind is absolutely clean, there is no dust in it. The divine is reflected in that clean mirror. This is a wonderful moment of peace, this is the unique experience of samadhi.

But you didn't go there to lose yourself, you went there to transform yourself, you went there to change yourself. You didn't go there to lose yourself, you went there to finish; you didn't go there to rest for a while, you went there to revolutionise your whole life.

Meditation can be done in two ways: the first is that you just want to forget yourself and the second is that you want to transform yourself. And you will get the fruits of whatever is the true reason within you. You will reap what you sow.

If in meditation you sow the seed of finishing yourself, then in the harvest you will find that you are finished; only pity remains. If in meditation you sow the seed of forgetting yourself, then you will find that even meditation has become an intoxicant; you forget yourself for a moment but then you are still the same. You return to your original condition, perhaps worse than before, because even that moment was wasted, it was useless.

So I definitely say that losing yourself in singing the song of the divine is an intoxicant - if you do it to lose yourself. But if you do it to end yourself, then it's not an intoxication, it's an awakening, it's consciousness.

And always remember that when you go in search of joy, of ecstasy, then you will not find it because that very search will become an obstacle. You will miss joy whenever you seek it, because you only get it when you don't ask for it. Joy and ecstasy are only for emperors and not for beggars. When you go with a bowl of alms you do not get joy; it comes to you when you stand up like an emperor. You will not get it as long as you ask for it. You will get it only when you stop asking for it. Then it will come rushing to you from everywhere. The most important rule of life, the most ancient religious law of life, is that you will not be able to attain joy and bliss when you keep running after it.

Try to understand it like this: you have forgotten someone's name. You say: "I know it, but I can't remember it. It's on the tip of my tongue". But if it's on the tip of your tongue, why don't you say it? The more you try to remember, the harder it is to remember. The harder you try, the more you forget. And you know you know it. You struggle and start sweating. What's the problem?

In reality, when you keep trying to remember you create tension inside you, and that tension affects the mind: it narrows, it shrinks, there is no space left in it. So you give up and you start reading the newspaper, or you go to the garden, or you go to tea. Just when you forget to try to remember the name, suddenly, like a flash, the name appears in your mind and you remember it. When you are making an effort you feel disturbed, restless. This effort causes tension.

When you give up the effort and are at peace with yourself, then automatically the name is remembered.

Ecstasy, bliss is your nature. You shrink when you make an effort. It is within you, you don't have to bring it from anywhere. But you shrink so much that there is no space left. You must have seen that the more you hurry, the more you delay. If you're in a hurry to catch the train, you keep putting the buttons in the wrong holes. In your haste, you can't close your suitcase properly. When you leave in a hurry, you leave your key or ticket at home, so getting to the station on time is useless.

And you also know that if you had done all these things without tension, without haste, then everything would have been done very conveniently. Every day you button your coat properly, there is never a mistake in it; but the day you are in a hurry the button is in the wrong hole. The coat is not your enemy, the coat is not trying to take revenge on you; the coat has nothing to do with you.

But haste upsets you, worries you and your hand becomes unsteady. When you do things with confidence and certainty then everything is done on time. But because of worry you get delayed. If you try to run fast, you will be late; the slower you go, the sooner you will arrive.

It sounds paradoxical but it is not, because patience is a great strength, and not asking for anything is a great self-confidence.

You get joy, bliss, ecstasy when you are not looking for it. Then the festival of ecstasy, of joy starts from all sides - from within and from without. Give up the search. Don't ask for it. Don't make meditation a means, but an end. Do not think that you are meditating to attain bliss. No, meditation itself is a bliss, a joy. You should not do it with the idea of attaining bliss. The bliss, the joy is in doing it. When the means becomes the end, then you have reached the destination. You don't have to go anywhere. Your godliness appears wherever you are. Where can you go? You don't know God's direction, you have no inkling of his whereabouts, where will you look for him? Where will you look for bliss? Where will you look for truth? Where will you look for deliverance? It is better for you to sit quietly.

Surely you have seen the statues of Buddha, of Mahavira, of Shankara. They don't seem to be walking, running or going anywhere, they just sit in silence. There is no searching expression on their faces. Look at Mahavira's face carefully: there is no hurry on his face. Does his face show the expression that he is searching for something? He is simply sitting. There is no search, no desire, no expectation, no future, just here and now.

If you have seen the statues of Buddha, Mahavira and Shankara, you will see that their whole message is "now and here". They are sitting peacefully, they are not going anywhere, they are not becoming anything, they are not attaining anything, they are not running for any desire. And then, everything happens in that moment! The sky rains.

The last question:

Question 5:

BELOVED MASTER, IS SINGING THE SONG OF THE DIVINE, LIKE PRAYER, ALSO AN EXPRESSION OF THANKSGIVING?

Prayer is the seed, bhajan, singing the song of the divine, is the tree. Prayer is hidden, unexpressed, bhajan is the expression. Bhajan is the dancing prayer, the singing prayer. Bhajan is the expression of prayer. If you want to see prayer, you will have to look at it in Mahavira and Buddha.

If you want to see bhajan then you better look at Meera and Chaitanya. Bhajan is prayer expressed. What remains within Mahavira and Buddha flows out of Meera and Chaitanya. What is static within Buddha and Mahavira has begun to dance in Meera and Chaitanya. Bhajan is the expression of prayer.

You can understand it like this. Suppose you are in love with someone. You can keep it to yourself, there is no need to say anything about it. It doesn't matter even if you don't say, "I love you". You can keep your love inside you. Normally women don't talk about their love to anyone, they keep it to themselves. There is no need to say that you love, because the very experience of love is enough in itself. But love expresses itself, sometimes in a song, sometimes in the touch of the hand, sometimes in the expression of the eyes, and sometimes also in silence. And when love expresses itself, flowers bloom, the seed does not remain a seed. Both are beautiful.

There are two kinds of people in the world. For some people prayer is enough - there is no need to say anything - they will reach God in their emptiness, in their silence. But it is not enough for the other kind of people. Unless it is more than enough, it is not enough for them, they have to overflow. They have to keep flowing, expressing their inner ecstasy. That's why Meera dances. Buddha did not express himself in this way, but Meera did; and both are beautiful, both ways are good. You must know your own nature. If you want to keep it to yourself, it doesn't matter, and if you want to distribute it, it doesn't matter either. And I don't compare the two. The seed is beautiful because from it flowers come, and the flower is beautiful because it becomes a seed. They are interconnected.

The expressed and the unexpressed, the manifest and the unmanifest, both are connected. You must discover your nature, your temperament, and choose what appeals to you. But remember that bhajan is expression and prayer is silence.

The question is: "Like prayer, is singing the song of the divine also an expression of thanksgiving?".

No, prayer is gratitude and bhajan is gratitude with ecstasy. Prayer says: whatever is given to me is plenty; I am fully satisfied and content with what is given to me. But bhajan says that whatever is given to me is more than is necessary, it cannot be contained, it has to be distributed. The bhajan expresses itself by dancing; it is not silent, it speaks. It has its own beauty.

Prayer is an unsung song, the picture hidden in the painter's mind that has not taken shape on the canvas. It is the statue hidden in the stone that has not been sculpted with the chisel.

Bhajan is the visible statue. The stone has been cut, the chisel has done the work. Bhajan is the song that is sung.

A friend came to see Rabindranath when he was about to die, just two days before he passed away. He said to him, "Yours has been a very successful life. Now there is nothing to worry about or regret". The two had been friends since childhood and were now both elderly. He said, "You can die in peace. I have achieved nothing in this life, I have wasted it, so I will not die in peace. You have sung so many songs.

Rabindranath has sung six thousand songs. No other poet in this world has sung so many songs.

The poet Shelley is very famous in the West, but his songs number about three thousand, while Rabindranath's number six thousand, and those six thousand songs can be set to music.

The old friend said to him: "You have been awarded the Nobel Prize; you have been showered with honours, you can die in peace. Of course I'll die without peace, but you can thank God as you say goodbye to the world".

Rabindranath listened to what his friend was saying. Then he said, "Well, I have not been able to sing the song I wanted to sing, it is still inside me like a seed. These six thousand songs are the fruitless efforts to sing that one song. I have tried many times to sing that song which is in me like a seed, but I have failed every time. You may have liked these songs, but they are the stories of my failure. My song has not yet been sung. I haven't sung it yet, and God has come to take me. A moment ago I was tuning my instruments; with great difficulty I was able to tune my sitar. People thought I was singing. No, I was tuning my instruments. Now I have matured enough, the instruments are ready, my spirit is ready, the time for singing has just come, but it is time to leave. Yes, I complain to God.

Rabindranath could not sit like Buddha under a tree. He wanted to sing the song of the divine.

Rabindranath has criticised Buddha a lot, not out of antipathy, but out of love and gratitude. But Buddha never appealed to Rabindranath: he was fond of him, but Buddha sitting silently like a stone statue did not appeal to him. But the fakirs bauls did attract him, the fakirs, the sadhus who danced with the ektara. This is the difference of individuals. Rabindranath respected the Buddha, he had nothing against him, but they were two different types.

The personality of the bhajan is different and the individuality of prayer is different. Prayer is silent, bhajan is speech, words, expression. Prayer is silent, quiet.

People who pray have said, Sufis have said, if your left hand is praying your right hand should not know. It should be done in the darkness of the night. If a husband prays, the wife must not know, otherwise it would be showing off, and showing off means ego. The person who prays is afraid that others will know.

But he who sings the song of the divine dances in the middle of the road. He doesn't care if others know it. He says it doesn't matter whether people know it or not. He destroys his ego by dancing. His ego is lost by dancing. They are two different ways. Prayer is only thanksgiving, bhajan is the expression of gratitude.

You must understand your inner condition. You can reach the divine through prayer or bhajan. The paths are different but the destination is the same. And you should always choose the one that suits you, the one you can enjoy. Always think of yourself, observe yourself.....

because you may find something about the other person very attractive but not suitable for you. Therefore, you should not accept it even by mistake. What is good for the other person may not be good for you. The other person's medicine may be poison for you.

Your medicine may also be poison for the other person. Actually, medicine is not medicine, poison is not poison - the poison that is good for you becomes medicine for you; the medicine that is not good for you becomes poison for you. So you should always observe what is good for you, what is harmonious for you, and then choose what is for you.

If you want to sit quietly like Buddha, if you want to go deep into silence without any body movement .... We have made the statues of Buddha and Mahavira out of marble. The reason is that they were sitting like this marble. When they were alive they were unshakable. But a marble statue of Meera will not be attractive. People have made it, but it is not attractive. The statue of Meera cannot be static, it has to be made of water - dancing, liquid, not static.

Meera is a movement, a physical expression of emotion, a dance. Mahavira is static. It is like a pond without any ripples. Meera is like a waterfall, like water falling from a hill, where every drop dances.

These are the big differences, but these differences are of paths. Ultimately, the pond is also lost, it evaporates into the sky riding on the sun's rays, and the river is also lost into the sky riding on the sun's rays after flowing into the ocean.

The destination is one, but the paths are many. The temple is one, but the gates are many. Choose your own door, do not follow others. A creed is created by following and religion is born by going according to your nature.

Enough for today.

The slavery of hope

H E WHO WEARS LONG HAIR ON HIS HEAD, HE WHO HAS SHAVED HIS HEAD, HE WHO HAS PULLED OUT HIS HAIR BY THE ROOTS, HE WHO WEARS OCHRE ROBES OR IS DRESSED IN VARIOUS ATTIRE, THIS IDIOT, ALTHOUGH HE HAS EYES, IS BLIND.

JUST FOR THE SAKE OF HIS STOMACH HE DRESSES IN DIFFERENT WAYS.

ALL THE LIMBS HAVE BECOME SICKLY, ALL THE HAIR HAS TURNED WHITE, THERE IS NOT A SINGLE TOOTH LEFT IN THE MOUTH - SUCH AN OLD MAN WALKS WITH THE HELP OF A CANE; EVEN THEN HE IS BOUND WITH THE MASS OF HOPE.

COLD-STRICKEN, IN THE MORNING HE WARMS HIMSELF WITH THE FIRE IN FRONT OF HIM OR WITH HIS BACK TO THE SUN. AT NIGHT, HE SLEEPS WITH HIS CHIN BETWEEN HIS KNEES, TAKES ALMS IN HIS HANDS AND LIVES UNDER A TREE; EVEN THEN HE DOES NOT GIVE UP THE SLAVERY OF HOPE.

HE CAN UNDERTAKE THE JOURNEY TO THE GANGES OR THE OCEAN, HE CAN PERFORM MANY AUSTERITIES AND FASTS, HE CAN GIVE IN CHARITY, BUT IF HE HAS NO SELF-KNOWLEDGE HE WILL NOT BE LIBERATED EVEN IN A HUNDRED LIFETIMES.

ONE MAY RESIDE IN THE TEMPLE OF GOD OR

UNDER A TREE, THE EARTH MAY BE HIS ONLY BED, THE DEERSKIN MAY BE HIS ONLY ROBE, HE MAY HAVE FORSAKEN ALL POSSESSIONS AND INDULGENCES - WHO DOES SUCH RENUNCIATION NOT MAKE HAPPY?

HE MAY BE ABSORBED IN SENSE ENJOYMENT OR IN YOGA, HE MAY BE ABSORBED IN THE COMPANY OF SOMEONE OR HE MAY BE ALONE, BUT IF HIS HEART DWELLS IN THE DIVINE, THEN IT IS HE WHO IS BLISSFUL, IT IS HE WHO IS BLISSFUL, IT IS HE ALONE WHO IS BLISSFUL.

There is a very old story about an ascetic who was doing sadhana in a dense forest. He was sitting with his eyes closed and continuously praying to God. He wanted to attain heaven. Hunger and thirst did not bother him.

A very poor young woman used to go to that forest to collect firewood. Out of kindness and consideration for the ascetic, she would pluck some fruits and bring him water from the pond in cups made of leaves, and put them near him. The ascetic could feed himself with these things.

Gradually, his asceticism became even more intense. She forgot her hunger and thirst and did not even touch fruit or water. That poor girl felt very unhappy and sad about it, but there was no way out. Lord Indra was also concerned and said that this person is going beyond the limits: does he intend to seize the throne of heaven? It is absolutely necessary to disturb his sadhana.

It was not very difficult to do so because Lord Indra knows the mind of man. A breeze came from the sky and turned that poor dark and ugly young girl into a dazzling beauty. It seemed as if a bolt of lightning came down from the sky and turned her ordinary body into a golden one. As she filled the pool of water for the ascetic, she saw her reflection in the water and could not believe that she looked like a fairy. She was fascinated by her own reflection.

She continued to look after the ascetic. Then, one day, the ascetic opened his eyes and told the young woman that he wanted to leave that place and go to other mountains, for he must tread a more difficult path; he cannot rest until he has conquered heaven itself.

The young woman burst into tears, tears falling from her eyes. She said, "What wrong have I done that you would prevent me from serving you? I have never asked you for anything.

thought the ascetic and looked at her face. He had never seen such beauty, not even in his dreams! The woman was at once familiar and unfamiliar. The contours were the same but now there was a glory in her. The body and the features were the same, but now they were radiant. It was like a forgotten melody, played again on a flute by some musician. The ascetic sat down and closed his eyes again. He did not go away.

That night the young girl could not sleep because she was happy for her victory and also regretful for having defiled the sadhu. She was happy that she had won, but she was unhappy that she had been an obstacle in the ascetic's path. She regretted that, because of her, he could not continue his upward journey.

I couldn't sleep at night. He cried and laughed. In the morning he made up his mind. He touched the ascetic's feet and said, "I have to leave. My family is going to another village.

The ascetic blessed her to be happy wherever she lived, and the young woman left.

After many years the asceticism was complete. Lord Indra himself came down, bowed down and said, "The gates of heaven are open to receive you".

The ascetic opened his eyes and said: "I don't want heaven".

Indra was very surprised. He could not believe that a human being could say that he did not want heaven. Then Indra thought that perhaps this ascetic had the desire to attain liberation. So he asked him: "Do you want liberation?

The ascetic said, "What shall I do with liberation?". Lord Indra was very impressed by this attitude.

He thought to himself that this was the height of asceticism - not even the desire to attain liberation was there. So, out of respect, he wanted to bow to that ascetic, but before he did so he said, "But there is nothing beyond liberation. What more do you want?"

The ascetic replied, "Nothing, except that young maiden who used to collect firewood in this forest. I want her.

Don't laugh. This is the weakness of man. Don't laugh, but think about it, because the gravitation of the earth is so strong! Do not think that this story is just a story; it is the whole agony of man's mind. And don't think that this choice was only before that ascetic, that it was only he who had to choose between the young woman and heaven. You too have the same alternatives. In fact everyone has the same choices: either you choose the pleasures that are transient or you choose the eternal. Either you lose the eternal for the transient or you dedicate the transient to the eternal. And, of course, most people will choose what that ascetic chose.

Do not think that you have done anything different. Whether Lord Indra has stood before you or not, whether someone has given you the alternative of heaven and earth or not, the fact is that the alternative is always there for you. And when you choose one you miss the other. He whose eyes are filled with the intoxication of earth remains deprived of heavenly consciousness. Heavenly gold cannot rain on hands full of earthly dust; heaven can only rain if the hands are empty. The divine can only descend if you are empty inside.

If you are filled with any infatuation the throne of your soul is already occupied. Then don't say that the divine has been unfair to you - this was your choice. Don't blame the divine if you don't find it - it means you haven't chosen it yet, because whenever someone chooses it, he finds it immediately. It doesn't take a second. But if you don't want it, the divine will not force you.

Truth is not imposed by force. You have the freedom to reject truth birth after birth, life after life. This is man's glory and also his disgrace. The glory is due to freedom, the freedom to choose. The misfortune is that we choose evil. But the choice of evil is included in that freedom. You cannot call freedom a freedom that can only choose the right and not the wrong; then that is not freedom. The meaning of freedom is that you have the right to deviate, to go the wrong way. The meaning of freedom is that you have the freedom to sin. The meaning of freedom is that you have the freedom to reject godliness.

Buddha was born, and on the fifth day after his birth, according to custom, the best of the pundits assembled and gave him the name Siddhartha. The meaning of Siddhartha is fulfilment of desire, fulfilment of hope, attainment of wealth, attainment of destiny. After waiting all his life, after hoping and dreaming and going through many disappointments, at last a son was born to Shudhodhana in his old age - he was indeed a "Siddhartha"! The experts had given him the right name.

There were eight great experts. The king asked them to tell him the future of the newborn.

Seven experts raised their hands and pointed with two fingers. The king did not understand and said: "I do not understand these gestures, so please tell me clearly.

The seven pundits said that there are two alternatives: either he will be a great emperor or he will renounce everything and be a great sannyasin. Either he will be a great emperor or he will be a great sannyasin.

Only one expert remained silent. He was the youngest of them all. His name was Kodanna. But he was the most intelligent. The king asked him: "Why are you silent? You have not raised your two fingers.

Kodanna said: "The two fingers can be raised at birth for

everybody because these two alternatives are for everybody: either this world or sannyas - these two alternatives are for everybody. Therefore, these experts have not said anything important about Buddha raising two fingers. Well, I raise only one: he will be a sannyasin!

On hearing this Shudhodhana began to cry. The unfortunate mind of man always behaves like this. He knew that Kodanna was an omniscient astrologer. He was young but very luminous and his words, his prophecies would certainly prove to be true. The other experts had spoken of the possibility of his being a great emperor, but Kodanna had ruled out that alternative. She said that the child would certainly be a buddha.

The king was happy when these experts told him that he would be emperor. He did not attach any importance to the other alternative of his becoming a sannyasin, because if one can be an emperor then why should he think of becoming a sannyasin? But Kodanna destroyed this hope by raising a finger.

The king tried to console himself with the thought that Kodanna is only one person and that there are seven experts who oppose him. Man always consoles himself in this way: seven will be right and one will be wrong. But only that one proved to be right, and it is good that only that one proved to be right.

Also at the moment of your birth, whether you call in the experts or not, nature raises two fingers.

Nature poses two alternatives: either to lose yourself in unconsciousness or to awaken in consciousness. Either you gather the outer wealth, you run the race to become a great emperor, or you gather the inner wealth, you rest in your being. Always remember the single finger of Kodanna. In real life no Kodanna will meet you with a raised finger. You yourself will have to raise your finger.

These Shankara sutras are very subtle gestures of renunciation and detachment.

HE WHO WEARS LONG HAIR ON HIS HEAD, WHO HAS SHAVED HIS HEAD, WHO HAS PLUCKED OUT HIS HAIR BY THE ROOTS, WHO WEARS OCHRE ROBES OR IS DRESSED IN VARIOUS ATTIRE, THIS IDIOT, ALTHOUGH HE HAS EYES, IS BLIND.

JUST FOR THE SAKE OF HIS STOMACH HE DRESSES IN DIFFERENT WAYS.

Always remember that the mind of man is very dangerous. Even in sannyas he seeks the world. It finds hypocrisy even in the temple; even in sadhana it finds sense enjoyment. Whatever the external activity, the mind still acts according to its old habit.

So Shankara says: Don't be fooled by someone who has long hair on his head. Long hair makes no difference. Don't be fooled by anyone who has a shaved head. Shaving your head, wearing your hair long or pulling out your hair makes no difference, it just doesn't matter.

So don't be fooled by the sight of such people. The Jaina Digambar munis pull out their hair, don't be fooled by them. There are people who wear ochre robes, do not be deceived by them. Don't worry if the other is cheated, but you should not be cheated, because it is very easy to wear ochre robes or to pull out your hair; it just takes a little experience. What difficulty is there in shaving your head or wearing your hair long? It just takes a bit of experience. But try to see what is going on inside the mind. Under these various guises of sannyas they are only carrying on business to fill their stomachs.

Ninety percent of sannyasins only fill their stomachs. If only one's stomach were filled, the world would be a better place. At least one would be honest: the shop could function as such without cheating others; there would be no need to pollute the temple. Ordinary clothes were fine, there was no need to defile the ochre robes. What was the need to tear out your hair? The barber could have cut your hair. All these external things don't matter if your mind is doing business.

If your mind is involved in the running of the shop, then this is just a hoax.

A few months earlier I received news that two Jaina munis - they live naked, have renounced everything and own nothing - left the village to answer the call of nature and started fighting. They were master and disciple. They attacked each other. Because of this quarrel and attack their secret came to light. Both had hidden money in the hollow stick of the pichie they were carrying; the fight was over the sharing of the money. Both were caught and taken to the police station. Their disciples in the village were worried and upset because it was also about their prestige. Somehow, they defused the matter by bribing the police so that the news would not spread to other places.

The naked man is also doing the same as the shopkeeper. So isn't it better that he sits in the shop? Then at least the nudity will not be contaminated.

No one forces you to renounce the world. Renounce it only when you feel like it; otherwise, this pretence of renouncing the world is nothing but a delusion.

HE WHO WEARS LONG HAIR ON HIS HEAD, HE WHO HAS SHAVED HIS HEAD, HE WHO HAS PULLED OUT HIS HAIR BY THE ROOTS, HE WHO WEARS OCHRE ROBES OR IS DRESSED IN VARIOUS ATTIRE, THIS IDIOT, ALTHOUGH HE HAS EYES, IS BLIND.

Why does Shankara say: THAT IDIOT, IN HIS EYES, IS BLIND? Who is he deceiving? It is not a question of deceiving others; the other does not care for him. He is fooling himself. The bottom line is based on what you are on the inside, not what you are on the outside. Life is determined by what you are on the inside, not by what you are on the outside.

Inside you are continuously counting money, outside you are chanting "Ram, Ram". This chanting is useless. Counting money is significant - the judgement will be based on that, because there is no one else doing the judging, the judgement is being done every moment by what you are doing inside you. If it had been someone else doing the judging, you could have asked for forgiveness, you could have asked them to give in. But there is no judge. There is no God sitting somewhere who can be appeased by you. Whatever you do, your action is your destiny. The result is hidden in your action. Your thought is the basis of your being.

There is a very sweet story about Mahavira's life. Mahavira was standing in a forest absorbed in meditation and a king who was his childhood friend was coming for Mahavira's darshan. On the way he saw another king, who had become Mahavira's sannyasin, standing near a rock doing austerities, tapasya. The three were childhood friends.

The first king felt very sorry for leading a worldly life. He thought, "Look at this king, Prasenchandra, how peaceful and silent he is. How blissful he is. How unfortunate I am. Mahavira has attained liberation and I am still counting money". The thought of renunciation arose in him.

When he met Mahavira he said, "I want to ask you a question. On the way I saw Prasenchandra doing austerities, tapasya. He is your disciple. Seeing him, I too feel like renouncing this world. And I want to know something: if Prasenchandra had died at the time when I was with him, where would he be reborn?

Mahavira said: "If Prasenchandra had died at that time he would have been born in the seventh hell".

The king was stunned to hear this. Prasenchandra was standing so peacefully, so quietly, immersed in meditation - and if he died he would be born in the seventh hell! Mahavira said, "Don't worry.

But if he dies now - only a few moments have passed between the two events - he will enter the seventh heaven".

The king said, "This looks like a riddle. Please explain it to me.

Mahavira said, "Before you came, the soldiers had passed by Prasenchandra. They saw him and remarked: 'This fool is standing here with his eyes closed. His sons are still too young and the ministers, to whom he has entrusted his kingdom, are busy plundering his wealth and he is standing here like a fool'. The soldiers said this as they passed by him, and when Prasenchandra heard that the ministers were plundering his wealth, that the people he had trusted were cheating him, for a second he forgot that he had given up everything. He forgot, he was not conscious, and the thought came to his mind: 'I am still alive, you fools. What do you think you are? I am still very much alive and I am going to separate the heads of these ministers from their bodies'. And unconsciously his hand tried to grasp his sword which was not there now, but because of the old habit he tried to pull the sword out of its scabbard. And another old habit was that when he got angry he adjusted his crown....".

Many of you also have the habit of scratching your head or scratching your forehead. So now, in his anger, when he tried to adjust his crown, there was no crown and he could only touch his shaved head. Instantly he became aware: what am I doing? I am no longer King Prasenchandra, I have renounced everything, how can I think of killing people?

Mahavira said, "When you were near Prasenchandra, inside him the sword was unsheathed, so if he had died at that time he would have gone to the seventh hell. But now that he has become conscious, he is laughing at his own stupidity. If he dies at this moment then he will be born in the seventh heaven.

Every action is the judge, and the decision of the action is within you, not outside you. You can be silent on the outside while a storm rages within you. You can appear very calm on the outside while inside you can be restless. You can be calm on the outside, while inside you can be ready to explode at any moment.

Your outside is not valuable. Your inner self is your existence.

Your every action decides the nature of your soul. Your every action creates you. There is no other judge but you.

That's why Shankara says: THAT IDIOT, EVEN THOUGH HE HAS EYES, IS BLIND - because he thinks he is deceiving others.

But all deception is deceiving yourself. You are deceiving yourself. You cannot make others lose anything, it is you who will lose. You may get some money out of other people's pockets, but with that money you will lose your soul. You will lose a lot and gain nothing. Even if you are able to cheat others, what will you get? At most you will snatch some money from the other person. That money will stay here, neither you will be able to take it away nor the other person will be able to take it away after death. It doesn't matter whether the money is in this pocket or that pocket. But by snatching it, by desiring it, you have perverted yourself, your mind has become dirty, you have sown the seed of sin within you. Then you must not expect to get any tasty fruit or any fragrant flower from this seed.

THAT IDIOT, ALTHOUGH HE HAS EYES, HE IS BLIND. JUST FOR THE SAKE OF HIS STOMACH HE DRESSES IN DIFFERENT WAYS. THEREFORE, OH IDIOT! ALWAYS SING THE SONG OF THE DIVINE.

ALL THE LIMBS HAVE BECOME SICKLY, ALL THE HAIR HAS TURNED WHITE, THERE IS NOT A SINGLE TOOTH LEFT IN THE MOUTH - SUCH AN OLD MAN WALKS WITH THE HELP OF A CANE; EVEN THEN HE IS BOUND WITH THE MASS OF HOPE.

Until the last moment of death, hope is not abandoned. You die, but hope does not die. Even in death hope lives, it remains alert and young. Even the man who is dying thinks that tomorrow all will be well. He dreams of tomorrow even when he is dying; people die dreaming.

You have to understand hope. What is hope? The illusion of

achieving what one does not have. This dream of what is not now, of what will one day be, is hope. And what is the awakening of hope? The awareness of what is. Hope disappears when you become aware of what is. Hope exists in the demand for what is not. The poor live in hope and the rich also live in hope.

When Alexander the Great came to India, he went to see a fakir called Diogenes because he had heard a lot about him. And it often happens that even emperors get jealous of fakirs.

Diogenes was also a fakir. He used to live naked like Mahavira. He was a unique fakir, he did not even carry a begging bowl with him. In the beginning, when he became a fakir, he used to carry a begging bowl. But one day he saw a dog drinking water from the river. He said to himself, "I must be mad! Why do I carry this bowl with me? This dog drinks water without any bowl. The dog has more sense than me; if he can do without the bowl, why can't I do without it? So he threw the bowl away.

Alexander heard that Diogenes was living in ecstasy, so Alexander went to meet him. When he saw Alexander, Diogenes asked him: "Where are you going?

Alexander said: "I have to conquer Asia Minor".

Diogenes asked him: "What are you going to do next? Diogenes was lying on the sand of the river. It must have been a winter morning like this one. He was sunbathing. He just lay there, he didn't even get up or sit down. He asked again, "What will you do next?".

Alexander replied: "Then we must conquer India".

Diogenes asked: "And after that? And Alexander said that afterwards he would conquer what was left of the world. Diogenes asked: "And then?"

Alexander said, "What then? Then I will rest.

Diogenes laughed. I'm resting now. You'll rest then! If you want to rest in the end, why go to all this trouble? I'm resting now. You can also rest on the bank of this river, there's plenty of room here. There is no need to go anywhere, you can rest here right now".

Alexander was very impressed. For a moment he felt ashamed that what Diogenes was saying was true: if he was going to rest after all, why was he planning it that way? And Diogenes was indeed resting. You can't say he was saying anything wrong: he was resting and happier than Alexander. His face was like a lotus in bloom.

Alexander possessed everything but had nothing inside. Diogenes had nothing outside, but he had everything inside. Alexander said to Diogenes: "You make me envious. If I am ever born again I will ask God not to make me Alexander but Diogenes".

Diogenes said: "Again you deceive yourself, why do you bring God? If you want to become Diogenes, what difficulty is there in you being Diogenes right now? It is difficult for me to be an Alexander because I may or may not be able to conquer the world. I may or may not be able to gather such a large army. But there is no difficulty for you to be Diogenes: get rid of your clothes and rest!

Alexander said: "What you say appeals to me, but it does not give me hope. I will come back. I will certainly come back. But now I must go, for my journey is incomplete. What you say is one hundred per cent correct".

This is very interesting. What you say seems right and yet hope keeps tugging at you. Just a few days before I was narrating the words of a great Japanese poet called Issa. His wife had died, he was very unhappy; then his daughter died, and when he was thirty-three all his five sons died and he was left alone. He was in great agony. His heart was that of a poet, he was completely shaken. He could not sleep at night; he was not in his right mind during the day. He asked himself: "Why is there so much agony in this world, what have I done, why did I have to face this misfortune?

Someone suggested that he go to the temple, because there was a monk there who could solve his problem. He went to the temple. The monk said, "Why is there so much agony?

is meaningless. Life is like a dewdrop that will disappear at any moment. You will be gone too. Your wife is gone, your five children are gone, you will be gone too. Don't waste your time. Life is like the dewdrop on the blade of grass that will fall any moment". Issa returned home. The monk's words appealed to her. Life is like that. He wrote a little haiku which is:

Life is a drop of dew, yes, I am perfectly convinced.

Life is a dewdrop, and yet and yet ....

"And yet" is hope. Even if you understand the fact, hope does not allow you to do it. Even if the intellect understands it, it does not affect life. At most the thought may come to intuit it, but it is not reflected in the emotions. And hope continues to weave its web.

ALL THE LIMBS HAVE BECOME SICKLY, ALL THE HAIR HAS TURNED WHITE, THERE IS NOT A SINGLE TOOTH LEFT IN THE MOUTH - SUCH AN OLD MAN WALKS WITH THE HELP OF A CANE; EVEN THEN HE IS BOUND WITH THE MASS OF HOPE.

Hope is the thread by which we live. It is a very fine thread. It can break at any moment, but it does not break. It has become a very strong shackle. If it breaks at one end, we hold it at the other end. If it breaks for the world, we begin to hope for heaven, for liberation. Hope continues. Hope is bigger than the world.

When you realise the agony of the world and detach yourself from it, then you begin to hope for heaven. Hope carries you even when you are tired and fall down. Many times this question must have arisen in your mind. When you see a beggar on the road with no hands, no feet, no eyes, his whole body wasting away, you wonder why he lives. What does he live for? But he is not the only one who is wrong. If you were in his place, what would you do? You too would go on living. You would hope that tomorrow everything would be all right thanks to some miracle.

Man goes on living in spite of suffering any amount of misery and distress. I want to tell you a unique thing: man does not give up hope even in great misery. Logically it seems that anguish will kill hope. But no, anguish cannot destroy hope. The greater the anguish, the greater is man's hope. Anguish does not destroy hope, it kindles it. Yes, hope is sometimes destroyed in happiness, but not in misery.

That is why the hope of princes like Mahavira and Buddha was destroyed, but the hope of beggars is never destroyed. The twenty-four tirthankaras of the Jainas were princes, the twenty-four Buddhas of the Buddhists were princes, all the avataras of the Hindus were princes. What can be the reason?

The irony is that hope may disappear in happiness, but it does not disappear in unhappiness. Hope should disappear in unhappiness, hope should disappear in misery, but the fact is that as misery increases, the mind keeps creating more and more hope. Hope springs up in misery, hope flourishes in misery, but is destroyed in happiness.

That is why a happy society becomes religious. The unhappy society may become communist, but not religious. There is a possibility of America becoming religious, but not India. India was religious when it was happy, when the country was happy; when its people were satisfied and contented hope disappeared.

When you have everything, you realise that everything is useless. And it's true, because how can you see the uselessness of something you don't have? The person who has money can see the futility of money. But the person who has no money, how can he see its futility? To realise the futility of something, you first have to have it.

A person who has knowledge can see the futility of knowledge, but a person who has no knowledge cannot see its futility. If you have the Kohinoor diamond in your hand, you realise its futility: you can neither eat nor drink it. But if you don't have it, you can still dream about it. Dreams never seem useless - you have no way of discovering their value. You can't see the worthlessness of anything until you possess it.

Hope lives in unhappiness, is nourished by it, but is destroyed in happiness. That is why a man on the edge of the road can be suffering and going through hell, and yet still have hope. If you ever visit hell you will find there the most hopeful people in this world. In spite of their agonies, they still hope to be free of it tomorrow.

I heard that a new prisoner entered a prison. He was taken to a cell where another prisoner was already living. That person asked him how long he was going to be in prison. The new prisoner replied, "Ten years".

Then you'd better stay near the gate, because I've been a prisoner for thirty years. I will stay by the wall. You stay near the gate, for you will soon be leaving. You will only be here for ten years.

Even in prison you are still waiting for the day when you will be released. People are still living, waiting for that day.

You must understand one thing in life: observe carefully the happiness you have, because only from happiness can you be free. If you have a beautiful wife, then you must enjoy beauty thoroughly; if you have money, then you must savour it properly; if you have position, observe it from all sides. You must carefully observe all that you have, only then can hope be destroyed. And if you observe what you do not have, hope will never be destroyed.

Religion cannot enter the life of a person whose hope has not yet been destroyed. Hope is the gate of irreligiousness; the annihilation of hope is the entrance of religion. And you must also know that the annihilation of hope is not despair. The defeat of hope is despair: hope is very much alive in despair. One may feel hopeless now, but after a moment one will be hopeful again.

Hopelessness is the defeated aspect of hope. It is the tired, exhausted hope. It is not destroyed hope, it is fallen hope.

When hope is destroyed, hopelessness disappears as well.

That is why Mahavira and Buddha seem pessimistic to the

Western mind, because they ask you to give up hope. They are being misunderstood. Mahavira and Buddha are not pessimists; they are neither optimists nor pessimists. They say that when hope is annihilated, hopelessness also disappears by itself because hopelessness is the shadow of hope.

Your shadow is cast when you walk in the sun. If you don't walk in the sun, the shadow is not cast. When there is no hope, hopelessness automatically disappears. The more you hope, the more hopeless or disappointed you will be, the more unhappy and miserable you will be. Then a new hope is born out of hopelessness and this game continues like night and day.

If hope is broken, then there is neither hope nor despair. Then you are at peace. The light of your consciousness keeps wavering in the strong wind of hope and despair. When there is neither hope nor despair, the strong wind stops blowing and the consciousness becomes stable, unshakable and firm. That stability, that steadfastness is very fortunate. That steadiness is samadhi.

COLD-STRICKEN, IN THE MORNING HE WARMS HIMSELF WITH THE FIRE IN FRONT OF HIM OR WITH HIS BACK TO THE SUN. AT NIGHT HE SLEEPS WITH HIS CHIN BETWEEN HIS KNEES, TAKES ALMS IN HIS HANDS AND LIVES UNDER A TREE; EVEN THEN HE DOES NOT GIVE UP THE SLAVERY OF HOPE.

THEREFORE, O FOOL! ALWAYS SING THE SONG OF THE DIVINE.

HE CAN UNDERTAKE THE JOURNEY TO THE GANGES OR THE OCEAN, HE CAN PERFORM MANY AUSTERITIES AND FASTS, HE CAN GIVE IN CHARITY, BUT IF HE HAS NO SELF-KNOWLEDGE HE WILL NOT BE LIBERATED EVEN IN A HUNDRED LIFETIMES.

Try to understand this:

HE CAN UNDERTAKE THE JOURNEY TO THE

GANGES OR THE OCEAN, HE CAN DO A LOT OF AUSTERITIES AND FASTING, HE CAN GIVE IN CHARITY, BUT IF HE HAS NO SELF-KNOWLEDGE THEN HE WILL NOT BE LIBERATED.

... Because it is easy to do these things - to fast, to give in charity, to live in discipline, to live by rules and regulations and in austerity. They are easy because the actions are always easy. You don't change and the deed is done.

Self-knowledge is difficult because knowledge means transformation. Knowledge means that you have to change and that the form of consciousness has to change. The meaning of knowledge is that the movement and the direction of your consciousness must change. The meaning of meditation, the meaning of knowledge is that your consciousness must not waver, it must be unwavering, stable and firm. It is difficult.

It is easy to do something. If you eat more then you are disturbing your body, if you fast even then you are disturbing your body; there is no difference between these two conditions. First you were disturbing the body by eating more, now you are disturbing it by fasting. If you go on accumulating money, you may as well give it up. You will know the uselessness of money only after you have collected it. Is it very revolutionary to give in charity something which is useless?

There is a story in the Kathopanishad - because of that story, that Upanishad is called Kathopanishad; katha means story. Nachiketa's father performed a great yajna, a religious ritual.

After the yajna he gave many gifts. Nachiketa is a little boy. He sits nearby and asks his father again and again: "Are you going to give it all away?

The father said: "All that I have I will give. Everything will be given in charity. Nachiketa saw that his father gave away only the cows that were incapable of giving milk.

People often give away in charity things that have become useless. The father distributed with enthusiasm and pleasure things that are useless. Nachiketa's intellect is fresh, the father's intellect is old. So what Nachiketa could see, the father could not see. Nachiketa said, "What is the use of giving to these cows that stopped giving milk long ago? The poor Brahmins, to whom you give them, will have to take care of feeding them. This is not a good deed at all". The father told him to shut up.

But like a little child, Nachiketa kept asking him: "If you are giving away everything of yours, who are you going to give me to? Who are you going to give me to? When he asked this question several times, the father became very angry and said, "I will give you to death".

Man gives what is of no use; you also distribute things that are of no use to you. I see that some things keep rotating - they keep passing from one person to another. They are of no use to anyone, so people keep distributing them. You give it to someone and they pass it on to someone else. It's giving for the sake of giving.

A friend of Mulla Nasruddin gave him a bottle of alcohol. Later he asked him: "How was it?

Mulla Nasruddin said: "Almost right".

The friend asked: "What do you mean, almost right? Either it's fine or it's not fine.

Mulla said: "No, it was almost good. If it had been absolutely fine, you wouldn't have given it to me, and if it had been less fine, I would have given it to someone else. It was almost good, so I drank it".

This is how you give things that are worthless. You give away in charity that which is worthless.

You don't have to try very hard to fast, it's just a little discomfort to the body. You can also do austerities because it satisfies your ego. But the only revolution is the revolution of self-knowledge. No one can be free without that revolution.

Self-knowledge is the only liberation. Knowledge is liberation.

But knowledge does not mean knowledge of the scriptures because, that is very easy. It is easier even than fasting and charity. There is no difficulty in reading the scriptures and there is no difficulty in filling the mind with the scriptures. You can memorise the Gita even when there is no song in your life. When there is no inner harmony in you, how can you sing the song of the divine? Yes, the Gita can be memorised without having any song within you.

When the music within is so deep that you are absolutely lost in it, only then does that music, that song become the song of the divine. Then one does not remember or think of Krishna and Arjuna or the words of the Gita. You become what is said in the Gita. You become that yourself. Then there is no need to remember all that rubbish.

The scriptures are valuable to those who are interested in scavenging. But scriptures are of no value to those who have become scripture. You cannot acquire knowledge until you yourself become scripture. You will have knowledge when your every gesture indicates the truth.

Even the wink of the eye, this small gesture will also express the truth. Whether you speak or not, the truth will be expressed through you.

You may undertake the journey to the Ganges. Poor Ganges, why do you trouble him? Someone asked Ramakrishna: "I am going to bathe in the Ganges. Do you think that bathing in the Ganges washes away all sins?

Ramakrishna was a very simple person. He used to say: "They are certainly washed away when you bathe in the Ganges. When you immerse yourself in it, the sins get separated from you and go and sit on the top of the trees on the banks of the Ganges. But after the bath, when you come out of the Ganges, those sins jump back on you from those trees. They had to leave you for the Ganges, not for you. If you do not come out of the Ganges, if you remain in the Ganges forever, only then can you get rid of sins."

The man said: "But I will have to come out of it at some point".

"Then there is no point in you going there," Ramakrishna said.

Will the Ganges deliver you from your sins? But if you have committed sins, how will the Ganges free you from them? If the Ganges goes on delivering people from all their sins, then the Ganges itself will become very sinful because then it will be burdened with all the sins committed by all the people.

Man keeps looking for excuses. Man sins, then tries to find some excuse to keep his conscience from pricking his conscience. By taking a dip in the Ganges he feels free from sin and is again ready to sin.

You will sin again and bathe in the Ganges again. The Ganges did not free you from sin; it actually made you an expert in sinning, because you found a cheap way to get rid of it. You didn't have to pay much. The actual journey is not very expensive, and besides most pilgrims travel without a ticket, they don't mind paying money for tickets. When the Ganges washes away so many sins, one more doesn't matter.

YOU CAN UNDERTAKE THE JOURNEY TO THE GANGES OR THE OCEAN, YOU CAN DO A LOT OF AUSTERITIES AND FASTING, YOU CAN GIVE IN CHARITY, BUT IF YOU DON'T HAVE SELF-KNOWLEDGE YOU WON'T BE LIBERATED EVEN IN HUNDREDS OF LIFETIMES....

THAT'S WHY, OH FOOL! ALWAYS SING THE SONG OF THE DIVINE.

ONE MAY RESIDE IN THE TEMPLE OF GOD OR UNDER A TREE, THE EARTH MAY BE HIS ONLY BED, THE DEERSKIN HIS ONLY ROBE, HE MAY HAVE FORSAKEN ALL MANNER OF POSSESSIONS AND

INDULGENCES - WHO DOES SUCH RENUNCIATION NOT MAKE HAPPY?

This is a very important statement. Shankara is raising a very serious issue. He is saying that if you have really renounced, then the proof of your renunciation will be your bliss. The bliss will prove whether your renunciation was true or not.

If the renouncer looks unhappy, then it means that his renunciation was false. If you say that you have lit a lamp in your house and still it is dark, then your lamp is false. If the lamp is lit, then there will be light in the whole house.

Shankara is saying that if you are living in a temple or under a tree and you feel unhappy and sad, then you have not yet reached the temple, then you have not yet met the temple deity. THE EARTH MAY BE YOUR ONLY BED. One who is so free that the sky becomes his covering and the earth his bed - that is why Mahavira was called digambar. The sky became his covering and the earth his bed.

WHEN, EARTH MAY BE HIS ONLY BED, DEERSKIN MAY BE HIS ONLY ROBE, HE HAS GIVEN UP ALL MANNER OF INDULGENT POSSESSIONS - TO WHOM SUCH RENUNCIATION DOES NOT DO GOOD?

Happiness is the yardstick. There is no other test of your renunciation except bliss. Your bliss will prove whether your renunciation is true or false.

You can give up your house, you can give up your money, you can take off your clothes, you can shave your head or leave your hair long, you can wear ochre robes and go to the Himalayas or sit on the bank of the Ganges, but if you are not happy, if you are not blissful, then all these things are nothing but a delusion. You may look like gold, but you are not gold, you are only brass.

Just as gold can be tested, your renunciation can also be tested by your bliss. True renunciation means happiness and worldly enjoyment means misery. A blissful person proves that his renunciation is true and that unhappiness, misery, is the result of worldly enjoyment.

That is why Shankara says:

HE MAY BE ABSORBED IN SENSE ENJOYMENT OR IN YOGA, HE MAY BE ABSORBED IN THE COMPANY OF SOMEONE OR HE MAY BE ALONE, BUT IF HIS HEART DWELLS IN THE DIVINE, THEN IT IS HE WHO IS BLISSFUL, IT IS HE WHO IS BLISSFUL, IT IS HE ALONE WHO IS BLISSFUL.

Then it makes no difference whether he is living at home or away from home, whether he is sitting on a throne or on a rock on a mountain, whether he is absorbed in sense enjoyment or in yoga, whether he is with someone or alone, whether he is in the company of family or society or alone, whether he is in a palace or in a hut.

IF HIS HEART DWELLS IN THE DIVINE, THEN IT IS HE WHO IS BLISSFUL, IT IS HE WHO IS BLISSFUL, IT IS HE ALONE WHO IS BLISSFUL.

Therefore, O IDIOT! SING THE SONG OF THE DIVINE.

To dwell in the divine, in Brahma. The definition of Brahma is satchidananda: to be absorbed in truth, awareness and bliss.

One who is authentic, and who is the same within and without; who tastes the same within and without; who is truth and consciousness; who is awake and not unconscious; who is blissful and filled with the fragrance of the divine; whose very breath is full of music; whose movements are like a dance; whose presence reminds you of the divine... if you approach him his freshness affects you, his bliss begins to dance in you. All your misery disappears as you look at him. His blessing means the attainment of all. When you feel this, when you feel a deep satisfaction, then that is the proof that he is absorbed in Brahma, that he is in a deep embrace with the divine.

There is something very interesting. You must have seen the image of Mahavira - he is very blissful.

You must have seen his body too. But look at the Jaina Muni. He looks so unhappy, so miserable.

There is no joy in it; it looks sad. It seems as if the bud has not become a flower, it has shrunk. But you say this shrinking is renunciation. He doesn't bathe, he doesn't brush his teeth, so he smells of sweat and his mouth stinks and he thinks this is renunciation.

When you are with him you will never feel like dancing for joy; when you are with him you will never hear the singing of the divine music of the flute that you have never heard before. Rather, you will feel a little uneasy when you return after seeing him. Perhaps his presence will create in you a self-condemnation; perhaps in his presence you will feel that you are a sinner. But his presence will not make you aware of the divine in you.

And that is the difference - with true sannyasin you will not feel self-condemnation, you will feel happy and joyful. With the true sannyasin you will feel gratitude. The real sannyasin will never show you your darkness, he will show you the light within you. You may be a great sinner but the real sannyasin will never give you any clue about your sins because it is not worth talking about; that subject has no value, it has no meaning. The glory within you is the real thing.

You are a sinner because until now you have not known your inner glory. If you become more conscious of your sins then your inner glory will be further suppressed. No, these sins are like the dream of the night. They are meaningless. You should be able to remember the godliness in you. But only that person can make you remember the divine, can remind you of the divine, that he himself is absorbed in it, that he is in the deep embrace of Brahma. In his presence someone within you will begin to awaken. In his presence - just as peacocks begin to dance when the sky is full of clouds - in the same way in his presence....

Buddha has said that many people's inner peacocks begin to dance when someone's inner space is filled with the clouds of the ultimate. Yes, you will dance in their presence. You should know that where you experience bliss that is the abode of Brahma, that is the temple.

HE MAY BE ABSORBED IN SENSE ENJOYMENT OR IN YOGA, HE MAY BE ABSORBED IN THE COMPANY OF SOMEONE OR HE MAY BE ALONE, BUT IF HIS HEART DWELLS IN THE DIVINE, THEN IT IS HE WHO IS BLISSFUL, IT IS HE WHO IS BLISSFUL, IT IS HE ALONE WHO IS BLISSFUL.

And that is the objective, that is the destiny that must be tackled from all points of view.

Therefore, O IDIOT! ALWAYS SING THE SONG OF THE DIVINE. SING THE SONG OF THE DIVINE, SING THE SONG OF THE DIVINE. OH IDIOT!

Enough for today.

Truth is not a debate

The first question:

Question 1:

BELOVED MASTER, YOU HAVE SAID MANY TIMES THAT A DIALOGUE IS NOT POSSIBLE THROUGH A DEBATE. BUT SHANKARA ANNOUNCED HIS UNIVERSAL VICTORY AND DEFEATED INNUMERABLE INTELLECTUALS IN A DEBATE ON THE MEANING OF THE SCRIPTURES. AFTER THE DEFEAT THEY HAD TO BECOME DISCIPLES OF SHANKARA.

PLEASE EXPLAIN WHAT KIND OF SCRIPTURAL DEBATE THIS WAS.

Through discussion and debate, through logic and debate, dialogue is never possible. Dialogue means the conversation of two hearts; debate means the conflict of two intellects. Dialogue means the meeting of two individuals; debate means the conflict of two individuals. In dialogue no one is defeated, both win; in debate both are defeated, no one wins.

But there was no alternative for Shankara. He had to debate, because at that time dialogue could only be possible after debate. Shankara did not debate to explain the truth. The fact was that people were so full of their own intellect, their ego, their erudition, that they were not willing to listen to any talk from the heart until their erudition and intellect were defeated. Shankara did not explain the truth to them through debate, but destroyed their ego through debate. And dialogue is possible only with the person who is willing to bow down.

Shankara's debate on the scriptures was only negative; it was like taking out a thorn with another thorn. A mind full of logic can only understand the language of logic. A mind full of scholarship can only understand the language of scholarship, it cannot even hear the language of love - and even if it hears it, it cannot understand the meaning and there is simply no question of understanding the language of msilence.

The scholarship of this country was at its zenith when Shankara was born. That very scholarship has ruined this country. It got stuck in the head and there was no way to get to the heart. To get to the heart it was necessary to cut off the heads first. This disease was so acute that it could not be treated with medicines, so an operation was necessary.

So Shankara was obliged to debate - that was his obligation. Shankara is not at all the debating or arguing type. It is not possible for Shankara to be argumentative. He is not at all interested in logic; otherwise he could not have sung songs like Bhaj Govindam. He wanted to sing the songs of the divine from his own heart. Had the time been ripe, had people been able to understand the language of the heart, then Shankara would not have argued or debated at all. Had he had the opportunity, he would have danced.

But the country was sick; scholarship was at its climax, people's heads were really heavy with learning and knowledge, so it was necessary to remove that useless weight from their heads. And scholarship can only understand arguments. Scholars can listen to the language of the heart after they have been defeated by logic. So Shankara defeated them in debate.

And remember that a person who has known the truth can use logic correctly, but logic can be dangerous if it is used by a person who does not know the truth. Logic is the end, logic is everything to one who does not know the truth, but if one knows the truth, one can use logic in the service of the truth.

Whoever knows the truth can make logic his servant. Truth can also ride on logic.

Normally, logic is like a sword in the hands of children. With it they harm others and themselves. But a knowledgeable person can use logic in a sensible way, like an adult uses a sword. He will not harm anyone with it, but will protect others from any mishap.

Shankara made correct use of logic. If used correctly, even poison can be turned into medicine. An intelligent person can always turn poison into medicine. And Shankara used logic in the service of truth. He went all over the country, from one corner to another.

He debated and used logic; he argued with people whose sick minds could not go beyond the intellect and who had forgotten the language of the heart. He debated whenever he saw that some genius was lost in words and could not find the door of truth. I would argue with people who were overloaded with scripture and struggling to get out of it. It was just prologue.

Whenever someone was defeated in the debate on the meaning of the scriptures, instantly Shankara made him a disciple. The really important thing is this: as soon as someone was defeated in the discussion, Shankara used his defeat. At the moment of that defeat, when the individual was stunned, when his ego was shattered, when his intellect and logic were not working, when he became helpless and began to sink, Shankara would immediately put the other boat in front of him. If the boat of your logic is sinking, let it sink. I have another boat, the boat of the heart - the boat of love, the boat of devotion.

In those moments he must have sung: O IDIOT! SING THE SONG OF THE DIVINE, SING THE SONG OF THE DIVINE, SING THE SONG OF THE DIVINE.

He has called these experts idiots. You must understand that he has debated so that your idiocy is cut off. All illusions disappear as soon as your idiocy is destroyed. And he used that moment of transition when your mind becomes thoughtless - all clouds disappear and for the first time you are looking at the open sky. Shankara did not debate to explain the truth. By debating, he removed the clouds so that the sun of truth could be seen.

There is no need to prove the truth, it proves itself. It is self-evident. And remember that if something has to be proven by logic, it can also be disproved by logic. Logic is just a game, it is not a force.

Everything that is proved by logic can be disproved by logic. Logic is like a lawyer; logic is like a prostitute; it is attached to no one - it can take either side, it can be used on both sides, for and against anything. Just as a sword belongs to no one, logic belongs to no one.

Your own sword can be used by your enemy to cut your throat. You cannot say, "It is my sword, how can it cut my throat?". The sword does not belong to anyone.

In the same way, logic does not belong to anyone either. That is why people who rely too much on logic will one day discover that it is not reliable at all. One day they will realise that they were on a paper boat.

One day they will discover that the logic that helped them stand on their feet has become the cause of their downfall.

If you believe in God you say there must be someone who created this world. Your logic is that this world must have been created by someone, so there must be a God. But then the other argument is: who created God? Because how can God exist without being created? There is no difference between the two arguments. One believes in God and the other is an atheist. But I don't see any difference between the two because they both depend on the logic that how can something exist without being created?

You get angry with an atheist and say: "Shut up! No one has made God. But the atheist just says that if God can exist without being made, why can't the world exist without being made? The logic is the same, the argument is the same, so nobody wins.

Logic never proves anything. What is, is beyond logic; what is, is self-evident. But if you go to Shankara with logic, he will counter all your logic. There are very few people who are as logical as Shankara. You may meet people who have known the divine - like Ramakrishna - but rare are the people who have known the divine and can refute the arguments of the atheist.

Ramakrishna could not refute the argument of an atheist. He knew no logic. He was a simple and pure person. Vivekananda could counter logic, but Vivekananda has no experience of truth. People like Shankara are unique. He has in him the qualities of Ramakrishna and Vivekananda. He has known just as Ramakrishna has known, and he can use arguments in favour of what he has known, just as Vivekananda can do without knowing.

But Shankara has been misunderstood. The irony is that all his life Shankara tried to destroy the ego of the pundits, and those same pundits also took him for a pundit! These pundits keep saying that Shankara conquered all. Shankara must be laughing his head off. The victory of logic is no victory at all. Defeating someone with logic means nothing. If someone is defeated in an argument, he simply keeps quiet, he does not feel defeated at heart.

If you make a lot of arguments to someone, they may not be able to answer you in the same way, so they will shut up at that moment, but in their mind they will still be waiting to get back at you.

Defeating someone with logic is like using the sword to make him surrender. He will give up for the moment, but he will wait for the right moment to take revenge. He who is defeated with a sword is not defeated at all. Only the one who is defeated with love is truly defeated, because no other surrender makes sense until you surrender from the heart.

So Shankara defeated with logic those people who existed on

logic. He defeated logic with logic.

But in that moment of defeat Shankara told them: "Your logic is useless, my logic is also useless. I have taken out your thorn with my thorn, but my thorn is not more valuable than yours. And don't try to keep my thorn in your wound, otherwise this too will cause you as much pain as your thorn was causing you".

It is better to throw out both thorns.

This was the meaning of being his disciple: to turn away from the intellect and go down to the heart. Truth is not to be sought with thought, but with emotion. Truth is not to be discovered with logic, scriptures and principles, but with the open heart. When the flower of the heart blooms, the sun of truth shines upon it. The rays of truth dance upon the blossoming flower of the heart. This was the meaning of discipleship. But to those who could not understand it, Shankara made them understand it in their own language.

Shankara is a unique person. And it is very easy to misunderstand a unique person because he is beyond common understanding. People thought he was also a logician, a great logician. But can a great logician say: "Sing! Dance! Sing the song of the divine"? It is not possible for a logician to say so. Such words can only be uttered by a lover of the divine from the depths of his heart. So remember this.

"You have said many times that dialogue is not possible through debate. It is never possible.

Shankara cleared the ground for dialogue through logic and debate. You were full of debates, so he humbled you with debates. You were full of arguments, so he humbled you with arguments. He cleared the ground with them and then sowed the seeds of love and devotion.

Many people have been thinking that Shankara is contradictory. It is not contradictory. It seems contradictory in the same way that you see someone in your neighbourhood demolishing his house.

He takes months to demolish it and then clean up the rubble; then he pours the foundations and builds a new house. Will you call this person contradictory? One day he demolishes his house and the next day he builds it. It may seem contradictory, but you know that to build a new house you have to demolish the old one. There is no contradiction in this contradiction.

The new house can only be built after demolishing the old one.

Shankara is not contradictory, but fights logic with logic. When the old house is demolished, then he invites to dance. You will say that this is contradictory - first he talks about thought and logic, then he talks about love and dance.

No, he used logic to destroy the old and built the new with emotion. He cleared the ground with logic and is now sowing the seeds of love. There is no contradiction.

You say: "But Shankara announced his universal victory". This announcement was also not made by Shankara; this announcement was made by people who were following Shankara but could not understand him. You cannot understand anyone by merely following him. It is very easy to follow someone, but it is difficult to be a disciple. It is very easy to follow or copy others, but it is difficult to understand someone and then develop your life according to that understanding.

So those who followed Shankara announced his universal victory. They are still doing it. Puri's Shankaracharya is still doing it, Karpatri is still doing it. They are still saying that Shankara defeated the whole world. Puri's Shankaracharya is still saying that he is Jagat Guru, master of the world. This is not Shankara's announcement, because Shankara knew that nobody wins and nobody is defeated with logic - it only means that the other person's logic was weaker than yours and you were more skilful. But tomorrow the other person can also become more skilled in logic.

Shankara knew that the victory of logic and argument is not a victory, it is only a deception. And Shankara does not try to defeat anyone with logic. His attempt is unique, but this unique attempt cannot be seen by those who follow him; they will only see that he has defeated another man. Those who follow him can only understand the language of the ego. They cannot see that in reality Shankara did not defeat the person but made him victorious, brought him to the path of the heart. A person was losing, sinking deep into logic - Shankara saved him and showed him the path of victory. Now that person will be victorious.

That is why people like Kumaril Bhatt, who was defeated by Shankara, became his disciple - he did not become his disciple in misery and distress. If Kumaril Bhatt had become a disciple after being defeated, it would have hurt his ego and he would have tried to take revenge for his defeat. Kumaril was as great a logician as Shankara. Debating with Shankara Kumaril realised that debating is futile. Shankara was not victorious, Kumaril was not defeated. Logic was defeated and emotion won.

It is necessary to understand this - debating with Shankara, playing with an expert player, Kumaril saw clearly that those things he depended on would collapse with the mere blow of a breeze. This does not mean that he accepted Shankara's logic. Shankara's skill is only that, through debate, he shows you that your arguments are useless, that my arguments are useless; logic becomes meaningless. Neither Kumaril was defeated nor Shankara won - logic was defeated. Because this defeat of logic came through the medium of Shankara, Kumaril bowed and fell at his feet.

And these debates were full of sweetness, these debates were full of love, there was no bitterness in them. They did not fight as enemies, it was like playing chess: an army of arguments was brought into play. Kumaril prepared the best of his logic and the best of his intellect, and Shankara destroyed all his arguments one by one. He did not try to put his own argument into Kumaril's mind, he simply negated Kumaril's arguments until a space was left, and in that space discipleship was born. The opponent saw that the person in front of him has brought no theory but the truth. He has destroyed all my arguments but has not established any new arguments in their place. There was an empty space left. There was an interval, there was emptiness, there was a void. In that state meditation took place. In that moment of meditation he bowed. Don't think that he bowed to Shankara; he bowed to the truth that was expressed through Shankara. Shankara was only an image, a symbol. Kumaril bowed to the truth. Kumaril bowed not because he had been defeated, but because he had awakened.

But the people standing behind, all they saw was that he was defeated and was bowing down. The people following him announced tha: "Shankara is victorious, he has defeated the world". Because of these stupid people Shankara's image was tainted. The unique approach of Shankara was lost and in its place arose a very ordinary tradition, a narrow path. The vast path of the open sky was lost - that openness was lost. Therefore, you will find that if a Shankara sannyasin is a logician, he will not accept Bhaj Govindam and such things.

There are people who say that songs like Bhaj Govindam have not been written by Shankara, that they have been written by others and have been given Shankara's name. They say, "How can Shankara write such songs?". Yes, Meera could write such songs, Chaitanya could write such songs, but how could Shankara write them... because he was a keen logician, it was not possible for him to sing such devotional songs. These people say that these songs have been made by others who have taken advantage of Shankara's name. They think that these songs are not authentic and believe in arguments that are really worthless.

Shankara used logic to destroy the old building and gave these chants to build the new one.

This process of his is not contradictory; if you think so, then you will not be able to understand him.

Shankara never announced his universal victory. Those who know the truth are not ambitious, those who know the truth are not selfish. Such announcements of victory are very childish: little children indulge in such things. Who has to win and who has to lose? Shankara sees that there is only the divine; the multiplicity of things is an illusion, unity is the truth. Who will win and who will lose? If someone wins it is only the divine that will win, and if someone loses it is only the divine that will be defeated. When it is he who wins and it is he who loses, then who will announce the universal victory? No, Shankara cannot make this mistake, and if he has made it then it is worthless. Shankara has awakened and has not defeated others.

No, Shankara made innumerable intellectuals really intelligent. Before this they had been involved with false intellect; they were guarding bad currencies. Now they were shown the real coins. You can only distinguish the bad coin after seeing the real one: there is no other way to prove that a bad coin is bad. Shankara showed the real coins and then the bad coins could be recognised. These debates were not like those held in the West. These debates were also not like the debates that take place in the East today. These debates were very sweet. They were the debates of the seekers of truth.

There are two kinds of debates: one is that whatever you say is right because you are saying it, because you can't be wrong. What you say doesn't matter, but it has to be right because you have said it. This kind of debate is futile, useless. If you seek the truth, then don't insist that what you say is correct. Then you say that from what you have known so far, this seems right to you: "I am willing to know more if there is more to know. I am open, not closed. I haven't come to any conclusions yet. But so far, wherever I have looked, this seems to be the most truthful. But if the truth is revealed to me, I am willing to accept it, to be transformed and to give up everything I knew before this". Debate then becomes the process of approaching the truth.

The East has used this type of debate. This tradition is thousands of years old. In the search for truth, intellectuals used to reflect and debate, not because they had found the truth, but because they were searching for it. This continued for thousands of years. Whenever a person showed the falsehood of the other, then he had the courage to prostrate himself at his feet, because in the search for truth the one who showed it was the master. So those who were defeated by Shankara became his disciples.

Discipleship means: you have taken me a step beyond where I was, you have made me see beyond where my eyes could see, you have made me see the open sky by carrying me on your shoulders.

The search for truth is quite another matter. If the aim is the search for truth, debate can also be used. That is why I say that even poison can become medicine.

There have also been debates in the West, but they are not like those in the East. In the West they are still fighting, debating, and you can never judge who has won and who has lost. They have never become anyone's disciples.

Shankara travelled to Mandala, the city of Mandan Mishra; Mandala was named after Mandan. On entering the city, he asked the women at the well, "Where is the house of Mandan Mishra?

They laughed and said: "You don't need to ask me because you can recognise it yourself.

The very atmosphere of that house will tell you. Even the parrots in the cage hanging in front of the house recite the words of the Upanishads. The aura of that house is ancient and sacred". The women laughed and said, "Stranger, you will be able to locate that house. No one need ask about it.

Shankara arrived at the house. Birds were singing at the door and reciting words from the Upanishads and the Vedas. Shankara entered and invited Mandan Mishra to debate with him.

Mandan Mishra was very famous. He was older than Shankara, and his prestige and fame were much greater than Shankara's. He also had more disciples than Shankara. He also had more disciples than Shankara. Shankara invited him to a discussion on the search for truth. He was welcomed and made to stay in the house. He was not an enemy. Mandan was then in his fifties and Shankara in his thirties.

Then Mandan said: "I am much more experienced than you. You are young. I am your father's age, so we are not equal, this debate is not equal. So I give you the advantage of choosing the judge.

You are young, so you choose the judge - he will decide who has won and who has lost.

It was not a fight at all, but a very affectionate contest. The older person welcomed the younger one as his own son and also gave him the upper hand. Shankara looked around for a judge who had the same reputation as Mandan but could not find one. So he decided on Mandan's wife, whose name was Bharati. Shankara said, "Your wife will do the judging".

You think this is a fight? This is not the language of enemies. If it is the wife who has to judge, there is a possibility that she will take her husband's side. This is quite natural if the debate is based on enmity. But this debate was about seeking the truth, and it was full of love.

The wife became a judge, and after debate ruled that Mandan had lost and Shankara had won. Bharati then said, "But wait, this defeat is incomplete. You have defeated only one half of Mandan - I am his other half. Now you have to debate with me. This sounded like a joke but it was a beautiful fact - the wife being the other half of the husband, only half of Mandan had been defeated and now the other half, the wife, had to be defeated. This wife who gave the judgment of her husband's defeat must have been unique. She told

Shankara, "Your victory is incomplete. You have to defeat me also for it to be complete".

Shankara agreed to debate with Bharati. But he realised that he could not answer the questions she asked him, because she did not ask him anything about Brahma or Brahma's knowledge. As he had already defeated Mandan on that issue. She had understood from the debate with Mandan that it was useless to talk to this young man about Brahma. She thought "This young looking person is actually a very ancient being".

And Mandan certainly knew more than Bharati. That is why Bharati had fallen in love with him, married him and cared for him. She had seen him defeated by Shankara on the issue of Brahma, so she asked Shankara questions regarding sex. Shankara was young. He was thirty years old and unmarried. He found himself in a difficult situation. He said, "I want six months time to answer these questions because I am single and celibate, I don't know love, I don't know sex. So if I answer now it will not be from my own experience and answers that are not based on experience cannot be true or correct." Just as Mandan has lost by talking about Brahma based on his knowledge of the scriptures, in the same way I too can talk about sex based on my knowledge of the scriptures and I will surely be defeated because I have no experience of sex. You will win because you have experience. I have only heard about it, mine is only second-hand knowledge. So I need six months to have that experience. Then I will be able to answer your questions.

These discussions were really full of love and affection. Bharati said, "All right, go for six months, get experience and come back".

It is a strange story. Shankara was in a great dilemma. He had taken the vow of celibacy - he had given this promise to his master. Now, if he married or looked for a woman, the whole pattern of his life would change. So, as the story goes, Shankara left his own body and entered another dead body. A king was dying, so Shankara entered his body and stayed in it for six months and understood the necessity of the body and the meaning of sex. When he returned after six months, Bharati looked at him and said, "There is no need to debate now. You already know. I am willing to be your disciple". Mandan and Bharati became Shankara's disciples.

In these incidents they were full of love and consideration for each other; there was no enmity between them. It is not that Shankara defeated the intellectuals - he gave real intelligence to these intellectuals and shook and awakened the defeated, gave light to the people who were living in darkness.

And those who bowed at his feet did not do so out of humiliation. They bowed out of gratitude and thanksgiving.

You say: "After the defeat they had to become disciples of Shankara".

Don't say "I had to". We have a habit of using the language of ego. Even if Shankara had refused, they would have become his disciples. They did not "had to" - they became disciples with gratitude and with great joy. That inclination was not made by being defeated. That bowing was out of deep understanding. That was surrender and not defeat; they found happiness in bowing at his feet. That bowing gave them self-esteem. In that bowing they understood for the first time the meaning of life, in that bowing they found the first glimpse of the divine.

Don't use the words "they had to bow". They bowed out of gratitude, out of joy, out of thanksgiving.

The second question:

Question 2:

BELOVED MASTER, THE FALL OF AN ORDINARY PERSON CAN BE UNDERSTOOD, BUT HOW CAN THE FALL OF A SEEKER WHO IS TREADING THE PATH OF RENUNCIATION, DETACHMENT AND AUSTERITY BE POSSIBLE?

A normal person cannot fall. Where can he fall? Where can a person walking on level ground fall? Only a person who is trying to climb to the top of the mountain can fall. It takes mountain tops to fall off. And there are hidden chasms and ditches near mountain peaks. But how can a person walking on flat, even ground, on the main road, fall? Where is he going to fall? He has already fallen.

An ordinary person cannot fall because he no longer has room for it. So you have not understood what you have said: "The fall of an ordinary person can be understood". How can an ordinary person fall... because he is living at the point from which it is no longer possible to fall. He is living at degree zero. He is already living in the abyss.

Only extraordinary people fall: those who try to reach the mountain tops, those who accept the challenges of heights, those who are not willing to live in the abyss, those who say that their life is meaningless until they have reached the golden mountain tops; those who do not accept to live in the darkness of the abyss, those who say: "We will fly through the sky and take a far journey". The longer the journey, the greater the danger of falling.

We have a word yoga bhrashta, one who has fallen from yoga. Have you ever heard the word bhoga bhrashta, one who has fallen from indulgence? Bhoga bhrashta is meaningless. Yoga bhrashta makes sense; it means that an attempt was made to climb the height but failed.

The danger of getting lost is always present in climbing. Maybe that's why many people don't try to climb heights. They forget about heights. They consider the abyss to be the height. In fact, they don't look at the summits, because looking at them they may have to accept the challenge.

I have heard that in countries where mountain birds come from far away, pet birds are also beginning to be willing to take up the challenge. In southern Europe, ducks come from Siberia to spend the winter. When the winter is over, these ducks return. Domestic ducks were also wild and free a few generations ago. When the flocks of wild ducks start to return, and the ducks from the farms and fields see them flying in the sky, they also start to flap their wings, they also try to fly a few metres and then fall down. Their wings are no longer strong. But when they see these mountain birds fly, birds like them, something in them challenges them and then they also remember the height of the sky and the unknown country. There is a faint memory of Siberia in their minds. Although they fall, they try to fly.

Whenever a Buddha or a Shankara passes among you, you also flap your wings a little in your fields and in your barns because their presence awakens in you the sound of some dormant music.

Then you will know that you can also fly to those heights, that that is also your destiny - but you flutter a little and forget everything after you fall. Or those among you who are very clever will say that this is not possible. You do not look at the Buddha at all. You turn your back on him. You do not look at Buddha directly, you only listen to the rumours about him. They don't look Buddha in the eyes because it is dangerous to do so. They sit in their tents and go on saying that all that is nonsense: nobody has ever realised the divine, there is no Brahma; all that is just tall tales to impress people. This man must have gone mad, or this kind of talk is very poetic. They simply cannot accept that there are such mountains, such heights, such virgin snow-capped peaks that few have ever reached, because they fear that if they believe it then they will also try to fly.

But they have no confidence in their own wings; they keep doubting. Will they be able to fly? Will they be able to reach? Or will they fall? With flight there is the possibility of falling, there is the possibility of slipping as you go along. But creatures that crawl on the ground cannot fall, where will they fall?

So do not say that you can understand the fall of an ordinary man. Have you ever heard of the fall of an ordinary person? Only the seeker who is treading the path of renunciation, detachment and austerity can fall, and that danger grows greater and greater as he approaches his destination.

Then there is danger in every inch. You can miss a little and fall. The mistake is small, the fall is big. If you make a mistake it doesn't matter, but if Mahavira makes the same mistake then he will have a big fall. Your mistakes don't matter because you live in mistakes, but if that mistake is made by Buddha....

Buddha was passing through a village. Ananda was with him. A fly landed on his shoulder while he was talking, and he brushed it off like any other person. Then he stopped suddenly as if he had made a big mistake, then he reached up and very consciously brought his hand to his shoulder and removed the fly which was now not there.

Ananda asked him: "What are you doing?

Buddha said, "I had removed the fly unconsciously, mechanically. I should have done it consciously.

Even a fly must be killed consciously, because if the act of killing it is done unconsciously, then other things are also done unconsciously. There was nothing to worry about: the fly had not died, there was no violence. But Buddha was certainly worried. Even this small black spot is too much on his white sheet.

But you can't see anything on your black sheet. That's why many people buy clothes that don't show dirt. Even a small stain is visible on a white sheet. The white Buddha sheet shows the stain immediately. That is why even the fly has to be removed consciously.

At night Buddha sleeps only on one side. Ananda asked him one day: "Whenever I get up in the night you sleep on the same side. Even your hands do not move, they also remain in the same position. Do you sleep consciously? Do you not relax in your sleep?".

Buddha replied: "He who wakes up does not sleep. You have to sleep consciously. I sleep, but there is someone inside me who is always awake, because if there is no wakefulness inside me, dreams begin.

And if sleep continues inside, the thoughts will continue during the day. If one is not awake at night, then it is difficult to be awake even during the day. Wakefulness must be natural all the time, day and night. The inner flow of wakefulness must continue".

So even at night Buddha sleeps consciously, he keeps his hands in the same position. He does not let unconsciousness enter even in his sleep. For Buddha, unconsciousness in sleep means falling down. The danger of falling increases as you get closer to your destination.

As the height increases, the summit gets narrower and narrower. Right at the top of Gourishankar on Everest, only one man can stand: there is only so much space.

Recently, when a Japanese women's expedition had gone to Gourishankar, the Chinese claimed that their seven-person expedition had also reached Gourishankar only two days before them. The Japanese refused to believe this Chinese claim, because seven people cannot be there at the same time.

The summit continues to narrow. This is your ordinary Gourishankar - what can you say about Buddha peaks? They become so narrow that even a person cannot stand. If you stand there with your ego, you will fall down; you can only stand there if you are absolutely empty. At that peak of fullness, of wholeness, only emptiness can be there. A little bit of ego will cause the fall.

Always remember that the danger of falling increases as you get older. But accept this challenge. It will show your inner strength and your inner depth. It doesn't matter if you have to fall a thousand times, but you have to reach the top, and you cannot be happy until you have reached the top. You can win anything, but you will remain a beggar until you realise the divine in you.

Happiness is not possible until you become what you are ultimately capable of becoming, until your future becomes the present; you cannot be in ecstasy until all your flowers bloom. That is why, for ecstasy, in Hindi we use the word prafullata, which means the blossoming of the flower. This full blossoming is ecstasy. So never accept anything that is even a little less than this blossoming, otherwise you will remain unhappy and live in hell.

A normal person does not fall, but lives in darkness, in pain, in misery. It is better to take the risk of falling, instead of living in misery it is better to glimpse happiness, instead of crawling on the ground it is better to fly in the sky for once. Flying even just once you will have confidence in your wings. Certainly you will fall and get up many times, but each fall is a lesson and each rise is a new strength. Falling now means that in the future your chance of falling will be less because you will become adept at getting up.

The journey is long and the destination is divine. Don't accept less, don't settle before and don't sit by the roadside with your eyes closed imagining you have reached the destination. This journey is uncomfortable, many people have done it, it is easy and comfortable to sit by the side of the road. To continue the journey means to gamble, to work hard, to strive. Life is a gamble and only high rollers can reach the divine.

The third question:

Question 3:

BELOVED MASTER, THE SO-CALLED SANNYASINS ARE DOING BUSINESS IN THE NAME OF RELIGION. AND YOU HAVE TOLD YOUR SANNYASINS TO CONTINUE THEIR SHOPS, THEIR BUSINESS. THIS SEEMS CONTRADICTORY. PLEASE CLARIFY.

There is no contradiction. The so-called sannyasins do business in the name of religion because they have been forced to give up their shops. They were not yet mature, they were still interested in running the shop, but they were forced to sit in the temple. So they turn the temple into a shop.

That is why I do not ask my sannyasins to give up their business or their shops. I say that if the temple has to be converted into a shop, then it is better to convert the shop into a temple. I don't force them to leave their shops, because I have seen that those sannyasins convert the temple into a shop. It is useless to stay away from the shop or business until you yourself have lost interest in it. The moment you lose interest in the shop, there will be no need to go away from it: you yourself will turn the shop into a temple.

Remember: if a temple can become a tent, why can't a tent become a temple? The process is the same in both cases. I insist on the second: if you have to change, then change the shop into a temple. And if you still have interest in the shop, in the business, it doesn't matter, please continue with it; then at least the temple will not be contaminated.

I want you to be mature. Be mature wherever you are. The basic thing is maturity. The most important fact of life is that if you are forced to give up something while you are immature, you can give it up physically, but mentally you will not be able to do it. Your mind will continue to desire that which you have had to give up. So you can live or go anywhere but that interest will create its own world. The seed is in your desire, not in your circumstances; it is in your mental conditioning.

Sannyas is the inner revolution. It is the declaration: "I am going to change myself from within".

And I think it is more convenient to change in the market than in the Himalayas, because in the market at every moment there is a challenge and at every moment there is a chance to fall and at every moment there is a struggle in which you cannot fool yourself for a long time. The market is a mirror. Every person you meet illuminates some corner of your mind.

Try to understand this. You will not be able to know many things about yourself if you don't know people. If you don't know anyone who insults you, how can you know whether there is anger in you or not? If no one insults you, you will think that you have no anger. You will only know the anger in you when someone abuses you. So, in a way, the person who has abused you has helped you to understand yourself, has helped you to realise that there is anger inside you that was kept bottled up. That dark corner came to light because of his abuse.

But the sannyasin who flees to the jungle does not have these opportunities to understand his inner characteristics because he is alone there, because there is no one to abuse him, no one to respect him, no one to seduce him with money. Nobody gives him any chance, he is alone there. Self-observation becomes difficult.

This world is the place where you can observe and understand yourself. Otherwise, God would have made countless jungles and kept a person in one jungle. But you will have to admit that the divine is smarter than you. Listen to him and beware of those so-called saints who pretend to be smarter even than God. They try to be very clever. They say they will do sadhana, spiritual practice, in the jungle.

But sadhana cannot be done in the jungle, it has to be in this world. You will only vegetate in the jungle. But here in this world the thorns will prick you the moment you walk on them. When you walk on these thorns and they are not able to prick you, that means now you are able to go to the jungle - now if you want to, you can go. Then I will not stop you. But then you yourself will say that there is no need to go to the jungle; for me there is a jungle in the midst of this very crowd. Wisdom will be born when you mature.

How is wisdom born? It is born out of conflict, it is born by accepting the challenges of life; by being defeated, falling down and getting up again. When you are mistreated a thousand times and get angry a thousand times, there comes a time when you will not be angry at being mistreated. The experience of a thousand times will make you realise that there is no point in burning with anger:

someone else is abusing, so why should I punish myself for it? Then surely one day you will not react when someone abuses you, you will not get angry. That very day the thorn in you will become a flower and you will be a changed person. The peace you will experience on that day no jungle can give you.

The peace of the jungle is a dead peace. If you become peaceful in the midst of these abuses, then your peace is real peace. The peace of the jungle is like the peace of a cemetery: the place is quiet and deserted, there is no one there. It is negative. If you become peaceful in this world, then it is positive. The peace of the jungle is like death, and the peace of the world is very much alive.

I tell you, if you want to reach the divine, don't run away. There can be no relationship of the divine with cowards or with escapists. The only way is the way of courage. There is the possibility of falling into courage. There is no other alternative.

Have you ever noticed that the children of rich families are not very bright or very intelligent? They can't be, because there is no challenge for them. Smart children always belong to families where they have to struggle to achieve even small things. The children of millionaires are usually mediocre.

Henry Ford used to send his sons to polish boots on the side of the road. He told them to earn their own money. He was a multimillionaire, yet he had his children polish other people's shoes. His friends told him that was too much. He replied: "I myself have made money shining shoes. People who were rich when I was a child have now become beggars. I was like a beggar, but today I am the richest man in the world. I don't want my children to become beggars, so I send them to shine shoes on the road".

It was very clever of him to make his children work like that. Usually the children of the rich have no life, they are absolute idiots, because there is no struggle and no challenge in their lives. And if there is no struggle and too much security, they become weak. The backbone is strengthened by struggle. The more you struggle, the more you strengthen the spine.

That is why I am not asking you to flee from the world. I am asking you to wake up from this world. Sannyas is not an escape from the world, sannyas is a great struggle and an awakening. And never avoid the challenge; always face the challenge until the work is completed. If you don't run away then you will awaken soon, because the energy that is spent in running away is turned towards awakening. I do not ask you for the peace of the graveyard. I ask for the peace that comes through work, through effort. I ask for the positive peace that comes from living to the fullest.

The fourth question:

Question 4:

BELOVED MASTER, IT SEEMS THAT BHAJ GOVINDAM IS WRITTEN FOR THE VANAPRASTHA STAGE. BUT YOU SAY IT FOR EVERYONE.

What does vanaprastha mean? Vanaprastha means "facing the jungle". Everybody faces the jungle. If not today, then tomorrow, if not tomorrow, then the day after tomorrow - one day that ultimate solitude which is called mercy has to be found. All are vanaprastha. At one time or another, everybody has to enter into that ultimate solitude; that inner jungle has to be found. Vanaprastha has nothing to do with your physical age; otherwise, how can you explain Shankaracharya? He left his body at the age of thirty-three. Long before that he had become a vanaprasthi and sannyasin.

You are intelligent, and this intelligence is your misery. You are smart and that's why you say this is only for old people. When you have nothing left to do in this world, when people forcibly retire you and when you are in your last stage, do you think you will be able to sing the song of the divine?

People don't want to give up anything until the last moment.

There is a medical school in London where a corpse has been

kept. Two hundred years ago, that man had given money to the faculty on the condition that he would chair the board of trustees not only while he was alive, but also after his death. So even today his skeleton is placed in the president's chair to preside over the board of trustees' meeting. Even after his death he presides. Even now he is the chairman. Do you think such people could be vanaprastha? You are asking about living persons, but he presides even if he is dead. Even now the trustees have to stand up and address him as "Mr. President". This is a trust deed which cannot be changed.

It is his legal right. The corpse is full of straw, but it still clings to that position. Now there is nothing but straw inside his body. He is full of straw, but he still holds on to the office of president.

You don't want to be vanaprastha; you find vanaprastha and sannyas unpleasant. You want to do these things at the end of life. But the person who wants to do them later can never do them then. Only the person who wants to do them now can do them. There is no other time except now.

Even unimportant things create obstacles.

A friend of mine had taken sannyas. He came yesterday and said that his wife would not let him wear orange clothes and a mala and he agreed not to! Listening to his plight I told him: "When you are defeated by your wife, you cannot win anywhere else. It's amazing that a man gives up so easily.

I tell you, now is the time. There is no other way for the moment to come, it is always now. If you can use this moment and your consciousness can turn towards the jungle - the jungle is just a symbol - if you can turn towards the solitude, towards the divine, then the result will be sannyas.

Vanaprastha is the preparation for sannyas. If you turn your back on the world, if you gradually lose interest in the world - happiness and unhappiness seem the same to you, when losing or winning is all the same to you - then it means that you have become a vanaprasthi.

It has nothing to do with the age of your body, it is related to your mental maturity. Some people are eighty years old but their mental age is not more than eight or ten years. But sometimes even a child of eight or ten has the maturity of a person of eighty. It all depends on the acuity and intensity of consciousness.

The words that were uttered by Shankaracharya at the age of ten years cannot be uttered by persons even at the age of one hundred years. The commentary on the Upanishads made by Shankaracharya at the age of ten cannot be made by persons of a hundred years. It all depends on acuity, depth and maturity.

Awaken all your energy and let it flow and you will find that vanaprastha has happened at that very moment, sannyas has happened at that very moment. But if you keep postponing it for tomorrow... today you want to see a movie so tomorrow you will go to the temple. If you have to postpone something then postpone the film, watch it in your old age, but you are postponing the divine till your old age! You give your youth to the world and your old age to the divine. From this your values are clear: your youth is spent on useless things and your old age is destined for the divine.

When you have energy you do evil, and when you have no energy you want to do good.

When you are unable to do anything, you set out to do good. You think of giving up when you are about to die, but you did not think of giving up when you had all the vitality. Who are you cheating? That is why Shankara says, "Blind in the eye". Who are you trying to cheat?

You must remember the divine when you have energy, because it takes a lot of energy for this remembrance. There is no greater action than this - it needs your totality, your every breath, your every cell. When you become weak and old, when you walk with the help of a cane, when you are not able to see properly, will you be able to remember the divine? Then your voice will become so weak that it will not be able to pronounce correctly the song of the divine. What is needed is intensity, a torrent of energy. For the remembrance of the divine you have to bring into play all the energy of your life, and that can only be done today. The day you understand this, it will be vanaprastha for you.

The last question:

Question 5:

BELOVED MASTER, CAN A PERSON WHO HAS COSMIC CONSCIOUSNESS REALLY ENJOY THE PLEASURES OR DOES HE JUST ACT AS IF HE DOES?

Only a person who has cosmic consciousness can truly enjoy. Only he can enjoy ultimate bliss.

He alone enjoys - the rest of the people are under the false notion of enjoyment. They are carrying false coins; in reality, they are suffering. Your happiness and pleasures are nothing but the misery and agony you have experienced. You say and think that you are experiencing happiness, but in reality you are experiencing misery.

Only the enlightened one enjoys. Ten tyakten bhunjithan - those who renounced, only they enjoyed.

Enjoy the divine. You are enjoying trivialities, and the supposed enjoyment of the trivial is causing you great misery.

One day a man came and placed a pile of money at Ramakrishna's feet. Ramakrishna said, "Please take it away".

The man said: "This is another proof that you are a great renouncer.

Ramakrishna said, "You are a great renouncer, not me, because I am enjoying the divine and you are renouncing it. You are collecting money and I am collecting the divine. So tell me, who is the renouncer and who is enjoying? I am the lover of happiness and you are the renouncer".

A person who does not care for diamonds and collects stones must be a renouncer. One who renounces the valuable and cares for the non-essential must be called a renouncer.

Cosmic consciousness is supreme enjoyment. It is entering into the supreme bliss of life. There is no greater bliss than this. Without it, all else is misery.

So don't ask: "Can a person who has cosmic consciousness really enjoy pleasures?". He cannot enjoy your pleasures because your pleasures are not pleasures. He is enjoyment, he is bliss, but his enjoyment is different from yours.

To know it you will have to give up your enjoyment and you will have to awaken your conscience.

At this moment you are in a dream; you have not experienced pleasure or happiness, you have only dreamt about it. But the enlightened one enjoys the truth. He enjoys bliss.

Enough for today.

The song of life

HE WHO HAS READ EVEN A LITTLE OF THE GITA, DRUNK EVEN A DROP OF GANGETIC WATER AND WORSHIPPED GOD, YAMA, THE GOD OF DEATH, CANNOT DESTROY HIM.

OH GOD, PROTECT ME FROM THIS TROUBLED WORLD WHERE ONE HAS TO BE BORN AGAIN AND AGAIN, DIE AGAIN AND AGAIN, AND FALL INTO A MOTHER'S WOMB AGAIN AND AGAIN, AND TAKE ME TO THE OTHER SHORE.

HE WHO HAS MADE HIS ROBE FROM THE RAGS OF THE WAYSIDE, WHOSE PATH IS FREE FROM THE THOUGHT OF SIN AND VIRTUE, WHO IS ABSORBED IN YOGA, SUCH A YOGI SOMETIMES PLAYS LIKE A CHILD AND SOMETIMES LIKE A MADMAN.

WHO ARE YOU? WHO AM I? WHERE DO I COME FROM? WHO IS MY MOTHER? WHO IS MY FATHER? CONTEMPLATE THESE QUESTIONS, AND THEN YOU WILL DISCOVER THAT THE WORLD AND ITS WORRIES ARE MEANINGLESS AND A DREAM, AND YOU WILL BE FREED FROM THIS BAD DREAM.

THE SAME DIVINITY RESIDES IN YOU, IN ME AND EVERYWHERE. BY BECOMING INTOLERANT TOWARDS ME YOU ARE BECOMING ANGRY IN VAIN. THEN, ABANDONING THIS IGNORANCE OF DISCRIMINATION IN EVERYTHING, SEE ONLY

YOURSELF IN EVERYTHING.

DO NOT WASTE YOUR ENERGY IN SUCH MATTERS AS ENEMY AND FRIEND, SON AND BROTHER, WAR AND TREATY. IF YOU WANT TO REACH THE FEET OF DIVINITY SOON, MAINTAIN EQUANIMITY IN EVERYTHING AND EVERYWHERE.

I heard a story. A wasp had its abode near the window of a large building. In winter it slept and rested, in summer it flew, danced and collected pollen from the flowers. It was very happy. But this wasp was special: it was a thinker. It thought a lot and despised other wasps because there was no thinking in their lives. Their lives were full of desires.

They never thought, never contemplated, never knew the scriptures.

Sometimes he also flew to that building. He loved that building. The people who visited the building seemed to him to be of the same type because they were thinkers. Actually, this building was a big library.

Professors, teachers, writers, philosophers and poets came there. People used to chase the wasp away, but it always came back.

Gradually he began to read and write. He started in the children's section and soon studied great books on philosophy. She began to read large volumes of science and poetry. She became very proud and could not tolerate the other wasps, they seemed insignificant to her. She became very selfish. She thought day and night. She forgot to dance in the sun, fly through the air and visit the trees. Now she used to sit absorbed in deep thoughts like: "Who made this world? Why was it made? Where did this existence come from and where is it going? All the time she was thinking about these serious questions.

One day I was reading a book on the science of aviation. In this book on aerodynamics it was written that the body of a wasp is heavier than its wings, so theoretically a wasp cannot fly because its wings are small and weak and its body is big and heavy. When he read this he was confused and perplexed.

Until now I didn't know that his body was big and his wings were small. It was the first time I knew it and, of course, you can't deny what the scriptures say. You can't go against what the scientists say.

He became very sad. That day he did not fly back to his hive, but crawled back. How was it possible for him to fly, to do something that was against science? He became very sad and stopped moving. He kept seeing the other wasps flying, going to the flowers, but he thought they were doing it out of ignorance: how can a wasp fly? Their wings are small and their bodies are big. He pitied those who flew because they didn't know the science. If they did, they would have stopped flying.

But one day a bird attacked the wasp with the intention of eating it for breakfast. In its nervousness and confusion, the wasp forgot the scriptures and flew away.

He sat down in a bush, rested for a while, calmed down and realised that he had flown! "I was thinking that a wasp can't fly but I have flown, so there must have been a block in my mind that was holding back my natural ability to fly and that was undone in the moment of danger". He had read about mental blocks in a psychology book. So he started flying again from that day on. He abandoned scriptural knowledge from that day on, and from that moment he became the wasp again - the natural wasp!

From that day on, he freed himself from knowledge and stopped despising other wasps. That day he experienced his true nature.

Religion is the freedom of knowledge, and in that freedom is ultimate knowledge. The scriptures are not meant to make you lame, but to give you the ability to fly. If the scriptures have made you lame, then it is certain that you have misunderstood or misinterpreted them. If the scriptures have made you sad, then you have either missed something in them or you have not understood them correctly. The scriptures that have robbed you of your natural ability to fly or flow are not your friend, you have made them your enemy.

A writing is a writing only if it gives you freedom. A writing is a writing if it makes you natural.

A writing is a writing if it does not fill you with condemnation towards others and is capable of making you realise that the divine is also hidden in them.

These phrases of Shankara are very important.

ONE WHO HAS READ EVEN A LITTLE OF THE GITA - take note of "a little" - ONE WHO HAS READ EVEN A LITTLE OF THE GITA, Drank EVEN A DROP OF GANG WATER AND WORSHIPPED GOD A LITTLE, YAMA, THE GOD OF DEATH, CANNOT DESTROY HIM.

You have read the Gita many times. This country has been reading the Gita for thousands of years; people have memorised it. Every person is full of the Gita and yet there is no liberation for him. He can only see death. And Shankara is saying that death disappears for one who has read even a little of the Gita - who has tasted the divine even a little, drunk even a drop of the water of the Ganges. And you have bathed in the Ganges!

... WHO HAS DRUNK EVEN A DROP OF WATER FROM THE GANGES AND WORSHIPPED GOD EVEN A LITTLE BIT....

You have worshipped much, you have recited many times, you have performed many yajnas, you have prostrated yourself at the doors of many temples. Even the stones of the temple doors are worn by the rubbing of your head, but no revolution has taken place in your life. Surely there must be some basic illusion, some mistake somewhere - you have missed something.

"Even a little" can give you deliverance if you can understand it, otherwise all the scriptures can become your prison. Even a single word can give you freedom if you understand it, otherwise the words will become a useless weight on your chest. It is not the scriptures that make you free, it is understanding. And understanding has to be created by you; the scriptures do not give it. You have to understand this. You have to create the understanding, only then can the scriptures make sense. If you don't have the understanding, then the scriptures cannot give you the understanding. They can only give you theories, and theories are worthless, because you don't care about theories, you behave very differently in life.

One day I told Mulla Nasruddin that I hadn't seen his children for a long time. He said, "I believe in family planning.

I was surprised to hear him because he had seventeen children and he said: "I believe in family planning".

I said, "What do you mean, I don't understand".

She said: "I believe in the family planning motto: Two or three children are the ideal number for the household. So I send the rest of the children to play in the neighbourhood. Now most of them have even started to sleep over at neighbours' houses. In my own house I don't have more than two or three children.

By sending your children to your neighbours, you can fulfil the theory of having two or three children at home!

Your understanding of the scriptures is also like that. You keep giving birth to children and then sending them to the neighbours. Man is capable of deceiving himself. It is easy to avoid theory but you cannot avoid understanding. You can avoid theory, because it is dead and you are alive. You can always save yourself from theory, but you cannot avoid your own understanding.

When the understanding is within you, you can run away anywhere but it will remain within you. So you must not give any importance to theory; you must give importance to understanding. The theory can be borrowed but the understanding has to be created by yourself. Theories can also be stolen from the scriptures, from the teachers, but you cannot get the understanding for free. You have to pay for it and fight inch by inch to get it. Theories are worthless, you get them for free. Theories are rubbish, and rubbish cannot be valuable.

WHO HAS READ EVEN A LITTLE OF THE GITA - a little of the Gita is enough. Even if you understand one word it is enough. Then there is no need to wait to hear the whole Gita. But the question is understanding.

There is a story in the Mahabharata that Dronacharya thought the boy Yudhishthira was the most intelligent of all the Pandavas and Kauravas, but after a few days of experience he found him to be rather clumsy. The other children were learning new lessons every day and progressing rapidly, but Yudhishthira was stuck in the first lesson. Eventually Drona's patience also ran out, so she asked him: "How long will it take you to learn the first lesson? Are you not making progress?

Yudhishthira replied: "What is the point of learning the second lesson while not understanding the first?

The first lesson was about truth. The other children had read it, memorised it and moved on to the second lesson. But Yudhishthira said, "Until I start telling the truth, how can I go to the second lesson? Please don't rush me.

Then Drona understood! Looking at Yudhishthira's mental condition, Drona understood for the first time that there can be no other lesson after the truth. Then he said to Yudhishthira: "There is no need for you to hurry. By learning, by understanding this first lesson, you will understand, you will know all the lessons. Just reading the lessons is one thing and living the lesson is a different thing altogether."

At the end of the story, when all the Pandava brothers were ascending to heaven, one by one they fell down. Only Yudhishthira and his dog - who was the truth - reached the gate of heaven.

The truth came to heaven and the one who accompanied the

truth came to heaven. It was his dog, who had always lived with him and had great integrity. Not even his brothers had such integrity, they fell by the wayside.

But the dog had never doubted, his faith was boundless. All his life he had obeyed Yudhishthira. Even Yudhishthira was surprised to see that all his brothers had fallen and only this dog could reach the gate of heaven with him. The gate opened and Yudhishthira was received, but the guardian said, "Only you can enter, the dog cannot enter. No dog has ever entered heaven.

Even human beings come here with great difficulty".

Hearing this Yudhishthira said: "Then I too cannot enter. This dog who was with me all my life, who has reached the gates of heaven where even my brothers could not reach, who has so much faith in me - I cannot abandon him at any cost, otherwise I would consider myself worse than a dog! I will not abandon him. Please close the door.

Then the whole of heaven laughed joyfully. All the gods gathered there and asked him to come in. Then Yudhishthira noticed that the dog was not a dog, it was Lord Krishna himself. It was his proof! If at that time Yudhishthira had abandoned the dog and entered the door without him, then he would have missed heaven. That was the test of his love, of his faith, of his integrity. Yudhishthira learnt only one lesson - the truth; that was enough to take him to heaven. Arjuna took a long time to learn it. Krishna pronounced the whole Gita, but even then Arjuna remained doubtful. Yudhishthira learnt only one small lesson in his life and that was the lesson of truth. Even the master had doubted his intelligence because he was stuck in the first lesson, but he soon realised that there is no other lesson after the first one.

He who has learnt one lesson has learnt everything. Don't try to learn it all, otherwise you will miss a little, A LITTLE OF THE GITA. If there is a little awareness of the divine, if you have heard even a little of the song of the divine, if your ears have heard even a part of that song, if even a word has reached your heart, then that will become the seed. It will sprout and become a tree, and you will be filled with limitless fragrance. Everything is hidden in that seed.

The pundits remain empty. They are able to memorise the Gita, but they cannot hear its chanting. Their minds are full of words, but their hearts remain impassive, untouched. They can repeat the Gita but there will not be a tear in their eyes, no music in their hearts, no dance in their feet - they will go on repeating like a dead person, mechanically, unmoved from within. There is not even a scratch in their heart, not even a shadow.

Then Shankara says, WHO HAS READ EVEN A LITTLE OF THE GITA. Here Gita does not mean only the Shrimad Bhagavadgita, because he who has read even a little of the Koran, he will also attain it; he who has read even a little of the Bible, he will also attain it. And he who has read neither the Bible, nor the Koran, nor the Gita, but has read a little of life, will also attain it. The whole emphasis is on the awakening of understanding: the one who has not spent his life sleeping, the one who has been awakened, has opened his eyes and has recognised a little of life.

If you can grasp even a little, you can grasp the whole sky. If you grasp one ray, you can grasp the whole sun. You can get the sun with the help of that lightning. If you are sitting in a dark hut and you can see a ray peeping through the thatched roof, you can find the whole sun in that ray. If you start with that ray, you will undoubtedly reach the sun. It is not necessary to have all the sunshine in the house, what would you do with so much? You will get indigestion.

Do not start accumulating scriptures, they will become your prison. Then your wings will not be able to fly, nor will your heart be able to dance, nor will you be natural.

It is the scriptures that make people more unnatural than anything else. If you can understand that, I would like to tell you that it is the scriptures that have made people irreligious. More people have been made irreligious by scripture than by anything else. As the number of scriptures increases, man becomes blind because he thinks that the understanding is in the book, and that he will be able to gain this understanding by just reading it. But if it were so easy to gain understanding, then the whole world would have been very understanding, very intelligent.

Every house has a Gita or a Koran or a Bible, but there is no understanding. Remember that you give up your effort when the scriptures are readily available. Don't get lost in the jungle of theories.

HE WHO HAS READ EVEN A LITTLE OF THE GITA, HAS DRUNK EVEN A DROP OF THE WATER OF THE GANGES ....

What will you do with the whole Ganges? It is not necessary; the whole of the Ganges is too much. One drop is enough for you. Which Ganges is Shankara talking about? He is not talking about the Ganges where you went for your pilgrimage.

Here the Ganges is a symbol: whoever has drunk a drop of piety, whoever has drunk a drop of innocence, whoever has drunk a drop of simplicity, has tasted the Ganges. There is no need to go to the Ganges, because there are many people who live on the banks of the Ganges and nothing has happened to them. They have lived there, they have bathed there, but nothing has happened to them. The Ganges we are talking about here is not the one you can see outside, it is the inner Ganges. One drop is enough. Even a drop is more than necessary, because our limit is no more than a drop; our being is no bigger than a drop. We are like a drop in this vast existence. A small drop of water from the Ganges will bathe us and make us whole.

But you must understand well that the Ganges means innocence, the Ganges means simplicity, the Ganges means inner virginity; the Ganges means becoming innocent as a child. By bringing back even a drop of your childhood, if you can look at the world again as you saw it in your childhood - with those fresh eyes, without thought, without any condemnation, without any judgement - if you can look at the world the same way you saw it when you first opened your eyes .... You just saw it, you didn't think about it, you didn't say whether it was good or bad, beautiful or ugly, a sin or a virtue, you just looked right. The whole world was before you and there was no thought inside you. If you look at it in the same way again, if you can recapture even a drop of your childhood, then you will have tasted a drop of the Ganges.

HE HAS DRUNK EVEN A DROP OF WATER FROM THE GANGES AND WORSHIPPED GOD EVEN A LITTLE BIT....

It's okay to worship too much. Too much worship means you don't know how to worship. Too much worship means you are repeating dead rituals, otherwise it is enough to say the name of the divine even once. And every day you are sitting with the rosary repeating "Ram, Ram". When will your life be full of Ram? How many times will you repeat "Ram"?

There are some people who keep count of the number of their chants. They say, "I have chanted this mantra ten million times". But if nothing has happened by chanting it once, what will happen by chanting it ten million times? Try to understand this.

A mantra is not mathematics. A mantra is not quantitative, it is qualitative. If something is going to happen, it will happen the first time. If it doesn't happen then, it won't happen even if you repeat it ten million times. If you have repeated it wrong the first time, you will repeat it more the second time, the third time even more, and so on. You can repeat it a million times or ten million times, it makes no difference.

It is a matter of calling properly; then a call of the heart is enough, then even a call becomes a revolution. The divine is not deaf. It does not want you to flatter it. Will it only listen when you repeat it to it? It can listen without you telling it, but it must come from your heart. It will never listen if you repeat it in your mind, because the divine is not related to your thinking, the divine is related only to your prayer of the heart.

I heard that it had not rained in a village for many years, so the whole village had gathered in the temple to pray.

A little boy also went to the temple to pray. Everyone laughed at him on the way. Even the priest said to him: "You fool, why are you carrying that umbrella? It hasn't rained for years, that's why we are going to pray.

That boy had brought an umbrella. Thousands of people had gathered to pray, but none of them had brought an umbrella. The boy said: "I have brought the umbrella because when we pray it will probably rain and I will need it on the way back.

People laughed, they said: "He's crazy".

Can the prayer of these people be answered? Only the prayer of this child could be answered. He had deep confidence; he had no doubt in prayer; his prayer was filled with deep confidence. But the elders planted doubt in the boy's mind. They said, "Go home and put this umbrella away. It won't rain that way. They go to pray, but they have no confidence that it will rain by praying. So why pray?

It's better to be an atheist and be honest about it. What's the point of being a theist if you're not honest? You have prayed many times, but did you think it would be answered? When it is not answered, you say that you knew beforehand that the prayer would not be answered. You have knocked many times at the doors of the temple, but have you done so wholeheartedly? With full confidence? Or have you gone in doubt?

If you went with doubts, then you should not have gone; that would have been honest. By going, who have you cheated? By going you have hurt yourself. Your prayer went unanswered. If your prayer remains unanswered again and again, then you lose confidence in yourself; then you pray with your lips and not with your heart.

AND YOU HAVE WORSHIPPED GOD EVEN A LITTLE
- yes, a little is enough. You must understand that Shankara's
emphasis is not on quantity - how much you have worshipped - but
on quality: How you have done it.

I heard that there was a lawyer who prayed every day. He prayed
the first day. The second day he would say, "Ditto". The third day he
would say again, "Ditto". He thought there was no point in repeating
the same words every day, so he used to say "Ditto".

People are very calculating in life. Even their prayer is calculating
and clever; they cannot be simple even when they pray. If you have
the opportunity, you can steal from God. Maybe that is why he hides
and is afraid to face you. Innocence itself is a prayer.

AND HAS WORSHIPPED GOD EVEN A LITTLE,
YAMA, THE GOD OF DEATH, CANNOT DESTROY HIM.

Whoever has tasted prayer even a little, goes beyond death. Only
people who are afraid die.

It is fear that kills. Only egoists die. Death is always of the ego.
Only those who have not known life die. Those who have known life
even a little do not die. Then the god of death stops talking about
you.

Whoever has understood even a little of the song of the divine
does not die. Then you may not remain as you are, but your
innermost being will always be. The mind, with which you have
been thinking, may not remain; the body, through which you have
enjoyed, may not remain; but your innermost being, where you have
experienced trust, cannot be destroyed.

Trust is eternal, because trust is the ultimate, the last, the most
intimate. Death has never entered there and can never enter. There
you are eternal, ancient. There you yourself are the divine. Whoever
has longed for the divine, whoever has sought the divine, has soon
realised that it is hidden within himself. It is not to be found in a
temple, but within oneself. It is not hidden in the mountains, nor in

the moon, nor in the stars.

When the first Russian astronaut, Yuri Gagarin, returned to Earth - and Russia is an atheist country - the first thing they asked him was: "Did you see God on the moon? And he replied: "I looked very carefully, but there was no God there". There is a very big museum in Leningrad where all the things related to atheism in the history of human beings have been collected. On the wall of that museum are engraved the words of Yuri Gagarin: "I went to the moon, I went into space, but I didn't see God anywhere".

If God had been in space, Yuri Gagarin would have known him. But Yuri Gagarin is wrong, and you are wrong too because you also think that the divine is somewhere outside. Both the atheist and the theist are wrong, because the theist thinks that God is sitting somewhere in the sky and the atheist thinks that if he is in the sky then we can look for him in the whole sky. But if we don't find him there, then...?

Yuri Gagarin should have looked for God within himself. The divine is there. The one who saw the moon and the stars through Yuri Gagarin's eyes, that is God. Whoever seeks God can never find him.

The divine cannot be seen, it is always the seer. It is not something that can be seen, it is the vision hidden within you. The seer is the divine. It is always the seer. You can never make him the object of your sight. But he who has heard even a little of the song of life.... I call that Bhagavadgita, the divine song. The song that Krishna has sung before Arjuna is the refrain of that ultimate song, it is the refrain of the song of life; it is a small part of that song. That song is written on every tree, on every rock, on every wave of the sea. The emptiness of the sky is its silence, the rivers sing the song of the divine. It is he who sees through your eyes; it is he who hears through your ears; it is he who throbs through your heart - there is nothing else but the divine. He who has understood even a little of the song of the divine, who has acknowledged even a little of life, who has drunk even a drop of simplicity, who has worshipped even a little .....

Worship means, the one who has made his ego bow even a little, who has bowed his head even a little. No matter to whom you bow, your bowing is enough. If you have bowed in a mosque, it is all right; if you have bowed in a temple, it is all right; if you have bowed in a gurudwara, it is all right. It doesn't matter whether you bow to a rock, a tree or the empty sky. It doesn't matter whether you believe in God or not. Mahavira bowed without believing and he succeeded.

And Buddha never accepted God, but became God. He knew the art of bowing down.

The point is not to reach God, the point is to destroy one's ego. Worship means, one who has finished with himself and who has said: "I am not". It is not necessary to say: "You are". The one who has said: "I am not", at that very moment has known that "You alone are". The divine appears as soon as the "I" disappears. This "I" is the only obstacle.

So, THE GOD OF DEATH CANNOT DESTROY IT.... Therefore, O IDIOT! ALWAYS SING THE SONG OF THE DIVINE!

OH GOD, PROTECT ME FROM THIS TROUBLED WORLD WHERE ONE HAS TO BE BORN AGAIN AND AGAIN, DIE AGAIN AND AGAIN, AND FALL INTO A MOTHER'S WOMB AGAIN AND AGAIN.

Man is powerless, and nothing can be done by man's resolve, for whatever you do will be less than you. The divine is immense, far greater than you. It is in you, it peers through you, but it is far greater than you.

It's like the ocean in a drop of water. If you taste the drop you get the salty taste of the ocean.

If you analyse one drop you will get the substance of the whole ocean. A drop is very small, but the ocean has shown itself through the drop just as the sky has shown itself through the window. The divine has also shown itself through you, but it is much vaster than you. The divine has shown itself through you just as the sky is seen through the window, the ocean is hidden in the drop, the tree is hidden in the seed.

You can't reach it with your effort; your effort is too little. It's like trying to reach for the sky with your hand. You can only reach it with His grace.

That is why Shankara says: "Oh God, please save me! I am sure I will drown. I can be saved only if you save me. My energy and strength are very limited. Even if I think, what can I think?

Even if I contemplate, what can I contemplate? - all thought will be mine. You are unknown, you are immense. To reach you, your help is needed".

That is why a devotee, a bhakta, is continually desirous of your support, your help. The day you start asking for their support you will find that you have it because you start growing; your shrinking stops and you start expanding. The day you ask for the support of existence you begin to become immense; your smallness begins to disappear from that very moment. You have given the invitation: "Come! Nothing more is needed.

Buddha has said: "I thought I was seeking the truth, but in reaching it I discovered that the truth was also seeking me".

The truth also seeks you. The divine also seeks you, seeks you, but you do not give the invitation. If by chance existence takes you by the hand, you give it your hand.

Have you noticed the little children? The father takes the child by the hand and leads him to the market.

The parent keeps holding the child's hand, but the child tries to free his hand because he wants to be independent, he wants to walk on his own. The parent wants to hold the child's hand, but the child wants to free his hand so that he can run on his own.

Man also behaves in this way. The divine takes him by the hand, otherwise man cannot even live. How can we breathe if existence does not pulsate in us? How can we live if existence does not pulsate in us? But we try to fend for ourselves. The ego always tries to stand on its own feet without the support of anyone else. It seems very insulting to ask someone for help. It seems pitiful to ask for someone's support. That is why, as man's ego is increasing, worship and prayer are disappearing.

Have you ever noticed that when you bow in the temple you feel a bit uncomfortable? You are afraid that someone will see you bowing. You kneel down, you put your hands together, but at the same time you make sure that nobody is looking at you, because people will say: "You are kneeling, you are bowing", and that will hurt your ego.

People are afraid to lean. It is very unfortunate, because everything that is great in life can only be achieved by leaning. It's like when you are thirsty and you are standing in the river but you don't bend down. You want the river to come up to your mouth. But if you want to drink water, you have to bend down, bow your head, pick up the water with your hands and drink it. But your ego won't let you bend down.

Most people deny the divine, not because they have come to know that it does not exist, but because if the divine exists they will have to bow down.

Friedrich Nietzsche wrote: "If God exists, we will have to bow down. That is why I say that God does not exist. How can I bow down? If God exists, he is superior to me. That is why I say that God does not exist, because no one can be superior to me". The ego is terrible.

Man is full of a terrible ego. The ego in the soul is like a cancer in the body. Yes, the ego is a cancer of the soul. Until you are free from this ego the song of the divine cannot be born in you, you cannot pray and you cannot worship. The divine cannot enter you as long as you are full of yourself. Come down from your throne, make space and invite it in.

OH GOD, PROTECT ME FROM THIS TROUBLED WORLD WHERE ONE HAS TO BE BORN AGAIN AND AGAIN, DIE AGAIN AND AGAIN AND FALL INTO A MOTHER'S WOMB AGAIN AND AGAIN.

Whoever has understood the fact of life has come to know that life is nothing but repetition; everything is repeated over and over again. You have been born many times, you have died many times, you have gained wealth many times, you have gained fame many times, you have succeeded many times and you have failed many times. You keep turning like the wheel of a vehicle, up and down, up and down.

It is a natural desire to be free from this repetition, because repetition is boring. That is why we have called this world the chakra, the wheel; we have called it the dushta-chakra, the bad, ominous wheel, because we go on turning in the same way - nothing new happens. You live today as you lived yesterday, tomorrow you will also live like that and the day after tomorrow you will also live the same way. It's always the same night, the same morning, the same anger, the same greed, the same attachment, the same birth, the same death, it's just repetition. There must definitely be a deep-rooted idiocy in us - that's why we don't wake up from our sleep - otherwise we would have seen that we keep repeating the same things over and over again. If we achieve nothing by doing them so many times, then it is certain that we will never achieve anything by repeating them countless times.

We have to get out of this vicious circle. That is why in the East, and especially in India, this great desire to get out of the circle of birth and death was born. This kind of desire was not born anywhere else in the world. In the West, religions like Islam, Christianity and Judaism are not inspired by this desire. They want to reach heaven.

Heaven means that there should not be all the miseries of this life, but all the pleasures. Heaven is only a further expansion of the worldly types of comforts and pleasures. But in India a unique desire was born, and that is the speciality of India: the desire for moksha, liberation. It is the desire for liberation and not for heaven. The meaning of the desire for liberation is that now we want neither misery nor happiness; we have had enough of both. There was nothing meaningful in them; now we want to be free from both. This desire for freedom from both is unique. That is why it is not possible to translate the word moksha into any language of the world. It is possible to translate swarga, heaven, and nareka, hell, but moksha is a unique word. No other language in the world has this word. It cannot, because first the desire has to be born and then the word to express it is born. First is the experience, and then the words are born to express it.

The experience of moksha is India's unique quest. No other quest has reached higher than this, and no other quest can reach higher than this. Only those people who have experienced happiness to the full, and have discovered that happiness is also a form of misery, a delusion of misery, can have the desire to be free from happiness.

HE WHO HAS MADE HIS TROP WITH THE THREADS OF THE WAY, WHOSE WAY IS FREE FROM THE THOUGHT OF SIN AND VIRTUE, WHO IS ENGROSSED IN YOGA, whose mind has been united, SUCH A YOGI SOMETIMES PLAYS LIKE A CHILD AND SOMETIMES BECOMES LIKE A MADMAN.

A person sitting by the roadside may look like a beggar, but if you look closely there is an emperor hidden inside. ... Because if you look closely at emperors you will find beggars inside. They keep asking for more.

There was a Mohammedan fakir named Farid. The people of his village asked him to request Emperor Akbar to open a school in the village, as Akbar held him in high esteem. Farid had never asked Akbar for anything. A fakir never asks, a fakir always gives. But since the villagers had insisted that he see Akbar, he could not refuse, so he went. He had never visited the palace before, but now he had to.

He got there very early in the morning and was told that the emperor was praying in his personal mosque. So Farid went and stood at the back. Akbar didn't know. He finished his prayer, raised his hands towards heaven and said: "O God! What you have given me is not enough, I want much more than this. Please make my kingdom much greater than this. Please increase my wealth and fame".

Farid could not believe his ears. The great emperor Akbar, who possessed such a vast kingdom, kept asking for more. He kept begging. So Farid thought, how could I ask a person who is still asking for more? - Because opening a school means spending some money, he will have much less. If he asks God, I can also ask him directly. Why have an agent in the way? He turned away. When Akbar got up he saw Farid coming down the stairs. He ran after him and asked him the reason for his coming. Akbar held Farid in high esteem and used to go to see him from time to time, but Farid had never visited Akbar. Akbar asked him, "Why have you come? Why are you coming back?"

Farid said: "I have come to see an emperor, to ask him for something, but instead I have seen a beggar, so I turn back. How can I ask a person who is begging, asking for more? I don't want to impoverish you. I had to come because the people of the village insisted that I ask you if you wanted to open a school. But now I will not ask you, I will ask God. When you keep asking him for so many things, I will be able to ask him directly.

Akbar told Farid many times that he would open the school, but Farid refused, saying: "You don't ask beggars for help. Only true emperors can help.

Your emperors are really poor beggars! They ask for more. But this country has produced such emperors who are not beggars; if you look at them you will find that they are more precious than all the precious stones!

HE WHO HAS MADE HIS TUNIC FROM THE RAGS OF THE WAYSIDE.

Yes, he has made his clothes out of the rags of the road, but in him moksha has been born, in him freedom has spread its wings.

WHOSE WAY IS FREE FROM THE THOUGHT OF SIN AND VIRTUE.

Note that religions say that if you sin you will go to hell and if you do a good deed you will go to heaven. But what will you do to attain moksha? Neither sin nor good deed.

WHOSE WAY IS FREE FROM THE THOUGHT OF SIN AND VIRTUE.

He who sees neither good nor evil, whose life has been liberated from choice.... Krishnamurti calls this choiceless consciousness. One whose life is filled only with consciousness, without choice, without alternative; one who does not choose, who neither says this is right nor says that is wrong; one who does not choose, who says that everything is the same, that there is nothing to choose - nothing is beautiful or ugly, nothing is sin or virtue.

This is a very unique idea that is related to moksha. That is why when the Upanishads were first translated, the thinkers in the West could not understand what the Upanishads were saying, because in the West it was thought that the purpose of the scriptures is to preach to do good deeds. The scriptures are to save you from sins and inspire you to do good. But the Upanishads say that the scriptures save you from both sin and good deeds, because when you are full of the thought of sin and good deeds then you are full of duality.

The scriptures are to take you beyond duality and make you one. Your mind is full of contempt while you keep saying this is sin. Your mind is full of praise while you say this is good. When you say this is good, it means you have chosen something. When you say this is sin, it means you have rejected something. And the divine is both in sin and in good deeds, and by rejecting something you have rejected the divine.

In the life of the enlightened one there is neither rejection nor demand. He neither accepts nor denies; his consciousness does not waver, it has become stable.

WHOSE PATH IS FREE FROM THE THOUGHT OF SIN AND VIRTUE, WHO IS ABSORBED IN YOGA....

A yogi is one who is united, who has become one; there is no duality for him. Heaven and hell, happiness and misery, sin and virtue will remain as long as there is duality. When only one remains, then heaven and hell, happiness and misery, darkness and light, all disappear. In that one is ultimate rest; in that one is ultimate bliss. In attaining that one, all is attained.

SUCH YOGI SOMETIMES PLAYS LIKE A CHILD - so innocent, like a child - AND SOMETIMES LIKE A CRAZY - so full of bliss, so drunk with ecstasy.

In a yogi you will find both a child and a madman. A child means one who has not begun to think and a madman means one who has gone beyond thought. The circle is complete in a yogi. He has become like a child, he does not think; and he has become like a madman, he has gone beyond thought. That is why it is difficult to recognise a yogi. You cannot put him in any category and you cannot make any judgement about him. You never know what he will do in the next moment because he doesn't do anything by himself, he does what the divine makes him do. It has put itself in the hands of the divine. It just keeps flowing; wherever the river of godliness takes him, that is his destiny. If he drowns in the middle, that is his destiny. He no longer has any goal of his own. Yogi' means ultimate freedom. Therefore, O IDIOT!

ALWAYS SING THE SONG OF THE DIVINE.

WHO ARE YOU? WHO AM I? WHERE DO I COME FROM? WHO IS MY MOTHER? WHO IS MY FATHER? CONTEMPLATE THESE QUESTIONS AND THEN YOU WILL DISCOVER THAT THE WORLD AND ITS WORRIES ARE MEANINGLESS AND A DREAM, AND YOU WILL BE FREED FROM THIS BAD DREAM. THEREFORE, O FOOL! SING ALWAYS THE SONG OF THE DIVINE.

THE SAME DIVINITY RESIDES IN YOU, IN ME AND EVERYWHERE. BY BECOMING INTOLERANT TOWARDS ME YOU ARE BECOMING ANGRY IN VAIN. THEN, ABANDONING THIS IGNORANCE OF DISCRIMINATION IN EVERYTHING, SEE ONLY YOURSELF IN EVERYTHING.

THAT'S WHY, OH FOOL! ALWAYS SING THE SONG OF THE DIVINE.

Do not waste your energy on the duality of enemy and friend, son and brother, war and peace. If you want to reach the feet of the divine, everything must be equal for you. To see everything as equal is the way to unity: in happiness and in misery, in victory and in defeat, in success and in failure. Then, gradually, you will attain unity.

You will remain two as long as you see duality, for you become what you perceive. When you don't see conflict, when you don't see duality, and you begin to see the one in a friend and an enemy, in good and evil, in sin and virtue, in heaven and hell, in blessing and curse - when you begin to see one, then you begin to become one. You become what you see. What you perceive becomes your nature. Therefore, going beyond duality is sadhana, spiritual practice.

How will you see it, how will you see the same thing in the person who abuses you and the person who praises you? But if you look closely, you will see that abuse and praise are only superficial; inside, there is only one. Try to see carefully that friend and foe, hate and love are only two expressions of the same energy. That is why love can become hate and hate can become love; a friend can become an enemy and an enemy can become a friend. If the two were absolutely different, this change could not have taken place. A friend today can become an enemy tomorrow. A person who was an enemy yesterday becomes a friend today.

Indeed, the energy is the same. The feet that take a person away from you are the same feet that will one day bring them back to you. The feet are the same. Moving towards and moving away are just two forms of the same energy.

Try to understand it. Try to seek it. Old habits will create obstacles. Old ways of thinking will create obstacles, but darkness disappears with continued effort and light appears. When you begin to see the one in the opposite also, you will experience a deep peace; some wholeness begins to come into you. You are no longer the same as you were yesterday. A new consciousness begins to be born in you. When the two disappear and only one remains, then you are ready for the divine.

And the divine is always ready. When you are ready, the cloud rains and you are full; the moment of bliss arrives.

But we must awaken from both, we must avoid duality, and we must see and hold on to the flow of the one.

You will achieve unity through disciplined equanimity.

Try always to see the one in the two; this should become your meditation, your sadhana. When you succeed you should be able to see that this is also a failure - failure will soon follow. And don't be angry when you fail, success will soon follow. They are two sides of the same coin. When success looks like failure and failure looks like success, the difference disappears and equality appears. Then your door to the divine will open.

The divine is always very close, but you keep away from it because of your differentiation. The divine is always before you, because what is before you is divinity. But your eyes are closed.

Because of the differentiation your eyes are closed, but they open when the differences disappear.

The difference is like the eyelid of the eye and indifference is like the opening of the eyelid. Therefore, O IDIOT! SING THE SONG OF THE DIVINE.

Enough for today.

The world is a school

The first question:

Question 1:

BELOVED MASTER, WHEN SHANKARA WAS VERY YOUNG HIS MOTHER DID NOT GIVE HIM PERMISSION TO TAKE SANNYAS. BUT ONE DAY WHILE BATHING IN A RIVER HE WAS CAUGHT BY A CROCODILE. AT DEATH'S DOOR SHANKARA ASKED HIS MOTHER TO GIVE HIM PERMISSION TO TAKE SANNYAS. PERMISSION WAS GRANTED AND SHANKARA WAS SAVED. PLEASE EXPLAIN THIS EVENT.

The event has no value - it is not even certain that it really happened - but its meaning must be understood. And always remember that the events in the life of the enlightened ones are not only events but symbols; some secret is hidden in them. They may or may not be historical, but they are spiritual. They may or may not have happened in the flow of time but they happen in the flow of consciousness. Don't try to understand the buddhas through history; understand them through poetic experience, otherwise everything is misunderstood. This is a parable.

"When Shankara was very young his mother did not give him permission to take sannyas". Many things are hidden in this. Mother' means, mother's love; mother means attachment.

It is difficult for attachment to give permission for sannyas because sannyas means the death of attachment. Sannyas means that a person becomes free from the family; now the mother will not be the mother, now the father will not be the father, now the brother will not be the brother. That is why Jesus has said again and again that whoever wants to come with me has to renounce his mother and father; whoever wants to come with me has to renounce his family. You cannot be part of Jesus' family until you renounce your family.

Sannyas means that this life between birth and death is useless, meaningless. If this life is meaningless, then the mother who gave birth also becomes meaningless. Not only did she give birth, but she created a dream.

Basically, sannyas is freedom of life. And freedom of life means freedom from the mother, freedom from the father, freedom from the family, freedom from society. All these become useless, meaningless. So how can the mother give permission? Will a mother ever give permission for sannyas? It is impossible. It is very difficult. Attachment cannot give permission for sannyas; a mother's love cannot give this permission. It is impossible to get permission to be free from life from the very source from which life comes.

"When Shankara was very young his mother did not give him permission to take sannyas". And remember, you can grow to any age but to your mother you will always be a child. You can never be older than your mother; you will always be younger than the mother who has given birth to you. You can be seventy years old, but to your mother you will always remain a child. "Shankara was very young" means that whenever a seeker asks his mother's permission to take sannyas, his mother always prevents him, thinking that her son is too young and wants to tread a difficult path.

"When Shankara was very young his mother did not give him permission to take sannyas. But one day while bathing in a river he was caught by a crocodile".

In the river of life misery takes hold of you at one time or another. You meet death in this river of life.

You don't go to the river to meet death, you go there to bathe, to enjoy swimming, to enjoy the freshness of the morning. No one enters the world to die, no one enters the river of life to meet crocodiles. One goes into life in search of happiness, in search of treasures - success, fame, prestige - but in this process one is caught by crocodiles.

Death catches you sooner or later. And if a person is wise, he soon understands that this river is the surface; death is hidden inside: "crocodile" means hidden death. On the surface the flow of the water seems so pure and peaceful, but deep down death is waiting. On the surface it looks very attractive, and the river also looks very innocent. Inside, death is waiting silently. Anyone who is intelligent, wise and aware can quickly understand this.

Shankara saw it at once. If you cannot see this for a long time, then it means that you have very little intelligence and understanding. Your mirror is covered with dust. Your intelligence is full of smoke, otherwise you could see it earlier.

In this story all that is conveyed is that Shankara realised that in this life nothing is achieved except death. And one cannot be free from the mother's love until the realisation of death.

Try to understand this a little bit. At one end is mother - mother means birth; at the other end is death - death means the end. Liberation from the mother is possible only if you can see death; birth can be meaningless only if you can see the end. So sannyas means realisation of death.

We keep postponing death in this world; we keep saying that it is always others who die, I will never die. Every day you see dead bodies being taken to the cemetery or the crematorium; you help others to take those dead bodies there, but it never occurs to you that you will die too. You always think that you will live forever and that only others will die. But one day others will also carry your body to the cemetery when you are no longer alive. Man lives on false hopes.

Sannyas means the awakening of the consciousness that "death is mine; the news of the other person's death is in reality the news of my death. The death of the other points to my death. And with everyone's death, I also die a little".

If you have a little understanding, then everyone's death will become your death. But if you don't have this understanding, if you are foolish, then you will think that it is always others who die; I will not die, I am immortal.

Shankara could see death. One is liberated from the mother as soon as one sees death, because mother means life. Mother means the one who brought you into this world. Death means that which will take you away. The imagination of the Hindus in this regard is unique. No other community on this earth is more imaginative, more poetic, than the Hindus. Their poetry is very deep.

Have you ever seen the statue of Kali? She is the mother and also death; kal means death - that's why her name is Kali. And she is the mother, so she is a woman. She is beautiful, beautiful like a mother. Nobody else can be as beautiful as the mother. Even if the mother herself is ugly, she looks beautiful. Nobody thinks of the mother's beauty. But the mother is beautiful... because if you see your mother ugly, that means you are ugly because you are her expansion.

So Kali is beautiful, very beautiful! But around her neck she wears a garland of human heads.

She is beautiful but she is Kali - Kal, death!

Western thinkers are perplexed by this symbol. They wonder why a woman should be depicted in such a horrible, terrifying way! And they call her a mother! How horrible! It is horrible, because death begins with the one who gives birth. It is horrible, because death has also come along with birth. The mother has given both death and life. So on the one hand she is as beautiful as the mother, as the source, and on the other hand she is like kal, death, as dark as death. Around her neck is a garland of human heads; in her hand she holds a severed head, dripping with blood, and she stands with her feet on her husband.

It is a very profound symbol: woman as life and as death! ... For death comes from where life comes from; these two are the two sides of the same coin. And no one else on this earth has realised this fact as the Hindus have.

When Shankara was conscious of death... whether he was really caught by the crocodile or not, you should ask the foolish historians; I am simply not interested. What difference does it make whether he was caught by a crocodile or not? But one thing is definite - that he saw death, and when he saw death, sannyas happened.

One cannot escape from sannyas after seeing death. So one remains stunned wherever one is.

Then life cannot be the same as it was a moment before this realisation. Ambition, fame, reputation... everything loses its charm. Death destroys everything. One has to die, so it doesn't matter whether one dies sooner or later - today, tomorrow or the day after tomorrow, it is only a matter of time. If death has to happen, it has already happened. And the arrow of death will pierce you in such a way that you cannot be what you were until now. This new change in you is sannyas.

If you ask me the definition of sannyas, I will tell you that sannyas is a state of being in which death has not occurred outside but within. One is alive but knows death; while living, one is very conscious of death. This is sannyas. One lives but does not forget death even for a moment:

this is sannyas. You know that the dewdrop is only momentary. The world is like the morning star:

will soon disappear. You live but you are not drunk with life. So life cannot make you forget the fact of death. You remain awake, you are conscious all the time. Death awakens you. The one who is awake is a sannyasin.

He who is lost in life and is taking dreams as reality is a worldly person, he is a householder. He who creates a home in dreams or who is creating dreams in the home is a householder. But the one who wakes up from the dream, whose dream is over, who wakes up and is conscious, realises that there is nothing here except death.

Any extended family, any place of life, is nothing but a cemetery, or a queue waiting to go to the cemetery. The queue moves towards the cemetery. Someone may be a little ahead and someone may be a little behind, but everyone goes to the cemetery. Attachment to life is over as soon as one sees this. To lose this attachment is sannyas.

Sannyas is not an effort for detachment. Sannyas is not a discipline of detachment. Sannyas is the loss of attachment - where attachment has ended. If the attachment has not ended, then one has to make an effort to attain detachment, but that is not sannyas. If attachment has not ended, only then one tries to attain detachment. But when attachment is over, then the empty space left by attachment is detachment. Then you become a sannyasin.

That's why I tell you there is no need to go anywhere for sannyas. If you can open your eyes wherever you are, if you become a little conscious, then you are able to see things as they are.

One night Mulla Nasruddin was returning home after getting drunk at the bar. He was walking merrily along the road humming a song when he bumped into someone. He lost his temper and shouted: "Idiot! If you don't apologise in five seconds, then ....".

The other person replied in a louder voice, in a threatening manner: "So?

Hearing the threatening voice, Mulla came to his senses and looked at the man closely: he looked like the boxer Muhammad Ali! All his drunkenness disappeared and he said: "Well, if five seconds is not enough, how much time do you need?

In this life you also go about like a drunkard, humming the song of dreams, and you don't see things as they are. It takes a hard blow to upset your dreaming mind, only then can you see the empty sky.

Then you will see that you are surrounded by death. What you think of as life is actually death.

What you consider happiness is in reality the mask of misery. What you consider wealth is only a game of falsehood. In the illusion of money you remain poor. And in the illusion of life you remain without knowing the real life. And time goes by, life goes by every minute and your energy diminishes.

This is just a symbol, that when death overtook Shankara then before he died he asked his mother to give him permission to take sannyas, and permission was given.

Yes, this permission is granted only when death is at the gates. Permission is not obtained before this, only when the mother realises that her son will only be saved if he becomes a sannyasin.

Otherwise, as it is, it will die. When it comes to choosing between a dead son and a sannyasin son, then the mother chooses the sannyasin son. This is the meaning, because a sannyasin son means a dead son. Sannyas means that one has died while living.

Jesus has said, "You cannot come with me until you are willing to carry your cross; you cannot come with me until you are willing to deny yourself; there is no way of resurrection until you are willing to die."

If this story is true, if this is how things really happened, then this symbol should be remembered.

Shankara, a small boy, is on the verge of death; a crocodile has grabbed his leg. His mother is on the river bank and Shankara asks her permission to take sannyas. He says, "I am dying, there is no hope for me to save myself. Let me die as a sannyasin. Give me permission for sannyas. The crocodile is taking me away - so give me the permission".

Even then the mother must have doubted. Even then she might have hoped against hope that her son could be saved. But death was driving Shankara away. A crowd of people would have gathered and said, "You had better give the permission now. He is dying, he is going away. You can't stop him from dying, so release him before he dies". Finally she gave permission after hearing Shankara's words that he wants to die as a sannyasin so that he will not be reborn, so that there will be no more attachment to life for him; he wants to die without attachment to life. Even then, it seems to me that the mother must have hesitated; her eyes must have been full of tears.

She must have prayed to God to save her son. But when there was no hope then very reluctantly, in a very helpless way, she must have said, "Since you are dying it is better that you die as a sannyasin".

But this incident may not have happened, because crocodiles don't care about such things. If men don't care, why should crocodiles care? It is said that Shankara was saved. The crocodile thought: Why kill this person now that he has become a sannyasin? No, crocodiles are not that smart! If Hitler and Mussolini are not intelligent, how can crocodiles be intelligent?

But this symbol is very precious. Man is saved only when he becomes a sannyasin; then even death cannot harm him. But only the one who tries to take over life dies; death cannot kill the person who renounces life himself. How can it be taken away from a person who is willing to renounce? Things can only be taken from the person who wants to save them.

That is why Jesus says: "He who saves will lose; he who is ready to lose has saved".

You must understand this. Shankara was saved. Did the crocodile leave him? No, it only means that death does not kill a sannyasin. There is no way to kill a sannyasin because, he says, "The self that could be killed by you was renounced by me. I have renounced the ego and all dreams of desire and ambition. I have killed myself with my own hands. Then only the inner nectar which was surrounded by death remains in its purity".

You know nothing of this nectar as long as you hold on to life.

That's why you hold on to life so tightly that it doesn't slip through your fingers. You are afraid of dying. You are afraid of death all the time. The more you try to hold on, the more afraid you become, because you know you can't cheat death. Yes, death is coming. Where can you hide from death? It comes from everywhere. If it came from a particular direction, you could avoid it, but it comes from everywhere. You could save yourself if it came from outside, but it comes from within. You can run anywhere, but death will come. You can hide anywhere, but death will find you, because death is hidden inside you.

Both nectar and death are hidden within you. As long as you continue to cling to the outer life, you will only see death within. The moment you accept the death within, you will begin to see the life within.

If you write on a blackboard with white chalk, the words are visible and clear. But if you write with white chalk on a white wall, then the words are not visible. If you accept that inner death, then in that blackness the little candle of immortality that burns within you will become a thousand times brighter. But if you don't accept the death, don't accept the blackboard, then you cannot see the white words. Always remember this contradictory statement: whoever has been able to see death well, has also seen the nectar.

"Shankara was saved" - because death cannot destroy you. It can destroy the so-called life. It can destroy what you call body. It can destroy what you call name and form. But death cannot destroy you. You are immortal, you are amrit putra. You have never been destroyed and you can never be destroyed.

You were never born and you will never die.

He who is born will die. Your body was born and will die. Your name and your personality were born and will die. But you were always in time beyond name and form, and you will always remain in time. You are ancient, you are eternal.

The meaning of sannyas is that I will renounce all that is transitory and go in search of that which will not be destroyed. I will give up the transitory and seek the eternal. Even if I finish this search it does not matter, because what is transitory cannot be saved for long. But even after giving up the transitory, if the impermanent remains - that which cannot be cut by any weapon and which cannot be burnt by fire - then it is worth saving. Sannyas is the search for this. Do not think that this event has happened. It is only a very valuable symbol, a parable.

The second question:

Question 2:

BELOVED MASTER, SAI BABA HAD COME TO NARAYANSWAMY'S HOUSE IN THE FORMS OF A DOG AND A LEPER AND NARAYANSWAMY COULD NOT RECOGNISE HIM. MY REQUEST IS THAT YOU COME TO MY HOUSE BUT IN THIS VERY FORM, BECAUSE I AM VERY FOOLISH.

If you have recognised me then you will recognise me in any form. And if you have not recognised me, how can you be sure of recognising me even in this form? Recognition of the form is not recognition. Bowing to the form is not bowing. Worship of the form is not worship at all.

If Sai Baba had gone in the form that Narayanswamy thought he recognised, then he would definitely have bowed down, he would have welcomed him, but that welcome would have been to the form and not to Sai Baba. In fact, a dog and a leper are more alive, more animated as far as the form is concerned. The form is only an outer covering. You must stop clinging to the cover. But I know why you are still clinging to the cover. It is because you also know yourself by this form.

I have heard that when Mulla Nasruddin went on pilgrimage to Mecca he took with him two people; one was a barber and the other a bald fool. They stopped for the night in the desert. As it was a new and unfamiliar place and seemed dangerous they decided to keep watch in turns during the night. The first shift was that of the barber. He stayed awake for some time, but soon felt sleepy, as he was quite tired. So, to keep himself busy, he shaved the hair off Mulla Nasruddin's head. He was getting bored, so he shaved Mulla's hair!

After the barber it was Mulla's turn to stand guard, so the barber woke him up and Mulla, out of old habit, put his hand to his head and then said: "My God, by mistake it seems you have woken up that stupid bald man instead of me! That shaven head gave him to understand that it was not him, but that stupid bald man. His head had a lot of hair so it must be the other person.

We identify with the shape. Have you ever thought about it? If you change your face at night while you sleep, will you be able to recognise yourself in the morning? No, you won't. Why? Because you recognise yourself through the mirror, there is no deeper recognition.

If you go to sleep at night as a white man and wake up in the morning as a black man - if a scientist changes the shape of your nose and the colour of your eyes, your hair, by doing plastic surgery at night - then you are also in the same condition as Mulla Nasruddin was.

What he said is not absolutely wrong. He is not saying the wrong things. He says: "My God, by mistake you have woken up the bald fool instead of me". You too will say and do the same.

You'll wake up screaming: "It can't be me, it has to be someone else!

We only recognise ourselves through form. Therefore, any recognition we have of others is also of the form. As long as you do not recognise your own consciousness, you will not be able to recognise mine either. Your recognition of me would be as deep as your recognition of yourself. I can come to your house, but that won't do any good. Unless you come to your own house, my coming to your house would not really mean anything.

The third question:

Question 3:

BELOVED MASTER, YESTERDAY, WHILE NARRATING THE STORY OF THE WASP, YOU TOLD US ABOUT A MENTAL BLOCKAGE. PLEASE TELL US HOW TO REMOVE A COMPLEX THROUGH SADHANA, THE SPIRITUAL PRACTICE?

You didn't even understand the story of the great intellectual wasp. In that story of the wasp it was clear that there was no blockage, no complex, but that he had read a book! There was no blockage in the wasp's life that had to be removed by sadhana. The wasp's only problem was that she had become an expert reader, and she had read in a book that a wasp's wings are small and its body is heavy, so a wasp cannot fly.

The authors of this book worked out the theory very well, but they did not see the wasp fly. According to their logic, it cannot fly, but the fact is that it does fly. The wasp was confused when it read this. Its state was like that of the centipede. It is a very old story.

A centipede with a hundred feet was passing by when a rabbit saw it and was very curious and puzzled too. He stopped the centipede and said, "Please tell me, how do you manage to move with these hundred feet, how do you synchronise them, which one goes first and which one follows? I find it puzzling, how do you manage them all?

Until that moment, the centipede had not even thought about its hundred feet. He had merely moved. He had never thought about this matter, but when the rabbit asked him, he himself looked at his hundred feet and was confused. He said, "My God, I had never thought of this. But now, since you have asked me the question, I will think about it, I will observe and experiment with it, and then I will report back to you."

But then he was so conscious of his hundred feet that he couldn't move and fell down. Such a small body with a hundred feet and such a small mind, how could he manage them all? He said to himself, "Silly rabbit! You have created a problem for me. Now I will never be able to move. Now I am aware of the question: how to synchronise the hundred feet? This question has never troubled me before.

Have you noticed that all the unimportant things become a problem if you start thinking about them? You can try this: for seven days, every time you eat something, start thinking about how you digest it. Scientists say it's a miracle. The food goes in, gets absorbed and becomes blood and bone, flesh and marrow, and all the fine nerves of the brain: thoughts and desires. And all this is transformed in the little factory of the stomach. And how? Well, if you think about it for seven days you will get indigestion and you will never be healthy again. If you experience like this, the stomach will become disordered. Like the centipede, you too will begin to wonder.

Life is bigger than your mind. Whenever you put your mind in it creates problems. Life is much bigger than you, and your mind is small. You couldn't even understand the story of the wasp, and you want to know how to eliminate the complex through sadhana? What did the wasp do? It did nothing. There is no question of doing anything, because it was only an illusion of the mind. The wasp had been flying until he read the book.

Writing was the cause of death. The wasp could not fly from that day on; it just sat down and got fatter as it sat down, and it became harder to fly. And when it became difficult to fly the scripture seemed quite correct. The other wasps flew, but she thought they were ignorant fools and flew in their ignorance. She thought she was very learned, and "These are ignorant fools so they don't know what is written in the scriptures; they are flying in their ignorance.

They don't know that scientists have said that a wasp's wings are small and its body is so big that it cannot fly". Man tries to cover up his idiocy and his diseases by means of knowledge. He is very adept at this task.

That wasp also had the impression of being the only sensible one; the others were stupid. They flew and therefore went against theory and scripture. They don't know what they are doing; they do what can't be done. But the wasp did not understand that what cannot be done, cannot be done even in ignorance. It was a fortunate moment when one morning a bird attacked the wasp and in the confusion of the attack it forgot all about the so-called knowledge, the Vedas, and flew away! But later, when he sat in the shade, he realised that he had flown, which means he can fly.

So these are certainly the tricks of the mind. The wasp did not think it was an illusion that it could not fly, and whoever had written this in the scriptures had written wrong. Even man does not doubt the written word, and this was just a poor little wasp.

If someone tells you something you may not believe it, but if they show you the same thing written in a book then you will believe it.

I have a friend who writes poetry. His poems are rubbish. If you listen to his poems, you get a headache. His poetry is the opposite of an aspirin: it gives you a headache. So nobody listens to it. Sometimes she read them to me. One day he told me: "Nobody listens to my poems.

People say they are too busy. If I see my friends, they disappear. If I go to the cafeteria, people don't sit at my table. What can I do?

I suggested: "Have the poems printed".

Who is going to read them? People are not willing to listen to them. Besides, printing them is quite expensive.

I said, "Printed words have a magical effect on people. But if that seems expensive to you, take this tape recorder and have them recorded on this. Then go to the coffee shop tomorrow with this tape recorder and tell your friends that you have recorded some poems".

When he returned after two days, he said, "What a miracle! Those fools were not willing to listen to me, but they listened to the tape recorder very carefully. This is the effect of the machine. You can deny the man but you cannot deny the machine.

In New York, an armed robber broke into a house, locked all the doors and opened the safe. When people found out, he stood with the gun in the window; it was very dangerous for someone to enter because he was at the window with the gun. Then someone went to a nearby house and phoned. The house phone rang, the robber put the gun aside, answered the phone and said: "Excuse me, I'm very busy". But in the meantime he was caught.

When asked why he had gone to answer the phone, he replied: "What could I do? The phone was ringing, so you had to answer it". So he put the gun down to answer the phone.

This is the magic effect of the machine. If someone knocks on the door, it doesn't matter, but if the phone rings - even if it's not your home phone - you will answer it.

That friend said to me: "Now they will surely print my poems and read them. They will even buy the book and read it. When I ask them to listen to me for free, they don't like it, but they listen to the tape recorder very carefully.

Certainly, printed words are very effective. If someone is talking to you about something and you don't believe it, if he shows you the same thing written in a book, you will immediately believe it, as if the fact that it is written in a book is a proof that it is true. In reality, ninety-nine percent of the things written in books are false, but they seem true because they are written in books. Yes, books are very effective.

The wasp was under the influence of books. He had no disease to be treated, no complex to be removed by yoga postures. There was nothing wrong with him except that he was under a false notion, a false idea. There is nothing to do with a false notion except to give it up. A bird attacked her and she got nervous, that was all she needed.

The guru is also like this bird that attacks you. If you become nervous and confused, at that moment you have the realisation. That is why one is afraid of a guru. He does nothing; he just laughs at you and at the same time feels sorry for you, because you are not sick but you imagine that you are sick. There is no doubt that you are unhappy, but you are unhappy for no reason.

Misery is only mental: you think you are miserable. You have to get rid of that thought. By nature you are always healthy. The divine has not left you, it is in your every cell. But somehow you think something is wrong. Nothing was ever wrong except this thought that something is wrong.

The wasp flew away. Not even then did he think.... Man's ego never thinks it is wrong, not even in the past. He thought there must be a blockage in his mind that he could not fly. Now that blockage is gone. At the moment of crisis, the blockage has been broken, the energy has been awakened and now he can fly. He didn't realise that there was no blockage. He was sitting there doing nothing and he had read about this blockage in psychology books.

Books are your death. Try to enter a little into life. Please say goodbye to the Vedas, the Koran and the Bible. Yes, you should say goodbye to them with these words: "Please excuse me now, enough is enough. Now let me live a natural life as it is".

To be natural is to be religious. You have become unnatural. You don't suffer from any disease, but you have the illusion of suffering from it. In reality the world is not, it is only an illusion. Only the divine is. That is why Shankara calls it maya, illusion.

If you have an imaginary illness, you want treatment and there are people willing to treat you. Then all sorts of problems start with the treatment, because the right medicine for the symptoms can be harmful, dangerous for the patient suffering from an imaginary illness. Of course, if the medicine itself is wrong, nothing happens;

then one problem leads to another.

But if you can diagnose the basic problem, then it will go away. The wasp was a bit too wise and that was his foolishness.

Now you ask: "Yesterday, while you were telling the story of the wasp, you told us about the mental block". No, I didn't say anything about it. You must have heard something else. And this is the problem, that when I say something you hear something else and you do something else, and later you will hold me responsible for it by saying, "You said it".

Sometimes people come to me and say "You said it", with such confidence that I also keep quiet, because if they didn't understand it before, how can they understand it now? I shut up: yes, I must have said it, otherwise how could you have heard it? I will have said it. But just because you heard it doesn't mean that I said it. Now you heard that yesterday, in the story of the wasp, I told you about the mental block. Not at all, I didn't say anything about it. The wasp was absolutely healthy; it could fly, it could dance, it could enjoy the spring, it could hum a song happily in the sunlight, but just by reading about the mental block in a psychology book it got the illusion that it couldn't fly.

Now you ask: "How to remove the complex by sadhana? You too are like the wasp: you have just collapsed after reading the scriptures, because it is written in the scriptures that you cannot fly.

Have more faith in yourself than in the scriptures. You are the judge, not the scriptures. Listen to your own nature, obey your nature; your nature will set you free. He who listens to his own nature and acts according to it is able to understand the scriptures also. Only then can the scriptures be understood in their right meaning. They do not mean what you thought they meant. But you always understand just what you want to understand. Even for your illness you take the support of the scriptures; then the illness becomes deeper.

What was wrong with this wasp, and why did it believe it so quickly? The evil was that he was already in the habit of running over the other wasps. He used to say, "These vagabonds are in the habit of wandering here and there, they don't think, they don't study the scriptures, they have no idea how to lead a high, pure and peaceful life. They waste their lives dancing on flowers".

The wasp already had the ego of being extraordinary. It considered other wasps to be very inferior.

This illusion was the cause of the problems he had with the scriptures. When he read that a wasp cannot fly he said: "This is absolutely correct and I am the only one who has attained this knowledge. All others are ignorant fools". The ego of this knowledge made her sit down. It was enjoying running over and condemning the other wasps. By doing this the ego was inflated.

Go and look at your so-called sadhus and sannyasins - they too are sitting like this wasp. They don't fly, they stay away from life, and they have a great condemnation for the people of this world. They say, "You will go to hell because of your attachments, because of your worldly involvements". They also think that it is because of ignorance that people are attached to this world. According to them, the whole world is ignorant; only one or two people who are sitting like corpses in the temple are full of knowledge.

I tell you that God wants you to go through this attachment. There is a secret behind going through the attachments: one gains maturity only after experiencing this attachment. These escapists who hide in temples are going wrong. They think only in terms of ego.

You like food, they like fasting, because then they can boast that they do not care to eat, while you like food like animals. You like comfort, and they deliberately put themselves in the sun or lie on a bed of thorns to torture the body. What madness! But their only pleasure is to condemn you, and that can be done very easily by lying on a bed of thorns. You cannot lie on thorns, you have not read the scriptures, but these people have read all the scriptures.

Your so-called sadhus and sannyasins do all kinds of austerities and renunciations just to satisfy their egos. They have not attained any heaven; it is nothing but ego gratification. To enjoy their ego-trip it is necessary for them to indulge in things which are just opposite to you. Whatever they do, they will do the opposite. And you are very impressed by these things, you think they have done miracles. You are an idiot, but they are bigger idiots than you. You are standing and they are upside down, and they say they are doing shirshasan, the headstand.

Man is made to walk on his feet, otherwise God would have arranged for him to walk on his head. There is no need to stand on your head, but the one who is doing it can certainly look down on you from above thinking that he is doing something wonderful, something great, and you are standing on his feet like ignorant fools. And the fact is that those people who have ego are very impressed by the display of such a kind of ego and they also start doing the yoga postures.

Now you ask, "How to remove the complex by sadhana?". I don't see any complex in you that has to be removed. You are just as you are meant to be - just forget the illusion of the complex. The day you give up this illusion of complex you will be surprised to realise that you were always without it and wasted your time under this illusion.

When Buddha became enlightened the first sentence he said was: "O Lord, the maker of the houses of desire. Now you will not have to make me any more houses, because I have grasped the source of desire and the source of desire is imagination. I have realised that all this was the web of my imagination. But now I have found the original source: the imagination! Now that journey of desire has stopped.

Your complex is in your imagination. Your desire is also in your imagination. Your world is also in your imagination. The truth is always as it was. Even now it is the same, even tomorrow it will be the same. The day you drop this web of imagination you will realise that you missed a lot of joy in vain.

But there are hypochondriacs - you must know some of them too - who keep creating illness after illness. They always run to the doctors. Sometimes they go to the allopathic doctor, sometimes to the homeopath, sometimes to the naturopath, sometimes to the ayurvedic doctor.

They are never calm, they are always running to different places for treatment, and everywhere they are told that they don't have any diseases. But they get very angry when they hear this and say: "We are suffering so much from these diseases, and you say that we have no disease at all! They can only be satisfied if they are told that they have a very serious and dangerous disease: "You are the first ones to suffer from it, and such a rare disease".

I heard of an old woman who always complained that she was ill, but nobody believed her because she wasn't really ill. And if the doctor treated her for a particular illness, she started complaining about other illnesses: either her head ached, or her hands and feet ached, or her whole body ached. Of course, there is no end to imaginary illnesses. At last she died, but before she died she told people that the inscription on her grave should be: "Now you must believe that I was ill". Now she has died, so people must believe that she died because of her illness.

A mentally unbalanced man was once brought to me. He was a healthy young man, but he suffered from the thought that two flies had entered his body through his nose while he was asleep.

Now they are still buzzing inside him and because of them he can't eat, he can't sleep, he feels uncomfortable all the time. He has been given all kinds of treatments, but they have had no effect. The doctors had told him there were no flies inside; the X-ray doesn't show them. He said: "The X-ray must be wrong, because I hear them buzzing all the time, I feel them moving in my bones! Your X-ray doesn't show them, but I'm still suffering". He was right to say that he was suffering.

I said, "Okay, let me try. Now lie down and close your eyes. Don't open them until I ask you to.

In the meantime, we'll try to get rid of the flies.

He liked it when I told him I would try to get rid of the flies. He immediately touched my feet and said: "You are the only sensible person I have met so far. The others laugh when I complain about the flies. One feels very bad if the doctor laughs at him. But you will certainly cure me.

I said, "Yes, I see the flies. It's surprising that the X-ray doesn't show them". I blindfolded him and made him lie down. I ran into the house and, with great difficulty, picked up two flies and put them in a bottle. He opened his eyes and saw the flies in the bottle. I said, "Look, I have taken them out".

But he said: "These are not the right flies. These are big flies, these are the small flies you find in houses. They are big flies and they keep moving inside me.

I said, "Well, I could only take these two out".

He said: "These two might as well have been there, but the real ones are still inside". What can you do with a man like that?

He who can imagine two flies can also imagine four. He can catch two, now he says that they are not the same as the ones that move inside him. Then I understood that if I catch two more flies, he won't accept them either. What to do with such a man?

You pity him because he suffers for no reason. The suffering is imaginary. If it had been real, it could have been treated. But suffering is so false that it cannot even be treated. One feels like laughing at it because it is entirely up to him to give up the illness. If he had believed that those flies were the same flies that were bothering him, he could have been cured. But he has found another way not to be cured, saying that they are not the same flies: "You have worked hard to get these flies but they are not the same".

Your illnesses and complexes are like that: they are imaginary, nothing is wrong with you.

It cannot be. When the divine is everything, how can there be anything wrong? It's just a web of imagination. If you can wake up - you can wake up this very moment - then there is nothing to do. Doing nothing is Bhaj Govindam. Bhaj Govindam means there is nothing to do: only by singing the song of the divine will the disease be cured.

If the disease were real, then it could not have been cured by Bhaj Govindam. By singing the song of the divine, how can the real disease be cured? How can cancer be cured by singing "Govinda! Govinda?

But the enlightened ones have said that if you even remember the song of the divine, then all the diseases will disappear, because there is no disease. At the moment of remembrance, at the moment of dedication to the divine, suddenly you will realise that there was never any disease - you are a pure buddha, you are without any name, without any form, without any taint. There is not even a black line on you. Everything is a web of imagination. Try to understand the story of the wasp again. It is your story.

The fourth question:

Question 4:

BELOVED MASTER, IS IT POSSIBLE FOR THE MIND OF A MAN TO BECOME LIKE THE MIND OF A NEWBORN CHILD?

No doubt about it. A lake is absolutely calm, quiet, but with the arrival of the breeze the waves start to rise.

But if the breeze stops, the waves will also stop and the lake will calm down. It will become like a mirror again. The lake is clean; with the falling leaves it becomes dirty, but when the leaves settle the lake will be clean and fresh again.

A child is born: the lake was still clean, there were no ripples, no sheets of thought, no waves of desire. Then, with the arrival of youth, storms arose, strong winds blew and the lake filled with waves. The mirror was lost. A terrible passion was unleashed. Then came old age and the storm passed: the lake became calm again.

A little understanding - let the leaves be still. A little understanding - let the winds of passion stop. The lake will become calm again; there is no difference in the nature of the lake.

When the mind becomes innocent again like the mind of a child, then we call that man a saint. A saint becomes like a child. That is why Shankara has said that the supreme yogi sometimes plays like a child and sometimes like a madman. Sometimes he looks as innocent as a child - he is absolutely empty, there is nothing inside him. And sometimes terrible unknown storms arise in him - then he looks absolutely insane, mad.

There is childlike innocence even in a madman, and there is madness like madness even in children. Little children get mad over little things. When they want a toy, they dance, jump and even break things because they want the toy right now. They may be very angry now, but after a while they will start laughing and forget all the anger. There is a certain similarity between mad people and children. That's why mad people have the innocent look of children and there is some madness in children's eyes.

The enlightened person becomes both at the same time. Sometimes he looks like a child and sometimes like a madman. Since he no longer observes any rules, he does not care about dignity, prestige, sin or virtue, so he looks like a madman to people. That is why he also looks like a child, because the child also knows nothing of dignity, sin or virtue. A child is before dignity begins, and a saint is beyond dignity. Between the two is the world where there are limitations: dignity, prestige, morality, rules, sin, virtue, luck, bad luck, worth doing and not worth doing - both extremes are there.

Certainly, the moment that was once in your life can come back again. You were a child - that child is lost, but it still exists in the crowd of your thoughts. When these thoughts subside, suddenly the child will be rediscovered. That is holiness.

The fifth question:

Question 5:

BELOVED MASTER, SOMETIMES SHRI SHANKARACHARYA SAYS THAT NOTHING WILL HAPPEN BY THE GANGES PILGRIMAGE AND SOMETIMES HE SAYS THAT EVEN BY DRINKING A DROP OF GANGES WATER, A MAN CONQUERS DEATH. PLEASE CLARIFY THIS CONTRADICTION.

The Outer Ganga and the Inner Ganga .... Nothing will happen if you undertake the journey to the outer Ganges, because the journey to the outer Ganges is an outer journey; it cannot send you to the inner. But if you drink even a drop of the inner Ganges, then you will succeed, because to drink even a drop of the inner Ganges you will have to go absolutely inside; only then will you be able to drink a drop of that water. Pilgrimage is not outside, outside is only the world. Pilgrimage is within, within.

The more you enter, the more you enjoy inside you, the closer you get to the pilgrimage. All pilgrimages like Girnar, Shikharji, Kaaba, Kailash, Kashi, are within you. Save yourself from the illusion of the outside.

But we have a habit of looking outwards, so when we try to look for the divine we look outside.

When we look for the temple, it means outside. Holiness is within you. It is hidden within the one who seeks it. It is the one who seeks it. Try to recognise your conscience; a drop of it is enough.

It is said that when the Ganges came down to earth only half of it reached the earth, the other half remained in the sky.

That means that when the Ganges came, only half of it came, half of it stayed inside. Heaven means inside, heaven means sinking into the deepest part of oneself. And hell means losing oneself in the other.

The great thinker of the West called Jean-Paul Sartre has said. "The other is hell".

Heaven is within oneself. You live in hell as long as you depend on others. When you acquire your freedom, your individuality, your autonomy, your being yourself, and you don't depend on others, you are no longer a beggar, and you become your own master - then it is heaven.

Begging anything from others means humiliation; that is hell. From the other you will only get misery in your begging bowl. You will never get happiness from the other.

Enter. The inner Ganges is the other half of the heavenly Ganges. Even a drop of it is enough. It is nectar. Nothing will happen by bathing in the outer Ganges. Fish and crocodiles live in the Ganges, other animals also bathe in the Ganges. Does it mean that all these creatures go to heaven? No, and you can't bathe any more than they do; you will just take a dip and go home. Who are you trying to fool? You are like a blind man who has eyes: you have eyes and yet you are blind.

Do not deceive yourself. The Ganges is within, all that is valuable is within. What is rubbish is outside, but the real wealth is inside.

The sixth question:

Question 6:
BELOVED MASTER, YOU SAY THAT ONE ATTAINS THE TRUTH WITH THE GRACE OF THE MASTER.
THEN WHY DO YOU ALSO ENCOURAGE EGO EFFORT?

Truth is attained by the grace of the master. But you cannot obtain the grace of the master without effort. The divine is attained by grace, but you have to seek the master; you have to have the capacity to be close to the master.

One must strive, but always remember that the ultimate is achieved without effort. This may seem contradictory to you, but these are the two wings, the two oars: effort and grace. The journey is completed with these two.

In this world there are two kinds of illusion. Some people think they will reach the divine by their effort. They never achieve it because their ego never disappears; the effort makes it even stronger: the doors remain closed instead of opening. There is also another type of people who believe that the divine cannot be attained through effort, but only through grace. They sit back and do nothing:

lose because of their laziness. Some lose through their ego and some lose through their laziness. The divine is found through tireless and yet effortless effort.

On your part, you must do it wholeheartedly; nothing must be left undone for you. You must put all of yourself on the line, only then will you deserve His grace. Then you will be able to say: "I have nothing more to put on the line, now please bless me with your grace". You will only have the right to ask for His grace when you have done all that it was possible for you to do and there is nothing left to do.

Grace does not come for free. Grace is a very valuable diamond that you cannot get for free. When you have put everything on the line, then prayer can come from your heart, then you can say: "Nothing happens because of me. It's all up to you now. At that very moment when you realise that nothing can be done by you and you say: "I have staked everything, I have thrown myself completely, still nothing happens. Now your grace is needed. Then you will certainly attain His grace.

The divine is always attained through grace, because your effort is so small and the divine is so vast. You will not attain it by effort, but by your effort you approach the point where the drop is ready to become the ocean.

The last question:

Question 7:

BELOVED MASTER, YOU SAID, AS LONG AS YOU ARE IN MISERY LIVE DEEPLY, FIND OUT ITS CAUSE AND WAKE UP. WHAT HAPPENS WHEN ONE WAKES UP?

Waking up or awakening means that the dream is over: what you have known until now no longer exists. That is why it is difficult to say what waking up means, because your language is the language of the dream. At this moment, everything that can be said to you or everything that you can understand is in the language of the dream. If I tell you that you will get happiness, then you will think of the happiness you have known in the dream. If I tell you that you will have no misery, then you will think of the same misery that you have known in the dream.

If you think, you will not succeed. That is why all the buddhas have kept quiet. When someone asked them what would happen after awakening, they kept quiet. They would say, "Wake up and see".

because this is beyond the language you know, or this is beyond your understanding that you have through language. Neither your happiness nor your misery is there. Neither your peace nor your restlessness is there. Neither your contentment nor your dissatisfaction - all that you have known so far is not there. The scriptures you have known so far are not there either.

The images of God that you created are not there either. Your notions of heaven and hell are not there either. When you are not there, your notions will not be there either.

There is something that cannot be described, that cannot be defined: you can call it Brahma, Vishnupad, Jinpad or Buddhahood, but even with these words you cannot know anything. If you awaken, only then can you know it. A mute cannot describe the taste of sugar, but he can enjoy it.

What will happen after the awakening? You will taste the divine, the taste that you have been trying to get all these past lives but have not been able to get - you have always missed it. It cannot be described. If you are bored with the way you have been living, then wake up. But if you still have a little interest in it, turn over and go back to sleep.

But one day you will have to wake up. Sleep cannot be eternal and slumber cannot be the ultimate rest and darkness cannot be the experience of ultimate truth. Sooner or later you will have to wake up - it all depends on you. But when you wake up you will regret not having woken up sooner: everything was within reach, it was just a matter of reaching for it.

Jesus says again and again: "Repent, the kingdom of God is at hand".

Enough for today.

The mirror of misery

ABANDONING SEX, ANGER, GREED AND ATTACHMENT, MEDITATE ON YOURSELF: WHO AM I? BECAUSE IDIOTS WITHOUT SELF-REALISATION SUFFER HERE THE ANGUISH OF DEEP HELL.

ONLY THE GITA AND SAHASTRANAM, THE THOUSAND NAMES OF GOD, ARE WORTH CHANTING; ONLY INCESSANT MEDITATION ON THE FORM OF VISHNU IS WORTHWHILE.

ALWAYS SEEK THE COMPANY OF GOOD PEOPLE, GIVE MONEY ONLY TO THE POOR.

ONE GIVES ONESELF TO A WOMAN FOR PLEASURE, BUT WHAT A PITY THAT IN THE END ONE HAS ONLY A WORN-OUT BODY. EVEN THOUGH DEATH IS THE ONLY CERTAINTY IN THIS WORLD, PEOPLE DO NOT STOP SINNING.

MONEY IS A DISASTER - ALWAYS CONTEMPLATE ABOUT IT. THE TRUTH IS THAT THERE IS NO HAPPINESS IN MONEY AT ALL. IT HAS BEEN SEEN EVERYWHERE THAT THE RICH ARE AFRAID EVEN OF THEIR OWN CHILDREN.

PRANAYAM AND PRATYAHAR, INTELLIGENT DISCRIMINATION BETWEEN THE TRANSITORY AND THE INTRANSITORY, DISCIPLINING SAMADHI WITH JAPA - DISCIPLINING ALL THIS WITH CAUTION, WITH GREAT CAUTION.

FULLY SURRENDERED AT THE LOTUS FEET OF THE MASTER, FREE FROM THE BONDAGE OF THE WORLD, HAVING DISCIPLINED THE MIND ALONG WITH THE SENSES, YOU WILL BE ABLE TO SEE THE DIVINE WITHIN YOUR HEART.

There is a Greek mythological story. There was a very handsome young man called Narcissus who fell in love with a young woman called Echo. It is worth reflecting on this name. People fall in love with the echo. You always fall in love where you hear your own voice, where your own ego is satisfied, where you find yourself in the hidden form. Your love is nothing but the extension of your ego. Echo also fell in love with him. Echo has to fall in love because she is the echo of your voice. There is no possibility or way for her to be separate from you.

But one day a misfortune happened. It had to be like that, because misfortune is certain in the life of those who let themselves be deceived by echoes, of those who fall in love with their own voice.

Narcissus had gone to the forest. There he saw his own reflection in the lake, which was absolutely calm, not a ripple in it. He was enchanted. In the lake, which was like a mirror, he saw his own face. But it was the first time he had ever seen it. It was so beautiful. Who doesn't like his own face?

People only love their own face. Narcissus was mesmerised; he couldn't move, he stood still. Attachment creates this kind of stillness. He was afraid to move in case the reflection broke. He didn't move from there. Echo continued to wait for him. And when Narcissus did not return, love died.

Echo... your voice can only resonate if you keep humming. If you stop humming, for a while the echo will be heard in the mountains and then it will be lost. Narcissus did not return.

They say that in that lake Narcissus became a plant: there is a plant called Narcissus that is found by lakes, streams and rivers. If you ever come across it, you should watch it carefully: it is always looking into the water, always looking at its own reflection.

This is a wonderful mythological story. If you enchant yourself, you lose consciousness; then you are no longer a human being, you become a plant. Then the humanity in you disappears, your inner soul is denied, you regress. A plant has no freedom. Man is free, he can walk. A plant cannot, it has no feet, it has roots. Narcissus became a plant - it means that anybody who gets caught in the ego reflexes, his feet become roots, he stops; his step stops and he loses his freedom of movement.

This happens to almost everyone. The Upanishads say that when a man loves his wife, it is not really the woman he loves, but through the woman he loves himself. A man does not really love his children, but in the children, through the children, he loves himself. The children are a mirror, the wife is also a mirror. And every man is Narcissus.

The gates of ultimate freedom cannot be opened with this kind of mental condition of man; in fact, it ends what little freedom he has. You should have had wings so that you could fly towards the divine - but you lost even your feet!

Do you understand the bondage of the tree? It can't move. It has to be where it is, it can't move an inch from where it is. It is helpless, it has no freedom to move.

Man can move, he can walk. A bird can fly. But there is a limit to the movement of the body; at a certain point it gets tired, and that tiredness will turn into slavery. And even if a bird can fly for miles, you can't measure the sky in miles. It will get tired, the body has a limit. And freedom can only be freedom when it is unlimited. The freedom of the soul is needed. When the soul has wings and can fly without any limit, without any obstacle, without any chain, then that is moksha, liberation.

The search is for this moksha. Your search for happiness is

actually the search for moksha. That is why every happiness of yours becomes misery, because when you find that instead of liberation you have bondage, then happiness does not look like happiness. When you seek money, even that is for moksha. You think that with money you will get a little freedom, that you will be able to move a little. The poor man's heaven is small; the rich man's heaven seems to be a little bigger, a little more comfortable. But when you get money you realise that your space, your heaven, has become even smaller than the poor man's heaven. Money has not given you any freedom, it has become a bondage. Now you can't even give it up.

There are stories about rich people, who after their death turn into snakes and keep their treasures. It is not necessary to know what happens after their death, because the fact is that even when they are alive they keep their wealth like snakes. Those who have money are always afraid of losing it, they are always keeping it. They don't enjoy it. They don't even own their money, they just keep it. Rarely does one meet a rich man who really owns his wealth. A poor man may be the master of his poverty, but the rich man is not the master of his money.

If you look closely, you will see that man wants money for freedom, he wants position for freedom.

If you have position, power, capacity, then you will be able to free yourself from some bonds and you will be able to go a little bit into the unknown and the unknowable.

Man desires freedom from all sides. Deep in man's consciousness the longing is only for moksha. That is why every kind of bondage disturbs him. Even when you fall in love you do so in the hope that this love will become a heaven, that you will be able to fly. You hope to get someone's support to attain freedom. But when you fall in love you realise that, never mind flying, you can't even move. You hoped to get the support of the other, but the other, the lover, ended all your freedom, and so love became a slavery. Freedom is only in dreams, and in reality love is only slavery.

The Prophet is a unique book by Kahlil Gibran. In it, a person asks: "Tell us about love". And the hero of this book, Al Mustafa, says: "Love each other but do not possess each other. Be close to each other but not too close. You should be like the pillars of a temple that support the same roof and yet remain far from each other. If the pillars of the temple come close, the roof will fall down. Keep a small distance from the lover so that there can be some empty space between the two of you. If this empty space is completely lost, then you will be encroaching on each other, attacking each other.

But all these things are written in books. In real life we take away all freedom from the person we love because we are afraid that their love may turn elsewhere: someone else may become the possessor of the love I have. We are always afraid of losing what we have. If we have money, we are afraid of losing it. If we have love, we are afraid of losing it.

Because of this fear, freedom becomes impossible.

The flower of freedom blooms only in a state of fearlessness. The only longing one has is for freedom. Everyone's inner quest is for liberation.

Wherever you get this freedom, you will rejoice. You will be sad whenever you feel the bondage. If you are sad then the reason is very clear: you wanted freedom but you got chains. You wanted heaven but you got a prison, you wanted wings to fly but even your feet were cut off, you wanted ultimate freedom and you gambled and lost everything you had for it. There is no chance of getting what you hoped for. That's why you are sad.

The meaning of the word god can only be moksha. That is why the great enlightened ones have not used the word god. Mahavira speaks of moksha and not of God, because there are many illusions with the word god and even the word has created prisons. Buddha also speaks of nirvana and not of God, because even the word god has created new bonds: to be a Hindu, a Muslim or a Christian. A Hindu is tied to being a Hindu, a Mohammedan is tied to being a Mohammedan. Someone is tied to a temple and someone is tied to a mosque.

Religion is the ultimate freedom. That is why there can be no temple or mosque of religion. The day you become truly religious you will see the divine in both the temple and the mosque. Then sometimes you will pray in the temple and sometimes in the mosque. Actually, there will be no need for you to go to the temple or the mosque; you will see the divine in your own house, you will see it everywhere.

You can understand this last sutra of Shankara only if you keep in mind that religion is the ultimate freedom.

ABANDON SEX, ANGER, GREED AND ATTACHMENT, MEDITATE ON YOURSELF.

Sex, anger, greed and attachment, these are the four bondages that keep your moksha, your freedom, suppressed. The basis of these four is sex, because sex creates attachment, attachment creates greed, and anger is born towards the person who creates an obstacle to our greed. The basic disease is sex.

You must understand the meaning of sex. The meaning of sex is the hope of getting happiness from each other. Sex means that my happiness is outside me. And meditation means my happiness is within me.

The journey will be very easy if you understand these two definitions well. The meaning of sex is that my happiness is outside myself, in another person; if the other gives, then I can get it. I cannot find happiness alone; it is miserable to be alone and it is a pleasure to be in the company of the other. That's why you don't want to be alone. You are afraid of being alone. You feel uncomfortable when you are alone, even for a short time. As soon as you are alone you start throwing all kinds of rubbish at yourself. You'll start reading the newspaper again - you don't care if you've read the same paper three or four times! Or you'll turn on the radio so that there's some noise to save you from loneliness. Or you'll play cards, or you'll run off to a hotel or a club, wherever.

A young man came to see me three days ago and told me that, because he is meditating, his fear of being alone is increasing, and sometimes he runs out of the house and goes to the bazaar, and being in the crowd of the bazaar he has a sense of relief that he is not alone. He comes home at ease.

You say you are very busy, but most of the hustle and bustle of your life is not necessary; that time can be used for your rest. It's not that work is very important, but you feel lost without work.

In the West, psychologists have a new concern. For the first time in human history, this concern worries people. The worry is that at the end of this century, in Western countries like the United States and Sweden, when all the work will be done by robots, man will have a lot of free time. So psychologists are worried about what man will do in his free time, because so far man does not have the ability to be empty or to sit quietly. Think about the situation: all the work is done by machines and there is no work for you!

Now you say that there is too much work and you want to have some time off to rest, although even now when you have time off you don't rest; you just can't spend the Sunday holiday sitting at home, so you go on a picnic. On Sunday you get bored and start thinking about Monday, you look forward to Monday, so you can start your work again.

But if your whole life turns into a Sunday party, will you be able to tolerate so much rest and peace? No, you will find ways and means to keep yourself involved and busy.

Psychologists say that we will have to find those kinds of jobs that may not be of any use, but will be given to people who cannot be idle. And they have come up with a unique idea. The government will give money to people who are willing to sit idle; it will pay you to sit idle! But those who work will not be paid, because you can't give two things at the same time: work and pay.

It seems very strange to us now, but Western countries are getting closer to this point. Eastern countries cannot imagine it, because there is so much poverty and so much conflict there. But at the end of this century, people who are willing to remain inactive will be called gentlemen and those who are not will be called non-gentlemen.

But only a person who has tried meditation can sit idle. That is why in the West people are now very interested in meditation. They are very anxious to know it. Nothing happens without reason; whenever something is going to happen the consciousness becomes anxious about it.

It is not by chance that people come to me from far away western countries. They have an acute desire to know the happiness of being with oneself, because one does not find, one cannot find happiness being with the other. It is always miserable to be with the other. But the problem is that we do not know the art of being alone. That's why we continue to tolerate the hell that the other makes us suffer. And there is no way out, because being alone is absolutely intolerable, more hellish. So we prefer to be with the hell of the other than to suffer the hell of being alone.

At least we can talk a bit with each other, no matter if it ends up in a fight.

Have you ever thought about it? If you are left alone, you think it is better to be in the company of the enemy than to be alone. You can fight with the enemy, you can abuse him and feel a little bit encouraged. But you can't do anything when you are alone; you sit there like a dead man. You have to do something. Then people start to go around the room.

I used to travel a lot by train. Very often I was alone with another passenger in the compartment, so I used to observe what the other person was doing. I didn't talk to him, because if I talked it wouldn't reveal his reality.

He would try to converse with me by asking, "Where are you going? I would reply in monosyllables and close my eyes. When I realised that I was incapable of making conversation with this man, then his true self would be revealed. I would watch him in silence. He would open the suitcase, then close it, then tidy it up again; he would open the window, then close it, and feel very restless. He would turn on the fan, then turn it off. He would go out and get tea. He would go down at every station and buy something to eat, or call the servant and talk to him.

But I understand his unease. He is unable to tolerate the solitude of twenty-four hours in the train. He cannot relax in those twenty-four hours, although he says he cannot even spend a minute in meditation because he is so busy.

If a man becomes absolutely peaceful, absolutely empty for twenty-four hours, he will surely become a Mahavira. In fact, twenty-four hours is too long because Mahavira has said that if a person becomes absolutely empty for forty-eight minutes he will become enlightened. Only forty-eight minutes, not even a full hour! I say twenty-four hours so that the Jainas will not get angry with me. Mahavira has said that if a man becomes empty for only forty-eight minutes, that is enough.

Only forty-eight minutes, not even an hour. The fact is that you cannot be at peace even for forty-eight seconds. You yourself will create a lot of disturbances.

Sex means happiness in each other. One never gets it, and that is the idiocy of man. Certainly there is some reason for Shankara to call you an idiot; he says so after much contemplation. You keep hoping against hope and you know it. You keep trying to extract oil from the sand. If you didn't know it means you were ignorant, and an ignorant person can be excused. But an idiot cannot be excused. A person who keeps hoping against hope is certainly an idiot. He knows that you can't get oil out of the sand, but he keeps trying because he can't sit idly by.

Watch your life carefully. Really, you're an idiot! Think: how many times have you had sex? How many times have you had sex? Have you ever felt satisfied? Have you ever been happy? But you are afraid to even think about these facts. You only stay involved in this way to get through your life. You will feel lost without it. So you go on with this game, and the name of this game is sex. In fact this is the only game; this is the whole world. You are too much entangled, too much involved in it. You know this path will take you nowhere - it has never taken anybody anywhere - but the mind goes on deceiving you, saying, "It may not have taken me anywhere so far, but tomorrow it may take me somewhere. I may be the exception. Everybody thinks like that.

It is said that there is a very famous proverb in Arabia which says that whenever God creates someone he whispers in their ear, amused: "I have made you very special, you are an exception. Other people are very ordinary, but you are extraordinary". That's why each person thinks he or she is unique. "The others are ordinary people, but I am special!

Because of this joke of God, each of you has the idea of being unique. You don't tell the other, but the other also thinks the same way. And without saying anything, you try to tell the other: the other also tries to tell you without saying anything. And those who say it out loud are put in asylums. But everyone has the illusion that this is an exception.

The Buddhas have said that after searching all the deserts of sex, no oasis of happiness could be found.

Mahavira has said the same. Shankara says, despite the long journey, no oasis could be found, not even the shade of a date tree. A date tree has hardly any shade, but even that could not be found. But you keep thinking that the others may not have found it; they may not have been able to find it, they may not know its location, or they may not have been wise enough to get a map, and because they didn't find it they keep saying it's impossible to find. Or they may think: "It doesn't exist and I didn't want it anyway".

You are always under such illusions and therefore you will never be able to get rid of sex. And if you do not awaken from sex, you will not be able to be aware of the divine. Only one who is able to awaken from sex can be conscious of the divine. It is no use chanting the name of the divine, because if the mind is full of sex, then your very chanting will be polluted.

When the mind is empty of sex, then there is no need to chant; then the call will arise of its own accord, every fibre of your being will be calling to the divine - this is not something you can do yourself.

This is not something that needs the support of your throat or your lips or your tongue. This will only be possible when sex disappears from your being. Suddenly you will find a perfume rising from your being. When the energy that is used in sex is released, it turns towards the divine.

Sex means the false hope of happiness in the other.

The divine means finding happiness within oneself.

And that is the only place of happiness. All those who have lost happiness have lost it in the same way that you have lost it. That is why Shankara says, "Oh idiot! But it is very difficult to see the idiot in oneself.

In Mulla Nasruddin's village a play was being performed. They needed a fool in the play, so they chose a political leader for this role. This leader was a great fool; if he had not been a fool he could not have been a leader! Anyone with a little common sense doesn't like to be a leader, because people throw shoes and rotten tomatoes at him, curse him, abuse him. But a leader doesn't care about all these things;

he only cares about staying in the chair. This leader was also of the same type, so people asked him to play this role.

The leader asked Mulla Nasruddin for advice on how to perform this role effectively.

Nasruddin looked him up and down and said: "Please come on stage as you are. There is no need to make any changes.

The leader was very angry. He said, "I know you keep spreading the rumour in the village that I am the number one fool. Now you have said it to me.

Nasruddin protested vehemently: "I may have called you a fool, but I did not say you are the number one fool. I know that you will never stop being the first, even if it means being the number one fool!

Leaders really always try to be number one!

You are so blind. You can't see what everyone else sees. What kind of idiocy is this that you keep wishing over and over again for the same experiences you've had a thousand times and still can't find happiness? When will you wake up?

He who is asleep in sex is really asleep, and he who has awakened from sex is really awake. And the journey of meditation begins only when you awaken from sex, because meditation means that happiness is within oneself. Admit defeat in the other. You have sought enough in the other; now repent and go home.

ABANDON SEX, ANGER, GREED AND ATTACHMENT, MEDITATE ON YOURSELF.

Shankara is deliberately saying that you can meditate on yourself only when you renounce these four.

If you give up sex, if you give up the hope of getting happiness from the other, if you can understand that happiness is not in the other, then the revolution has taken place, because as soon as you realise that happiness is not in the other, you will have no attachment for the other.

We are attached to those things from which we hope to derive happiness. We care for them, we guard them, we protect them and we guard them so that we do not lose them, so that others do not take them away from us. We are attached to the things that give us the hope of happiness. We keep hoping that tomorrow we will get happiness, so we keep these things for tomorrow. We don't learn anything from the experience we had in the past and we keep waiting for tomorrow.

The question of greed does not arise if there is no attachment. Greed means the desire to get more pleasure from things that have given you some pleasure. If you have ten rupees and you want a thousand, that is greed. If you have a house and you want ten, that is greed.

Actually, greed means the desire to multiply that which has given you pleasure. Attachment means to take possession of the thing that gave you pleasure and greed means the desire to multiply that thing.

But why would you try to multiply the things that did not bring you happiness? There is no reason for it. What does anger mean? When someone puts obstacles in the way of your desires that you think will bring you pleasure, you get angry. When you try to earn money and someone puts obstacles in your way, anger arises. When you try to marry a particular woman and someone puts obstacles in the way, then anger is born. You were about to win the election when another person also contested the election with his banner, then anger will arise. Anger means when someone puts obstacles in the way of your desire.

Thus, anger, greed and attachment are the shadows of desire.

People come to me and say they want to give up anger. I tell them that is the wrong question. Someone wants to know how to give up greed and someone asks how to give up attachment, but hardly anyone asks how to get rid of desire. This means you don't even know the basic problem of life. How can you find the solution? How can you cure yourself if you haven't even diagnosed the disease?

Many people want to get rid of anger because it is so annoying. Because of it people quarrel and enmity is born unnecessarily. It is quite clear that anger creates a lot of trouble and unpleasantness, but this is like trying to get rid of your shadow while walking in the sun. For that I will have to say to you, "Don't walk in the sun," and your answer is, "It is impossible. I will walk in the sun but there must be no shadow. I will live in this world of desire but there must be no anger".

Many times the desire is not fulfilled because of this anger. When one says a wrong word in anger the whole plan is disturbed. So you want to get rid of anger. But you also want this so that your sexual desires can be fulfilled more conveniently. But anger is nothing but the shadow of sex.

That is why Shankara has mentioned sex first. The second is anger, because he who has lust also has anger. When you have desire, competition will be born, enmity will be born. You want to have money. The whole world wants to have money. The day the desire to earn money arose, you became the enemy of all those people who also had the desire to earn money. The seed of enmity is sown from that moment. Anger follows the desire immediately. It may take years to express itself, but the journey has begun. When you ask for something, when you desire something, anger is born. This anger is so unpredictable.

You are sitting happily when a car drives by and you would like to have that car. Of course, you haven't talked about it with anyone; you can say, "What's going on? There is no dispute, no conflict....".

But I tell you that this is the beginning of anger in you against all those who will be obstacles in your path. The shadow of anger is forming in your subconscious. Soon it will enter the conscious, because you will have to fight to get this car, you will have to compete with others to get this car and this will create enmity. If you have desired to have something that belongs to someone else, then anger will surely be born.

But this anger will not be born if, by desiring and having something, the other person does not have to lose what he possesses. But there is only such a thing, and it is the divine. No matter how much you attain, it is never taken away from others. If I attain the divine, it will make no difference to your attainment of the divine. In fact, if I attain it, you will be helped to attain it; then you will be able to attain it sooner, because I have opened the door.

If one has made it, the other can make it too. The ladder is there, all it takes is a little effort.

Now the trust and confidence is there. If a person has achieved it, then he can show you the way, and he is called a guru, a teacher. The one who has achieved it is called a guru. He will be able to guide you.

The divine is the only thing that does not diminish if one attains it. The divine is not a matter of economics. If one attains it, it does not diminish; in fact, it is available in greater quantity. If one person attains it, everyone is enriched. The attainment of one looks like the attainment of all.

When Buddha attained, when Shankara attained, when Christ attained, that day the divine rained down upon the whole earth. Yes, nothing could be done for those who had kept their pitchers upside down; they could not get anything. But the other pitchers were filled. When Krishna attained thousands of pitchers were filled, when Buddha attained thousands of pitchers were filled, when Shankara attained thousands of souls danced. This festival of ecstasy was not Shankara's alone.

Try to understand this. Happiness is only what can be shared. Happiness is what is shared, what is spread. Happiness is what you don't have to take from others to achieve. In fact, if you attain it, others will attain it too. That is what we call bliss; that is what we call great happiness.

What you call pleasure is something very superficial. It is like the story of the Puranas. A kite got hold of a dead rat and flew away. As soon as it got hold of the rat, the other kites started hovering around it and attacking it. They pecked at it and it began to bleed profusely. The kite was surprised by this attack, but did not leave the dead rat. But when the other kites attacked, the rat accidentally fell. As soon as the rat fell, all the kites fluttering around it left it alone and started chasing it. The kite sat in a tree and began to think.

That kite must have been smarter than you. Shankara could not call him an idiot. He thought like this: "First I thought all these kites were my enemies, but they left as soon as I released the rat, which means there was no personal enmity with me. The cause of their attack was this rat. The mistake was mine, I was holding the rat. I should have thrown it away earlier. But I was stupid enough to think that they were angry with me".

Ramakrishna used to tell this story often, and he used to say that holding a desire is like having this dead rat in your mouth.

Yes, all around you anger will be born, enmity will be born. You can go on saying that you have never harmed anyone: "I live quietly in my house, I only care about my family. I have nothing to do with others, so why do people make enemies of me? But indirectly you care about others and others care about you. You married the beautiful woman in whom the whole village was interested. Now you say, "I live with my family". But the whole village has become your enemy because you married that beautiful woman.

In ancient India there was a custom, which continued until the Buddha's time, not to marry off the prettiest girl in the village or town, because her marriage to one man would create many problems. Instead, she was made the bride of the whole village - nagar vadhu. She was made a prostitute. It was the only way to keep peace in the village.

You must have heard the name Amrapali. She was nagar vadhu, everybody's wife. The most beautiful woman in the village was not allowed to be the wife of only one man because then people would start fighting, so it was better for her to be everyone's wife. But fights are inevitable when it comes to sex. There used to be fights at Amrapali's doorstep too, because Amrapali could only be available to one man for one night, and all the men from near and far were eager to be with her.

There must have been queues of people at his door, there must have been competitions between rich and poor and kings; there must have been much suffering because of him.

But this was the only solution.

If you have a dead rat in your mouth, it is only natural that all the other kites will attack you. Abandon the rat and you will suddenly find that the whole world has become friendly. With the disappearance of sex and desire the whole world seems friendly, there is no enemy. There was no enemy; the fight was because of the dead rat. You thought it was because of personal enmity: it was because of the dead rat in your mouth.

That day, the kite must have been meditating, sitting alone in the tree. He could understand that there was no happiness in having that rat; it was the source of unhappiness. It was the cause of enmity.

Anger cannot disappear unless desire disappears. People ask me: "How do you get rid of anger? I tell them: "It is difficult. You are asking the wrong question. You want to cut the branches and save the root. This will create more branches. You have to cut the root.

That is why first of all Shankara says that lust is the root. Then anger, its shadow. Then greed, its growth, its by-product. Then attachment, its ultimate conclusion. After renouncing them, meditate on yourself. One can meditate on oneself only after renouncing them, because then the mind is not on others.

When desire disappears, the mind is not attracted to the objects of desire. When there is no anger, then all the issues of anger disappear. When there is no greed, then the anxiety involved in greed also ends. When you are free from all this, then the inner journey begins. And this inner journey is the only pilgrimage; the other pilgrimages are only delusions. The one who goes within has really attained the pilgrimage. The others who wander outside are deluding themselves.

MEDITATE ON YOURSELF: "WHO AM I?" BECAUSE IDIOTS WITHOUT SELF-REALISATION SUFFER HERE THE ANGUISH OF DEEP HELL.

Do not think that people without self-realisation will suffer only after they go to hell. People try to deceive themselves by saying that they will be miserable when they go to hell, as if they will be happy here. Will they suffer only when they go to hell? What will they get here?

I have heard that lately, when people go to hell, Satan asks them: "Where did you come from?

"From the land," they reply.

He says, "Then you can go to heaven. You have already suffered hell on earth".

Now the latest news is that those people who sin in hell are being sent to earth to be punished.

In hell people are told that if they sin they will be sent to earth!

Shankara is saying that you are suffering hell here; what makes you think that you will go to hell in the future? These are just ways of deluding yourself. You think you will suffer in hell, but are you not suffering now? You have gained nothing but misery and unhappiness. You are full of suffering.

Ask yourself: "Who am I?". But this can only be asked after the disappearance of the four. If you then ask: "Who am I?", you will get the answer. Actually, then there is no need to ask the question. Just close your eyes. Don't ask: "Who am I? - You don't have to utter those words because now there is nobody else to talk to, there is only you. Who are you going to ask, "Who am I?". You are facing yourself.

Better to see and recognise - what is there to ask? But Shankara says for the sake of saying.

Shankara was very fond of a story. A disciple used to ask the master: "What should I do to achieve self-realisation? The master would go deaf when he heard this. He used to answer other questions, he used to hear everything, but when the disciple would ask, "What should I do to achieve self-realisation?", suddenly the master would go deaf. He was busy with other things and never answered.

Finally, one day, the disciple grabbed him and shook him, and asked him: "You answer all my questions, but only when I ask you this: ....".

The master said: "I answer but you don't listen. This is the only way to self-realisation, to be silent. I keep quiet so that you will listen, so that you will understand".

This is the only secret: if one becomes quiet inside. When the dead rat falls, inner silence is natural. At that moment you become aware of who you are.

ONLY THE GITA AND SAHASTRANAM, THE THOUSAND NAMES OF GOD, ARE WORTH CHANTING; ONLY INCESSANT MEDITATION ON THE FORM OF VISHNU IS WORTHWHILE.

ALWAYS SEEK THE COMPANY OF GOOD PEOPLE, GIVE MONEY TO THE POOR ALONE .... OH IDIOT! ALWAYS SING THE SONG OF THE DIVINE.

Until the four disappear and you can ask in your wordless inner space "Who am I?"... until then keep on chanting the Gita and the thousand names of the divine. Keep meditating in the form of Vishnu, be in the company of good people, give money to the poor - distribute as much as you can, and hear as much as you can about the truth. Sing the songs of the divine. Keep making all these preparations until the time comes.

ONE PLEASURES ONESELF WITH A WOMAN FOR PLEASURE, BUT WHAT A PITY THAT IN THE END SHE HAS ONLY A WORN-OUT BODY.

You go in search of happiness, but you only get sickness. You go in search of life and you meet death.

ALTHOUGH DEATH IS THE ONLY CERTAINTY IN THIS WORLD, PEOPLE DO NOT STOP SINNING.

Death is absolutely certain. Everything else may be uncertain, but death is not. Dying is the only certainty. Even then people do not stop sinning. Everybody has to die and yet they are always ready to sin for a very small amount, as if they are going to live here forever, as if it is very inconvenient for them to live here forever without this paltry sum of money.

People think of the waiting room at the train station as their home. They pack their luggage as if they are going to live here forever. But the bell is about to ring and the train is approaching, so they will soon have to pack their bags and board the train.

I'm sure you've seen in train station waiting rooms that people don't even open their beds or suitcases, they just sit and wait, because why bother opening them when you have to leave soon? This life is also like a waiting room. It's just an overnight stop, and everyone has to start their journey in the morning.

If this could be seen, then it would be difficult to sin. Who are you sinning for? Why do you have to do it? In the end it all stays here. So why sin? You are able to sin because you live as if you are going to be here forever. You can only sin when you think you are not going to die. But you will sin less and less as you remember death. That is why I consider the remembrance of death as a good deed. Sin becomes impossible in the life of a person who remembers death.

MONEY IS A DISASTER - ALWAYS CONTEMPLATE ABOUT IT. THE TRUTH IS THAT THERE IS NO HAPPINESS IN MONEY AT ALL. IT HAS BEEN SEEN

EVERYWHERE THAT THE RICH MAN IS AFRAID EVEN OF HIS OWN CHILDREN. THEREFORE, OH FOOL! ALWAYS SING THE SONG OF THE DIVINE.

PRANAYAM AND PRATYAHAR, INTELLIGENT DISCRIMINATION BETWEEN THE TRANSITORY AND THE INTRANSITORY, DISCIPLINING SAMADHI WITH JAPA - DISCIPLINING ALL THIS WITH CAUTION, WITH GREAT CAUTION.

PRANAYAM AND PRATYAHAR.Pranayam means that you should not think that you are small.

Expand your energy, expand its dimension. You are big, you are immense. But you think you are small - it is only your belief that you are small.

Look carefully: where do you begin and where do you end? You are not limited only to the body, because if this sun that is millions of miles away ends, then you will also end up here.

You are connected to it. You are also connected to the moon and the stars, which are billions of kilometres away.

You cannot live without the Earth's atmosphere, you breathe in it. Those who know say that it is not correct to say that we are breathing in it; it is really more appropriate to say that it is breathing in us. The breath that was mine now will become yours in a moment, and before I have finished saying this it will become that of another person. The body that is yours today was sometimes in the trees, sometimes in the animals, sometimes in the birds. When you are dead, the water will flow into the river, the dust will become dust; again the plants will grow, again the trees will grow. Perhaps your children will eat the fruits that grow from your dust.

Everything is connected, everything is united, there is nothing separate here. We are not small islands. There is one big continent, and we are its different parts.

Pranayam means to expand. The process known as pranayam in

yoga is actually the method of expansion. Breathe in so deeply that you fill all the pores of your lungs; then release the entire breath. As you go deeper into this process, you will suddenly discover that it is not you breathing, but the divine breath in you. This is only one method. This is how pranayam happens. The bio-energy expands with this method, and it seems that we are small particles of a vast consciousness, we are drops of a vast ocean. Then even a drop is filled with the grace of the divine. The ocean in your little cup also begins to churn.

PRANAYAM AND PRATYAHAR.... Pranayam is to expand your life energy, and pratyahar is the return to your home - going back, coming in. Pratyahar is to return to your inner self, from where you have come. Pratyahar is like the shrinking of a tree - if you become a sapling and then a seed, shrinking. If you start shrinking inside, going deeper and deeper inside, then you will find the original source from whence you have come. If the Ganges returns to Gangotri, to Gomukh, the source, then that is pratyahar. Pratyahar means to regain your source. Zen monks say: "Come and meet your original face, the face that was yours before you were born". To know your face when you were not yet born is pratyahar.

PRANAYAM AND PRATYAHAR, INTELLIGENT DISCRIMINATION BETWEEN THE TRANSITORY AND THE INTRANSITORY.

And to keep on knowing, thinking and seeing at every moment what is meaningful and what is meaningless. This must not be forgotten for a moment, because as soon as you forget, you cling to the useless and forget the meaningful. It doesn't take long to catch the rat dead.

But you stop as soon as you become aware of it.

DISCIPLINING SAMADHI WITH JAPA.

Here Shankara is saying something very beautiful. He is saying, DISCIPLINING SAMADHI WITH JAPA, disciplining enlightenment with chanting. Patanjali says that eventually samadhi must be without japa. Nanak says, AJAPA JAPA, chanting without chanting. Buddha and Mahavira also say that everything must disappear, only emptiness must remain.

But Shankara says japa-samadhi, to discipline samadhi with japa. He is saying that emptiness must be there, but the dance of the whole must not be lost. The whole must be present in emptiness. Thoughts should disappear but emotions should not disappear, because with the disappearance of emotions you will become dry. You will become peaceful but no song will be born out of that peace. Then Meera will not dance and Chaitanya will not sing songs of the divine. You will become silent, you will achieve it, but you will not be able to express it. Your song will remain buried in you; no one will be able to hear it. Your bliss will not overflow; its waves will not be able to drown others in it.

That is why Shankara says that one has to become thoughtless but not without emotion. One has to attain knowledge, but without losing devotion. It is a unique coincidence, but it happens. It is an impossible event but it happens. Thoughts disappear but emotions do not. Thought and worry disappear, but the heart dances with joy.

DISCIPLINE SAMADHI WITH JAPA - DISCIPLINE ALL THIS WITH CAUTION. Repeat again, DISCIPLINE ALL THIS WITH CAUTION.... And, O IDIOT! SING ALWAYS THE SONG OF THE DIVINE....

FULLY SURRENDERED AT THE LOTUS FEET OF THE MASTER, FREE FROM THE BONDAGE OF THE WORLD, HAVING DISCIPLINED THE MIND ALONG WITH THE SENSES, YOU WILL BE ABLE TO SEE THE DIVINE WITHIN YOUR HEART.

The divine is not far away. It is in your heart. You don't have to go anywhere in search of it, you have to come back to your own home. You have never lost it, you have only forgotten it.

He is always present even in that forgetfulness. You have forgotten Him, you turn your back on Him, and yet He is present.

In reality, who are you? Only the divine is. You have forgotten it and that is why you think "I am". When you remember him you will disappear; only the divine will remain.

YOU WILL BE ABLE TO SEE THE DIVINE WITHIN YOUR HEART.... Therefore, O IDIOT!

ALWAYS SING THE SONG OF THE DIVINE.

In reality, Shankara is emphasising an integration between meditation and devotion. He wants a harmony between meditation and bhajan. He wants an impossible bridge to be created between meditation and bhajan.

There have been many bhaktas, devotees, but they have not experienced shunya samadhi.

They are always filled with the image of god; duality always remains. There have been many gyanis, self-realised people; duality disappears in them and only advait, non-duality, remains. But with the disappearance of duality also the sensitivity of the heart dries up.

Shankara says, try to bring that moment - which may come, which has come at times - when you can become empty like the gyani and whole like the bhakta.

The synthesis of knowledge and devotion is the ultimate event. It is the event. There is nothing higher than this - where bhakti and gyan unite; where devotion becomes knowledge and knowledge becomes devotion; where samadhi sings, where samadhi blossoms, where samadhi is not a desert, it becomes greenery; where the mind is totally finished and the heart fills it. There is the temple of the divine.

YOU WILL BE ABLE TO SEE THE DIVINE WITHIN YOUR HEART.

The devotee is not separated from the divine. The day the bhakta comes to know this, then it is only piety.

Many have realised the divine; then their inner bhakta is gone, only the divine remains. And many have tried to save their bhakta; then the bhakta remains and the divine remains - a duality remains, a distance remains. Is it not possible that you become a bhakta and the divine at the same time, that your kirtan, your divine chanting, continues automatically - that you dance and also watch?

It is possible. And that is the Shankara hypothesis. Such a unique personality flourished in Shankara, where the culmination of knowledge and devotion met together. If the saying "Fragrance in gold," has ever been actualised, it is in Shankara.

BHAJ GOVINDAM, BHAJ GOVINDAM, BHAJ GOVINDAM MOODHAMATE.

OH IDIOT! SINGS THE SONG OF THE DIVINE.

Enough for today.

A moment is enough

The first question:

Question 1:

BELOVED MASTER, YESTERDAY YOU EXPLAINED THAT PRANAYAM IS THE METHOD THAT EXPANDS BIOENERGY AND PRATYAHAR IS TO RETURN TO THE ORIGINAL SOURCE.

FIRST IT'S EXPANSION, THEN IT'S RETURN TO THE SOURCE. WHY IS IT SO?

Because life is made of contradictions and there is no other way for life to exist. The breath goes out and then comes in, have you ever wondered why? If the breath has to go in, why does it have to come out? But if the breath stays in and does not go out, the result will be death and not life. If the breath stays out and does not go in, even then it will be death and not life.

Life is movement, movement between two opposites. It is like the flow of a river between two banks. The breath goes out, it comes in; it goes in and then it goes out. Every moment is pranayam and every moment is pratyahar. When the breath goes out it is pranayam; when the breath comes in, it is pratyahar.

If your consciousness becomes accustomed to this kind of rhythm, if this kind of movement continues in your consciousness, if you thus expand limitlessly outwards, if you thus reach the emptiness within you - if there is emptiness within and limitless expansion without - if you constantly flow between these two shores, only then will you become divine, because the divine is like this: emptiness within, wholeness without.

All this existence is the pranayam of the divine. Creation is pranayam and destruction of the world is pratyahar. When the breath goes out, creation takes place; when the breath comes in, the destruction of the world takes place.

If you can understand it correctly then you will see this everywhere in life. Birth is pranayam, death is pratyahar. In birth you expand, in death you shrink, you return, and life is between the two shores of birth and death. Birth is not life, death is not life either; that which is flowing between birth and death, the unknown which is dancing in the beat, which is absorbed in the rhythm, that is life.

The mind tends to be logical and life is contradictory. Life is illogical. Those who wanted to know it through logic lost their way and never reached it. Logic will say that pranayam and pratyahar are contradictory, tell us only one; knowledge and devotion are contradictory, tell us only one; emptiness and totality are contradictory, tell us only one. But remember that life is always contradictory because life is bigger than contradictions; life is capable of absorbing contradictions. Logic is very small, it is the method of the small mind so it can only absorb one and not the opposite. Therefore, the opposite is left out.

So when Buddha said shunya, emptiness, it does not mean that the whole was not included in it. Buddha's emptiness included the whole. But Buddha's followers said that if it is emptiness then it cannot be the whole. When Shankara said totality, emptiness was included in it. But Shankara's followers said that if it is the all, how can it be empty?

That is how the follower misses the point, because the follower lives by logic and by the mind, and those who know have known the contradictions together. But they also feel difficulty in expressing the contradiction because they have to explain it to you. If the contradictions are said at the same time then you think they are incoherent things. Your mind keeps trying to make life logical and calculative. But life is not a calculation. Life is a flood that flows with such force that it breaks all boundaries and limits of arithmetic. Life is a flood.

The second question:

Question 2:

BELOVED MASTER, YESTERDAY YOU TALKED ABOUT HOW TO BE WITHOUT PASSION, HOW TO GO BEYOND PASSION. PLEASE TELL US THE ALCHEMY OF BEING WITHOUT PASSION, SEX, EVEN IN DREAMS.

Don't worry about dreams. You must achieve it in your waking state. What you achieve in wakefulness, automatically appears in dreams, because dreams are the echo of wakefulness. Whatever you do when you are awake, you keep hearing its echoes again and again in your dreams. Nothing new appears in your dreams. Everything you do in waking life repeats itself.

If during the day you collect money, at night you count it. If you are full of passion during the day, at night you dream of sex. People who are devout are devout even when they sleep. Those who are empty and peaceful during the day, remain empty and peaceful even at night. The night is the shadow of the day, it only follows the day. Do not worry about changing the night. If lust disturbs you in your dreams during the night, then it means that some deception is going on during wakefulness.

Understand it. Dreams can give you an indication; they clearly indicate what your understanding does not comprehend during the day. You may behave like a saint during the day, but this saintliness is like the crane standing on one leg and pretending to be very holy. It looks so white, so austere; it stands like a yogi and looks so pure. But don't be fooled by her appearance: she only thinks of fish and is quietly waiting to devour them. It has done all these manipulations, these postures, for the fish. So the crane may fool others, but it does not fool itself. It knows why it stands still and holds its breath.

But man is more dishonest than the crane. He deceives not only others, but also himself.

When others begin to believe him, he also begins to believe in the deception he is using.

There is a contradiction between your waking and your sleeping. You don't feel any lust during the day because you have repressed it so strongly. You simply don't allow it to emerge. It's not that it's finished, it's that you don't let it express itself. You keep repressing it inside your chest. At night, when the repressor goes to sleep, the repressed wave arises and begins to roar and that becomes the lust of your sleep. Those who have repressed it during the day will see it in their dreams.

Sleep is the indicator. It is your friend. It is telling you that it is useless to suppress anything; it will appear in the night. "You can suppress us during the day, in the night we will reappear". You can deceive others and deceive yourself, but "you cannot get rid of us".

Now you want to know how to get rid of lust even in dreams. You think that you are free from lust during wakefulness, that you have it only in dreams. This is an illusion, a wrong notion. The dream itself is the proof that you are not free from it during wakefulness. The moment you are free of it during wakefulness, you will not even see it in your dreams. The dream is only your subtle history.

You ask how to suppress in sleep what you have been able to suppress in wakefulness. But then there will be no way to free yourself. You must understand that whatever is repressed will always be present and will express itself at one time or another. It is like a sleeping volcano. The flames don't come out, but so what, you will burn and burn inside. This disease will spread like a cancer in your existence.

No, try to understand your dreams. Your dreams are telling you that during the day you have cheated yourself and suppressed something. So now try to find out what you have suppressed.

Try to understand this profound rule about the mind. The mind is like the root of a tree. If the roots are deep in the earth, then the tree continues to flourish; new leaves, flowers and fruits continue to sprout. But if the roots are taken out of that dark depth and put into the light, then the tree dies.

This is exactly what happens with the mind. Whatever the disease of the mind is, bring it out into the light. Light is death to disease.

But you do just the opposite. Your so-called religious gurus have been telling you just the opposite.

They say you have to suppress it so much that you can't even see the root. But the deeper the root, the more dangerous it is. Then your life will become poisonous. You must uncover yourself and put it before your eyes. Don't run away and don't hide. Dig up your roots during the day and look at them in the light.

I call this meditation. Meditation is not a method that can be done once and then forgotten.

Meditation is a continuous process of awareness. You have to be conscious twenty-four hours; while you are standing, while you are sitting, be conscious. When a beautiful woman passes by on the road, a licentious person will look at her. But if you are a gentleman you cannot look at her openly. Try to look at her indirectly. You make the excuse of looking at a shop which is in her direction.

But if you have repressed yourself very deeply, then you don't look anywhere, neither at the shop nor at the woman; you keep your head down without looking to the right or to the left. Then, at night, you will see that beautiful woman in your dream because you really wanted to see her. And this is also possible, that you have acquired the habit of walking with your head down and your eyes looking down. Out of habit, your eyes must have looked down automatically as soon as you became aware of the presence of the beautiful woman.

You may have formed your character in such a way... that you have decided the rules of behaviour for yourself which you follow mechanically. Outwardly you may not know that a woman has passed, but your look down shows that a breeze blew inside you, something fluttered inside you, a ripple arose in you that made your eyes look down. This downward glance was your way of saving yourself from that woman. You passed by.

For this behaviour the world will call you a gentleman or a saint. You will get a lot of respect. So your ego will be satisfied, it will be nourished. You will try to be more religious. For that you may even go to the extent of blinding your eyes. But who are you trying to fool? Can you fool your innermost self? In the darkness of the night, in your deep sleep, when your knight, your saint sleeps soundly, then all your repressed feelings and desires will come to the surface, and create your dreams. Don't think that there is something wrong with dreams. A dream is your friend; it is trying to tell you that you have deceived yourself and that you will gain nothing by this deception. The dream proves that you have repressed your lust. So wake up and recognise your instinct.

The real question is not to look or not to look at the woman passing by; the real question is, are you aware of the wave that arose in you caused by the desire to look at her? It does not matter whether you look at a woman or not look at her, what matters is that the wave of passion arises in you. If you repress it, you will dream of her, but if you are conscious of the passion that arises in you when you look at her, you will not dream of her. If you keep looking at the passion, the desire that arises in you every moment, then you will not dream of it.

Yesterday I was reading a song written by a friend of mine, Kumar Barabankvi, who is an Urdu poet.

One line of the poem is: "The destination seems to be near, while the road is deserted and lonely". Yes, as one begins to approach the destination, the roads of the mind become deserted and lonely.

Even dreams are not there. The markets and even the shadows of the market disappear; there will be no more friends and enemies and even their wavering shadows will disappear.

"The destination seems to be near, for the road is deserted and lonely". When all your inner paths seem lonely, then you must know that the destination is not far away, it is quite near.

As long as your inner ways are full of dreams it means that you are in the market place. The world may be calling you a saint and you may be thinking that you are a saint, but the worldly man in you is not dead, he is only hidden; and the hidden worldly person is more dangerous because he is like a hidden disease. If it is manifest it can be treated, but if it remains hidden it cannot be treated. And what can a doctor do if the sick person continues to deny that he is sick?

This is not the problem of ordinary people, it is the problem of the so-called great mahatmas.

During the last days of his life, even Mahatma Gandhi used to have sexual dreams. He was a very honest man, though he was going astray. Because if, in spite of a lifelong effort, lust arises in your dream, then it means that the effort was being made in the wrong direction. He had worked very hard, he was not lacking in effort, and he was very honest about it. But with honesty and integrity alone you cannot reach your destination. You can't get to the destination with integrity alone and you can't get to the destination by just walking the right paths. You only get to the destination when you put together integrity, effort and the right paths.

If you try to extract oil from the sand in all honesty, you will not succeed. Your honesty is not enough for this purpose because there is no oil in the sand. You can keep trying with full faith, with all your integrity, but it will be of no consequence. On the other hand, another person with less integrity may succeed in trying to extract oil from oilseeds. But a person without faith and without integrity may have the oilseeds, but he will not get the oil because he is not making any effort to extract it. That is why a revolution in life only takes place when integrity and the right path come together.

Till the end of his life Gandhi used to be disturbed by dreams. But I must say that he was an honest person, he was not like the so-called sadhus and saints who are disturbed by dreams but never talk about them to anyone. But Gandhi talked about it openly. His followers did not want him to do so, because it hurt their ego to know that their guru had such dreams. His followers considered him a "Mahatma". That's why they were very worried about what they would say if they found out about his dreams. That is why they asked him not to talk about it openly.

During his last days, Gandhi began to sleep naked with a young woman. At this, some of his followers fled. Of those who fled at that time, some of them now claim to be the heirs of Gandhism! Yes, these are the very ones who had fled, the ones who had opposed Gandhi, saying: "I have never heard, I have never seen such a thing".

But none of them could understand Gandhi's agony. His agony was that he had wasted his whole life in the vain effort to be celibate. During his last days he came to know the scriptures of Tantra which say that if you want to be free from passion you have to awaken, you have to be conscious.

If you have to wake up, then you have to be in that situation, it's no use running away from the situation. That's why, to create that situation, he slept with a naked girl for a year, so that in that situation, if passion arose in him, he would see it, recognise it. All his life he had repressed it, so now he had to make a great effort to discover it. Sleeping with a naked girl was the effort to awaken the passion he had previously repressed.

Escapism is not the solution to life. Life is solved by facing it, by confronting it. You have to face all the problems of life. Don't ask what you have to do to free yourself from lust in dreams. Know that the passion that appears in your dream is due to your suppression when you are awake. Do not suppress it when you are awake. You must discover it and see it in your waking life.

It will not be easy for you to do it because it will hurt your ego. You will say, "I am celibate! I am a sannyasin! How can there be passion in me? But it is there; whether you see it or not, it makes no difference. Your false pride is meaningless, you will have to give up your false attachment. You must realise that you can be free from passion only by observing it.

Try experimenting with this for a few months. Don't repress anything. Whatever comes in through the eyes, let it come in, all of it. Don't condemn it even a little bit, because condemnation causes suppression. Suppose you have a sexual thought and you say it is bad, it is sin, immediately suppression will start. Even if you don't say it is bad, that it is a sin, but you see it very reluctantly, you feel it would be better if you had not seen it, even then suppression will begin.

You say to existence: "My God, what are you showing me? Immediately the suppression has begun.

Every time you make a judgement about whether it is good or bad, or complain or regret, or feel a sense of guilt or try to evaluate, suppression begins.

So you should look at each thought as if you had nothing to do with it. You should see it just as you see the flowers on the tree, or you see the clouds floating in the sky, or you look at the people passing by on the road. You have nothing to do with them. Just observe without any prejudice or bias, then all the instincts appear in their real form. You have repressed them in many lifetimes, so when they appear in their full form, for a moment you may feel that you have gone mad. "What is happening to my morals, my religion, my character? Everything is going down the drain, my reputation that I have built up with such hard work will be shattered." But don't panic about this, stay calm. This takes courage, and this kind of courage is really austerity. You don't need courage to stand in the sun or naked in the snow. Those things come with a little practice. The greatest courage is to be able to see yourself as you are inside. And this creates the transformation, creates the inner revolution.

Just observe, and when you begin to observe the dreams will begin to disappear, because whatever you see during your waking life will not show up in your dream. Then there is no need to show you what you have already seen. Your nights will become dreamless. And if your night becomes dreamless, then you will attain samadhi.

Patanjali has said that there is very little difference between sushupti, dreamless sleep, and samadhi - very little difference. Both occur when all dreams have disappeared - the difference is that sushupti is unconscious and samadhi is waking.

Have you ever noticed that in the morning, when you wake up, you can remember that you have dreamt, that you have dreamt all night long? That means that there is a consciousness in you that sees the dreams, that recognises them and remembers them. If all the dreams disappear, then this consciousness that was absorbed in seeing dreams will now see samadhi, because now there are no more dreams, the road is without travellers, the road is lonely and deserted. Now you can see the lonely road. In the morning, when you wake up, you will say that you have seen sushupti and not dreams. And to see sushupti is samadhi. The path was lonely, there was no crowd. There were no people, so the path could be seen. The sky could be seen when there were no clouds. The sky is covered with clouds because of dreams; sushupti is covered and sushupti is samadhi.

Every night you reach where Buddha came. Every night you reach where Shankara lives. But there is a great crowd between you and samadhi. There is a great fair between you and samadhi. And it is you who have picked up this crowd and this circus. You go on picking up this rubbish by dealing with life in the wrong way. Deal with it every minute. Take a good look at whatever comes in front of you. Don't hesitate for a moment to see it rightly. Then it will have no reason to appear in your dreams.

You see it in your dreams only because you didn't see it well during the day, so it insists on coming back again and again.

Have you ever noticed that if you experience something thoroughly you don't remember it afterwards?

If you take a good look at someone, at anything, then you will be free of him or her; your mind will no longer think of him or her. If you live intensely, deeply, then no love or affection can bind you. But incomplete experiences will always haunt you because the mind wants to fulfil them. Incomplete experiences of life always accumulate in you. Now, please don't repeat this behaviour and don't ask me how to stop it in your dreams. You must know from your dreams that you suppressed it when you were awake; now don't stop it even when you are awake.

I am not saying that you are going to satisfy whatever passion arises in you. I am not saying that, because many times you have tried to satisfy it but it has not been fulfilled. You have been doing it birth after birth. Anger has not disappeared by getting angry. Lust has not disappeared by indulging in sex.

Greed has not disappeared by being greedy. This is the conflict. If you indulge in it, it becomes stronger because it becomes a habit. You got angry today, you got angry yesterday, you got angry the day before yesterday... and so the chain of anger becomes stronger. Then you become an angry person by habit. Then any little excuse will trigger your anger.

If you do it, if you indulge in it, it becomes a habit, a practice. If you repress it, then it hurts you inside. But there is a way between the two: don't fall into it, don't suppress it; just observe, just see. This is the thread of witnessing. Don't be a doer, just be a witness, just be an observer. If you are angry, you are either taking your anger out on the other person or you are suppressing it inside. Both are wrong. If sexual desire arises, you either impose it on the other person or you repress it within yourself. Both are wrong. Don't impose it on the other person, because by imposing it on them you also drag them into the mire and filth of passion. The other person has enough problems and you have added to them.

No, don't force anyone, because if you force the other person, he will also force you. If you make someone the object of your passion, then he will also use you in the same way. That is why passion is a bondage. You bind the other and the other binds you. You enjoy the other and the other begins to enjoy you. You bind someone and he binds you. So don't force your passion, anger or anything else on anyone, and don't repress it either. If you have been kind to the other person, be kind to yourself and don't repress it.

And between these two there is a very subtle journey. Just look at it well, watch it well, don't let it hurt anyone. And as you continue to watch you will feel awakened and become aware.

People who bow down to a temple or a mosque should know that life itself is a prayer if you remain conscious, attentive. There is no other prayer, no other meditation, no other worship.

Life itself becomes worship if one is full of awareness.

The third question:

Question 3:

BELOVED MASTER, YOU SAID THAT DESIRE ALWAYS CREATES MISERY. SO DO DESIRES FOR GOOD DEEDS, FOR RELIGION, FOR GOD ALSO CREATE MISERY?

Desire itself leads to misery; it doesn't matter what you desire. The object of desire can be anything - you can want money or you can want religion - desire is desire.

Desire means that you are not satisfied, that you are not happy where you are and how you are.

You think if you get more money you will be satisfied, if you get more religion you will be satisfied. Desire means that you are dissatisfied and discontented. Desire is anguish born out of dissatisfaction. No matter what kind of dissatisfaction it is, there is no satisfaction. What is desired is all the same. Some people build a good house on this earth and some people build a good house in heaven.

One day, while I was driving along a road, a woman came and gave me a brochure with a picture of a beautiful building with a garden full of flowers and a stream. On it was written: "Are you looking for a nice bungalow?

Out of curiosity I turned it over and discovered that the bungalow was not from this land, it was some propaganda of the Christian missionaries. That beautiful bungalow with the garden and the stream is in heaven. In that brochure it was written that if you want such a building in heaven, no one can take you there except Jesus.

Even if you desire the sky, you will be the one who desires it. It is the extension of your mind - it will be in your language and in your colours. One day you should sit down and make a list of the things you want in heaven. You will be surprised to read the list: it will contain all the earthly things. You will want to have a Rolls Royce, you will want to have the most beautiful actress, you will want the Taj Mahal. Yes, make this list and read it. Don't be afraid. You can tear it up later. Don't show it to anyone. It will surely reveal to you the things you want to possess.

If God is willing to give you heaven and if He tells you to ask for anything, what will you ask for? Your desires will reveal to you that your heaven is but an extension of your world here. It may be a little refined. Even in heaven you will ask for those same worldly things, but there they will be permanent; here they are temporary. The differences will be merely in detail.

An actress ages here, but in heaven she will always remain young, because in heaven women are never more than sixteen years old. Urvasi was sixteen years old millions of years ago, and even now she is sixteen years old; she will always remain sixteen years old. This does not give any information about Urvasi; this reveals the man's desire. He wishes a woman to be no older than sixteen. In heaven streams of wine flow; it is not sold in bottles, it flows in streams. Here there can be prohibition, so what? You can swim in the wine like a fish, you can drink all you want, because there is no prohibition there. If there are rules and regulations in heaven and if you have to take a license for alcohol then it's not freedom. No, there is not even a policeman at the crossroads.

Heaven is nothing but the net of your dreams. Your desire for God is out of sheer misery, pain, disturbance of mind - the same reason people want money, the same reason people want fame and position. So God is your ultimate achievement. And your so-called sadhus and sannyasins also say that God means the ultimate position.

You will be surprised to understand the language of the sadhus and sannyasins. They say, "What is the use of money? It will definitely be taken away from you sooner or later, so you'd better be in search of that currency that will never be taken away from you". But if you analyse their language, you will be surprised: the one who seeks the coin that will be taken away from him is a sinner, a materialist, a libertine. He will go to hell because he seeks temporal money. And those who seek the money that is not of this world are saints, virtuous.

What is the difference between these two? The only difference there seems to be is that the one who seeks the transitory is not very clever, and the one who seeks the intransitory is cleverer, more dishonest and cunning. When little children pick up pebbles, you tell them not to be so foolish; they should pick up precious stones and diamonds. Your advice shows that the child is still very innocent and you have become worldly wise and very calculating.

I see that, compared to your so-called sadhus and sannyasins, the people you consider worldly are more simple and innocent. Your sadhus and sannyasins are more cunning and dishonest because they seek unlimited and eternal wealth. But the desire is the same, there is no difference.

What I say is very different, what Shankara says is very different, what Buddha says is very different. They are not saying that you should desire the truth, that you should desire the divine; they are saying that when all desires disappear then the divine is attained. This is totally different: when all desires disappear, the divine is attained.

Therefore, you cannot desire the attainment of the divine, because that very desire will become the obstacle. When all desires disappear without any condition - when there is no desire in the mind, when there is no passion - then only the divine remains. You cannot desire the divine. When desire is abandoned, then godliness is attained, but the divine cannot be desired. The very desire for God is wrong. If you expect to get something in return then you will get nothing, then you have not realised the divine at all.

Godliness is the result of the disappearance of desire. But to attain it, if you deliberately give up all desires, then you cannot attain it. You cannot claim anything from it, you cannot become the claimant. This is not a business; it is a prayer of the divine. Try to understand this.

When there is no desire left in you, you say: "I am satisfied as I am, I don't want anything else, I don't want to be anywhere else. It's enough for me to be here, I'm lucky". And you sing and dance because you are very happy as you are. There is no desire; you have become an emperor, you are no longer a beggar. Then this emperor meets the supreme emperor. To meet the emperor you have to become the emperor. Only an equal can meet the equal. If you desire even God, it will lead you to misery.

That is why you will find many fakirs in your temples and mosques who are unhappy and unfortunate.

You are unhappy because you didn't get money, you didn't get fame, you didn't get position.

They are unhappy because they have not yet reached God. But the unhappiness continues.

Desire means misery, because desire is not satisfied. The nature of desire is dissatisfaction.

Buddha has said that desire cannot be satisfied; it is not that you are not able to satisfy it, it is that its nature is dissatisfaction. You can do anything, but it is never fulfilled. It cannot be fulfilled.

Fulfilment is not its destiny. The moment a person realises that desire cannot be fulfilled, he ceases to desire the divine as well. He gives up all desire, he drops it, and at that moment of dropping it he discovers that the one he was seeking is within him. He could not see it because desire had made him blind.

That is why Shankara says that the divine is within you. The day you come home after you have given up all the running around, all the desires, when you sit in your own house in a relaxed way with gratitude in your heart, you will hear a new music inside you. The music has always been there, but you couldn't hear it because of the noise of desire. It was a very subtle sound - it went on day and night, but you were not at home and the divine was at home. You never went home, you never found the time. You had a chain of desires to follow, one after the other.

You simply don't have time to go home and see who lives there.

You don't have to go anywhere in search of the divine, you have to come back to your own home, and that is pratyahar.

The fourth question:

Question 4:

BELOVED MASTER, THIS PRATYAHAR SEEMS LIKE AN IMPOSSIBLE EXPERIMENT. IS IT POSSIBLE FOR THE GANGES TO RETURN TO GANGOTRI AND IS IT POSSIBLE FOR THE TREE TO RETURN TO BEING A PLANT AND A SEED? AND BOTH SHANKARA AND YOU

ARE ASKING US TO DO SO.

The return of the Ganges to its source, to Gangotri, and the tree becoming seed seems impossible to you, but that is what is happening every day. The tree turns back into seed every day. Look at the seeds hanging on that gulmohar tree: the whole tree has become seed. And every day the Ganges returns to Gangotri through the dark clouds; it rains in the Himalayas and the Ganges returns to Gangotri. This happens every day.

You wonder what to do. Actually, this happens unconsciously; you just have to see that this happens in wakefulness. Many times you go home but you are not aware of it. You have become so used to staying in guesthouses that even when you go back to your own house you think it is a guesthouse.

A friend of mine has to travel day and night for his job. He only stays at home for four or five days at a time and he can't sleep because he has got used to sleeping with the noise of the train. He has been travelling for twenty years. He told me he had a lot of problems because he couldn't sleep at home. So I suggested to him that it would be better for him to rent a house near a railway.

This appealed to him. He said he had been to many doctors, but no one could give him the right advice. So he rented a house near a railway track and he is very happy because now he can sleep at home. A train passes every ten or fifteen minutes. He is very happy. It's difficult for you to understand his situation, because when you travel by train for the first time you can't sleep.

Habit... we are all slaves to habit!

You have lived so much away from home that when you return home it is not home, you just don't recognise it. Home also seems to you like a boarding house, a place where you spend the night and start your journey again in the morning. Every day the Ganges returns to Gangotri, and you say it is difficult. You are already at your original source and you say it is difficult.

How can you go away from your original source? Where will you go? You must have gone in your thoughts; you cannot go in reality. It is as if you go to sleep in Poona and see Calcutta in a dream; when you wake up in the morning, do you have to take the train back to Poona?

In your dream you were in Calcutta, but that doesn't mean you have to take the train in the morning. When you wake up in the morning you will find yourself in Poona.

Moving away from oneself is just a thought, an idea. If you ask me, and if you can understand it, then I would like to say that the Ganga has never moved away from Gangotri. The seed never became a tree; it only saw the dream of becoming a tree. It was a dream that the Ganga went out of Gangotri and went towards the sea, because one cannot go away from one's own nature.

You say that it is very difficult to return to one's own nature. I tell you that it is not only difficult but impossible to get away from your nature. No one has ever gone away. In this very moment you are the buddha, in this very moment you are the jinna, in this very moment you are the divine.

But your thoughts... you think otherwise. You say this does not appeal to me: I, who run a pan shop, how can I be a buddha? But how can the pan shop become an obstacle to being a buddha? Does one become a buddha merely by sitting under a bodhi tree? I say that sitting in your bun shop you are a buddha. Because you have a pan shop or anything else... you can do anything, but you cannot stop being a buddha.

A fish can get out of the sea, but how can it get out of the divine? ... Because the sea has a limit - it has a shore, a beach - but the divine has no limit, it has no shore; it is unlimited. So it's just your idea that you're running a frying pan shop. Yes, by all means do it, but this should not make you think that you are no longer a buddha. If you become so mindful, then the Ganga goes back to Gangotri. This awareness, this consciousness ....

Many obstacles will stand in your way. First of all, the world will stop you: the shop will stop you, money will stop you, position will stop you. If you somehow free yourself from them, then the temple and the mosque will stop you, the Vedas and the Puranas will stop you, the Gita and the Koran will stop you. You will be able to go home only after you have freed yourself from them.

Many obstacles will stand in the way, but you have to free yourself a little from them. I call this awareness. Shankara has called this care, great care. If you are awake then nobody can stop you. A tent is very weak. The temple and the mosque also cannot stop you; books and ledgers, nothing can stop you; the Vedas and the Koran cannot stop you.

"Many obstacles stood in the way of the beloved. Even the temple and the mosque became obstacles, but thank God we were able to move forward with a little care."

The fifth question:

Question 5:

BELOVED MASTER, YOUR MEDITATION TECHNIQUES INCLUDE YOGA AND BHAKTI. ARE BOTH NECESSARY FOR PRATYAHAR?

Life is of two kinds. One is based on necessities and the other on abundance, on opulence. Look at the peacock dancing: is the rainbow colouring of its feathers necessary? If you cut off its feathers, will there be any difficulty in the peacock's life? In spite of this, the peacock will be able to live, because the life force is not related to the feathers, nor is the obtaining of food. There will be no difficulty in reproduction either; these colourful feathers are not a necessity. They are the symbol of excess, of abundance, of opulence.

These birds are singing. If you sew up their beaks, nothing will change. These birds will be able to go on living. They will not be able to sing; the songs were not necessary, they were born out of abundance.

Why don't you dance, why don't you go about your business and go home? You sing, you love: if you don't sing and you don't love, what difference does it make? Doing your business is enough to survive, will you die if you don't love? Those who don't love also live, those who don't sing also live - perhaps they live better because that saved energy is spent on earning money. But the splendour of their life will be lost.

Living out of necessity is the way of the miser. Here I am not teaching you to live by necessity, I am teaching you to go beyond necessity, to live life in abundance.

I also know that the divine can be attained by gyana knowledge alone and there is no need for bhakti, devotion. The divine can also be attained by bhakti alone, there is no need for knowledge. But then the attainment of the divine will be like a business. You only do what is necessary. If you can do something by spending two paisa, then you hesitate to spend even three paisa. You remain miserly even in the path of the divine. But I want to teach you to be a little carefree, happy-go-lucky!

I also know that people have attained knowledge and there is no need for bhakti, there is no need for everybody to dance like Meera. But even then I will say that if you can dance then a new form of the divine will appear before you which is not of mathematics, which is of poetry. Yes, the divine can be reached by knowledge, by dryness, by mathematics, but if you reach the divine by necessity, then even this relationship is calculated. If even in this relationship you have not jumped, you have not melted and you have not flowed, you have not enjoyed the ultimate bliss, then it means that this was also a business.

People have attained it only by bhakti; knowledge is not necessary. But I say, why try only for the necessary when you can have in abundance? When you can have in excess, when life can become the ultimate luxury, why be miserly and calculating? If you want to dance, you cannot be calculating. A calculating person cannot be a good dancer.

When will you get rid of your stinginess, when will you be able to flow without hesitation?

According to me, the ultimate fortune is in abundance. Look at the peacock: existence has put so many colours on its feathers, it has worked so much on them!

If a scientist were to create a peacock, one thing is certain: he would not make feathers, because, according to him, they are absolutely unnecessary. It will have a tube to eat, a stomach, genitals to reproduce, but no feathers. There will be no poetry, no song, no dance. The colours of life are lost because of these stupid people, because everywhere they advise to do only what is absolutely necessary.

Look at existence. The divine does not agree to have only what is absolutely necessary. It does not stop at the necessary, it keeps flowing towards the unnecessary. Birds sing, it is not necessary; trees blossom, it is not necessary; fragrance flows from flowers, it is not necessary. The rivers flow swiftly to the sea, and the sea keeps roaring and its waves keep crashing against the shore. It is not necessary. Think of what is necessary. If God had been an economist, he would have made only the necessary things in this world. Then this world would not have been good for living; it would only have been good for committing suicide. There would have been no pleasure in living in a world that had only necessary things.

You will attain through knowledge, you will attain through bhakti, but it is completely different to attain through both knowledge and bhakti. It is a different enjoyment. But it all depends on you, the choice is yours. If you like to live in small yards and you are afraid of the open sky, then you can live in small and dirty rooms.

But I tell you that the open sky, the vast sky is also available with this very effort. Do you think you are so small? Why do you talk about what is necessary? Let your knowledge increase to the point where it becomes bhakti, and let your bhakti be so deep that it reaches the point where it becomes knowledge. Rather, touch both ends so that nothing is left untouched. Try to make the most of what you have in this world.

The sixth question:

Question 6:

BELOVED MASTER, I AM LISTENING TO YOU DAILY; I AM ALSO UNDERSTANDING YOU. TEARS WELL UP IN MY EYES, MY HEART IS BEATING LIKE AN EARTHQUAKE, AND IT SEEMS AS IF THE DAY OF SELF-REALISATION HAS ARRIVED. BUT IT DOES NOT COME. THE NEXT DAY THIS EXPERIENCE REPEATS ITSELF AGAIN. I DON'T KNOW WHAT THE MEANING OF THIS GAME OF SUN AND SHADOW IS.

There is no sun or shadow. It's just an illusion of your mind. We are never happy with what we have because the mind keeps asking for more. Has there ever been a time in your life when you didn't want more than what you had?

I am distributing self-realisation, and you receive it every day. It rains on you. Your eyes say the right thing because tears come out of them. They can recognise because they are more sensitive than your mind. And your heart is also giving the right indication because it starts beating. But your head is very strong; it is still thinking that yes, something is happening but it is not yet complete, self-realisation has not yet happened. But what is self-realisation? When will it happen? When you agree that yes, now it has happened, how will you know? What criteria do you have for it?

The mind deceives you. Thoughts will always deceive you. So listen to your tears and listen to your heart. The mind will say, "Yes, it has happened, but not yet completely". But what is complete?

What is full? Even if you are before the divine you will say: "Yes,

I have attained it but not fully". You can make some additions even in God: the nose should have been a little longer, the ears should have touched the shoulders like Buddha's and Mahavira's. The ears are small, they should have been longer. The ears are small, they should have been longer. Do you think that if you meet the divine you will be able to accept that you have it in its fullness?

The mind never says it has everything. The mind has a habit of saying, "Yes, I have it, but there is still so much to be had". Don't listen to the mind. Trust your tears; they are more innocent, simpler and more natural, more internal, more sincere, more primal. Trust the beating of your heart because it is here that the dance begins for the first time. And the mind is of man, of civilisation, of society. It is borrowed, it is from the scriptures. The mind has been given to you by others. But no one has given you tears; you brought them with you. The heart is yours, the sensations in it are yours, the sensitivity is yours; no one has given it to you, though others have taken it from you and created many obstacles in their way.

And if you can listen to your heart and your eyes, if you can listen to your inner life, then you will not be worried about tomorrow and you will not be worried about self-realisation. This moment of bliss will make you very fortunate. You will be filled with gratitude and a deep prayer will arise in your heart. Then you will be grateful to the divine for giving you more than you deserve. It has given it to you when you did not expect it. Then you will not think it is a game of sun and shadow. Today is enough for today. Tomorrow, when it gives you again, you will thank it again.

And don't compare today with tomorrow, because all this comparison is of the mind. Every moment of life is unique. Tomorrow again will be tomorrow; again it will be showered. But don't compare because no two moments can be the same, at the same time. All these comparisons are of the mind. There is always one moment at a time.

In existence there is no possibility of measurement or comparison, and if you keep moving forward like this - grateful, thankful, full of deep gratitude - then you will be able to achieve self-realisation. Self-realisation is not something you are going to achieve all of a sudden; just keep moving forward, increasing, deepening. Self-realisation is not an object, it is a process. Self-realisation is not something you can achieve by just grabbing. Self-realisation is your transformation. It is your development.

And there is no end to self-realisation. That's why the soul is called limitless: it keeps increasing, it keeps growing. You never reach a point where you can say enough is enough. It is limitless. The more you see the divine, the more vast it becomes. New doors open, new flowers bloom; there are thousands of lotuses of consciousness, and there are thousands of petals on each lotus, and each petal has thousands of colours. You will continue to see, you will continue to go deeper into it, and you will continue to increase.

Do not keep an account of the past, for if your mind is filled with this account then you will miss out on what you are receiving now. Don't worry about tomorrow, because He has given you today and He will give you tomorrow too. If He has given you today, why won't He give you tomorrow? Don't worry about tomorrow. Let the past be the past. Don't think about tomorrow, today is enough.

If this confidence penetrates deep within you that today is enough, this moment is enough, then this very moment will become one of bhajan.

Question 7:
OH IDIOT! SING THE SONG OF THE DIVINE, SING THE SONG OF THE DIVINE.